Revision Guide

Cambridge International AS and A Level

Business Studies

Peter Stimpson
Peter Joyce

CAMBRIDGE
UNIVERSITY PRESS

CAMBRIDGE UNIVERSITY PRESS
Cambridge, New York, Melbourne, Madrid, Cape Town,
Singapore, São Paulo, Delhi, Mexico City

Cambridge University Press
4381/4 Ansari Road, Daryaganj, Delhi 110002, India

www.cambridge.org
Information on this title: www.cambridge.org/9781107604773

© Cambridge University Press 2013

First Published 2013

Printed in India by Sanat Printers, Kundli

A catalogue record for this publication is available from the British Library

ISBN 978-1-107-60477-3 Paperback

Contents

iv Contents

Introduction

Purpose of this revision guide

Cambridge International AS and A Level Business Studies Revision Guide has been written to support students working towards this important qualification. The guide follows exactly the order of topics contained in the current Cambridge International AS and A Level Business Studies syllabus produced by Cambridge International Examinations and the endorsed textbook *Cambridge International AS and A Level Business Studies* published by Cambridge University Press (Stimpson/Farquharson ISBN 9780521126564). The guide is so comprehensive that it will also prove to be invaluable to students following other similar courses such as AQA AS/ A level and IB Business and Management.

The Revision Guide has four main objectives:

1. Explain important subject content, concepts and techniques using easily remembered approaches
2. Give a clear understanding to students of the key skills that each type of examination question requires
3. Allow for practice at planning and answering examination questions
4. Encourage students to *avoid* the most common errors in their answers but *include* the most relevant points of analysis and evaluation.

What makes this book different?

✓ It is written by two experienced examiners with many years of teaching and examining experience in Business Studies

✓ It does not just focus on subject content – it is not designed to be a textbook – but also gives clear guidance on how students can improve skills so that they can do better and achieve high grades by preparing appropriate answers

✓ It contains student answers and answer plans to over 37 exam-style questions – with invaluable comments and advice from the authors on these

✓ The sample student answers and student plans given for the exam style questions are written by the authors.

 Note

Cambridge International Examinations bears no responsibility for these answers or for the comments offered.

✓ It uses a variety of different presentational styles to make it easier to revise and learn important material and essential Business Studies concepts.

The style of each chapter follows the same format and the key features are:

Chapter section	Purpose of each section	How to use each section
Revision objectives	Outline the key objectives to be reached as you work through the chapter	These objectives serve as a checklist of your progress through each chapter
Bullet points, diagrams, and mind maps of important subject content	Key subject knowledge that is presented in an easy to recall style	Use these as summaries of the important subject knowledge covered by the main textbook
Notes with key definitions, formulae and common errors to avoid	Summarise the main terms and formulae in advanced level Business Studies and the common mistakes to avoid	Test your knowledge against these definitions and formulae and make sure you avoid the common mistakes!
Progress check questions	Test your understanding of the subject content covered by each topic	If in doubt about any of these go back and re-read the topic or the textbook
Exam-style questions	Allow practice at answering typical examination questions	Author's comment allow to see what is important and compare your own answers against sample answers
Multiple choice questions	Identifies areas of misunderstanding that might still exist	Make sure you can answer all of these correctly!
Revision checklist	Final check that all key points have been revised and learnt thoroughly	Do not proceed on to the next chapter until you can tick all of these points

Explanation of the features in each chapter

Each chapter title is drawn from the headings used in the specification.

Top tip Obtain a copy of the syllabus (you are studying) and keep it in your Business Studies file.

Tips on how to revise

Different people revise in different ways and the aim of this section is not to make you change the way you revise – *if it works well for you and you get the results you are capable of.*

However, there are some important steps that anyone can take to improve the effectiveness of the revision period.

Place
- ✓ Find a quiet place to study – but sometimes, testing yourself with friends can be a useful checking process and can lead to discussion of important ideas and common problems
- ✓ Make sure you are sitting comfortably – perhaps, at a well lit desk
- ✓ Avoid studying in an area where there will be distractions – such as television!

Planning
- ✓ This is very important as it is so easy to waste valuable revision time
- ✓ Allow plenty of time for revision – especially if you are taking more than one AS or A level subject
- ✓ List all of your exam subjects and the amount of time you think you will need for each one
- ✓ Divide each subject into major topic areas (use your copy of the syllabus to help you) and allocate sufficient time to revise each one – allow more time for the topics you find most difficult
- ✓ Vary your revision plan – do not revise one topic or even one subject for a whole day but include other subject areas to avoid becoming bored with just one
- ✓ Build 'time off' into your plan – allow 5 or 10 minutes break each hour and go out of the room you are in and take some exercise
- ✓ Write up your plan, display it somewhere visible and do your best to stick to it!

Methods of revising
- ✓ Reading notes and textbook are important but rarely enough by themselves – this is rather passive revision

- ✓ Make definition lists, bullet points of key factors; write out a summary of existing notes, make spider or mind map diagrams, test yourself using e-versions of multiple choice questions, test yourself with a friend revising for the same subject – these are all active forms of revision
- ✓ Use the 'look, cover, write and check' technique for learning important topics. This involves:
  1. study the topic for a few minutes
  2. cover up the book and notes
  3. write down all you can recall about the topic
  4. check what you have written against the book and notes.
- ✓ Study your past test and mock examination scripts to identify what went wrong – things to avoid – but also what went right – things to repeat and build upon during the 'real' exam
- ✓ Practise writing answers to past examination questions – or questions in this book – and either ask your teacher to mark them or check them against the 'student's answers with author's comments' at the end of each chapter.

Last minute tips
- ✓ Don't leave all your revision to the last minute!
- ✓ Use your summary notes, checklists, definitions sheets, spider diagrams etc., to check final facts and understanding
- ✓ Sleep well – do not stay up all night trying to cram in yet more knowledge! It's more important to get a good night's sleep before any examination.

Top tip Use the Student CD-ROM in the *Cambridge International AS and A Level Business Studies textbook* published by Cambridge University Press (Stimpson/Farquharson ISBN 9780521126564) as it has many multiple choice questions and mind maps to aid your revision.

Examination skills

- ✓ How can you use the skills and knowledge you have been building to perform to your best abilities in examination?

The answer to this question is: show the key examination skills in your answer that are relevant to the question set.

What is meant by 'examination skills'?

They are also known as 'assessment objectives' which means the ways in which an examiner will assess or mark your answer. Your answers need to demonstrate the following:

Knowledge with understanding

This means, does your answer contain accurate and relevant Business Studies subject knowledge which shows understanding of the part of the course that is being examined? *ALL* of your answers must contain evidence of relevant knowledge as without this there can be no marks awarded for any of the other skills either. A most effective way of showing knowledge is to accurately define the Business Studies term used in the question. So, if the question asks:

'What is meant by the term 'price skimming'?' then a full and accurate definition of this term will gain marks.

Even if the question is a more challenging A level question, for example as found on the Cambridge Paper 3 Case Study, then a definition can be an excellent way to start an answer – and gain important marks for knowledge in the first sentence! For example:

'Evaluate a marketing plan for the successful launch of Product X in your country'.

A definition of 'marketing plan' would help you show good subject knowledge and it would also direct you to what factors to include in the rest of the answer!

Application

This skill requires you to make a clear link between your answer and the business in the case study (Example: Cambridge Papers 2 or 3) or in the stem of the question (Example: Cambridge Paper 1). A 'clear link' does not just mean mentioning the name of the business or the names of the owners/directors of the business. True application of an answer means that, for example, your knowledge and understanding are being used to analyse the problems *this* business may be facing or how an important decision will impact on *this* particular business.

For example, if the question is: 'Analyse the advantages and disadvantages of the piece rate system of payment for cooks in Jamie's restaurant', then an example of part of an answer which is *not* applied would be:

'The piece rate system encourages faster working by employees and this may reduce the quality of the finished product'. This argument could apply to *any* business, not just a restaurant.

Here is an example of part of an answer that *is* applied:

'If cooks are paid piece rate then they may concentrate on preparing meals too quickly so food may not be cooked properly causing customers to complain'.

Application is a very important skill to demonstrate in Business Studies examinations as different businesses will respond in different ways to problems or ways of resolving them or be affected in different ways by external events. Without demonstrating this skill of application you may lose about 25 per cent of the total marks but, in addition, you are likely to lose marks for the skill of evaluation too.

Analysis

This skill requires that answers contain more than just knowledge. Analysis can be demonstrated in several different ways in answers to Business Studies questions. For example:

✓ Using the theoretical concepts and techniques included in the Business Studies course to explain the advantages and disadvantages of business decision
✓ Examining the impact on a business of information provided, for example, economic data or information about competitors' actions
✓ Selecting information presented in different forms, such as graphs, tables and charts, and identifying trends and changes and explaining their impact on a business
✓ Drawing together ideas and information.

If the question is: 'Analyse the likely impact on Business B's profits of an increase in its selling prices' then an example of one part of an analytical response would be:

'An increase in prices means that the gross profit margin on each unit sold will be higher, assuming that the costs of making it did not increase too. If the business sells the same amount as before, then total gross profits will rise'.

Evaluation

This skill requires students to draw conclusions from the arguments used, make judgements which are supported or make recommendations that are justified by preceding analysis. To be really effective – and to earn good marks – the evaluation should be rooted in the context of the business featured in the data or case study – which means the judgement made must be applied to the business.

Before evaluation can be effectively demonstrated, the answer must show evidence of knowledge, application and analysis. Evaluation cannot just 'appear' in an answer without the building up of relevant and applied arguments, based on subject knowledge, to support it. Many examples of questions that require evaluation – and students' answers to them – are contained in this book.

How will I know which skills are being examined?

Top tip

Questions consist of:

'**Command word**' + **Topic** being examined + **Context** (for example, case study).

Spend time thinking about what each question is asking before writing answers!

The 'command words' are the important word or words that appear in a question that indicate to students which skills are being examined. It is very important that you understand these command words so that you do not:

- ✓ waste time developing an answer with examination skills that *are not* being examined in a question
- ✓ throw away marks by not showing evidence of the skills that *are* being examined.

These are the main command words that will be used on Business Studies AS and A level examination papers:

Command words	Skills being examined
State List Define What is meant by…	Knowledge
Calculate for this business… Explain how this business… From the data outline…	Knowledge } Application }
Analyse Explain why… Explain the advantages and disadvantages of…	Knowledge } Application } Analysis }
Evaluate Discuss Assess Recommend and justify… Do you agree…	Knowledge } Application } Analysis } Evaluation }

Top tip

Spend time analysing questions to decide which is the best way to demonstrate evaluation in an answer. For example: 'Recommend' requires a justified recommendation, 'evaluate the factors' requires a prioritisation of factors, 'Discuss' requires a balancing of arguments and so on.

Understanding mark schemes

Have you seen examples of mark schemes for the Business Studies examination papers?

Top tip

Ask your teacher for examples of mark schemes from past Cambridge examination papers.

Mark schemes are the documents used by examiners to guide their assessment of examination scripts. Although the schemes contain details of the subject knowledge that students are expected to show in their answers, this is not their only purpose. They also give details of the number of marks to be awarded for each examination skill – and these are normally divided into 'levels' that denote the quality of the answer. It's demonstration of skills that get the marks – the higher the skill, the higher the mark!

Keys to examination success – the day of the examination

Assuming you have done your very best during the Business Studies course and that you have followed the revision tips above, what are the best ways to prepare for the examination day itself?

- ✓ Check the time of the examination and leave for the exam in plenty of time.
- ✓ Take all of the necessary equipment with you – for Business Studies, two black pens (one could run out of ink!), a calculator and a ruler should be sufficient. Your exam centre will want these in a 'see through' plastic case.
- ✓ When the exam starts, read the instructions carefully and ask the invigilator if any of these instructions are unclear before you start writing.
- ✓ Read through case study material very carefully – do this again after you have read the questions because a hurried start in answering the first question nearly always leads to poor marks if the case study material is not understood and key points from it are not incorporated in your answer.
- ✓ Look at the marks available for each question and the 'command' word – these will indicate to you which of the examination skills are being tested. They will also give you an indication of how long to spend on answering each question.
- ✓ Divide the total time up – you may need to make a note of this – between the questions in proportion to the marks each one carries.
- ✓ Write as neatly as you can. It is recommended that you leave a line between each paragraph and at least two lines between each separate answer.
- ✓ Plan answers to the longer questions.
- ✓ Allow ten minutes at the end to read through answers to correct any glaring errors or to add a key point that has been missed out.

Now that you have read this introduction you are well prepared with important advice on how to face (your) examinations! However, first, you have to actually do the revision and the remainder of this book will, we hope, make your revision more effective and will help you gain the final grade that you deserve. Good luck in your examinations!

Peter Stimpson
Peter Joyce

Acknowledgement

The following is reproduced by permission of Cambridge International Examinations:

Syllabus Name and Code	Paper and Question Number	Month/Year	Chapter/Page in Book
Cambridge International AS and A Level Business Studies 9707	Paper 31, Section B, Q6	June 2010	Chapter 7, Page 42
Cambridge International AS and A Level Business Studies 9707	Paper 11, Section B, Q5	November 2010	Chapter 8, Page 48
Cambridge International AS and A Level Business Studies 9707	Paper 21, Q2(d)	November 2010	Chapter 10, Page 60
Cambridge International AS and A Level Business Studies 9707	Paper 22, Q2(c)	November 2010	Chapter 15, Page 93
Cambridge International AS and A Level Business Studies 9707	Paper 32, Section A, Q1&3	November 2010	Chapter 18, Page 112
Cambridge International AS and A Level Business Studies 9707	Paper 21, Q1(d)	November 2009	Chapter 21, Page 129
Cambridge International AS and A Level Business Studies 9707	Paper 21, Q1(c)	November 2009	Chapter 22, Page 134
Cambridge International AS and A Level Business Studies 9707	Paper 31, Section A, Q2	November 2009	Chapter 24, Page 146
Cambridge International AS and A Level Business Studies 9707	Paper 3, Section A, Q3(a)&(b)	November 2008	Chapter 25, Page 150
Cambridge International AS and A Level Business Studies 9707	Paper 23, Q2(b) (I)&(II)	June 2011	Chapter 27, Page 165
Cambridge International AS and A Level Business Studies 9707	Paper 31, Section A, Q2	November 2010	Chapter 28, Page 171
Cambridge International AS and A Level Business Studies 9707	Paper 33, Q1	June 2010	Chapter 32, Page 194
Cambridge International AS and A Level Business Studies 9707	Paper 32, Q4	November 2010	Chapter 33, Page 200
Cambridge International Business Studies 9707	Paper 31	June 2010	Chapter 34, Page 205
Cambridge International AS and A Level Business Studies 9707	Paper 33, Section B, Q6	June 2011	Chapter 35, Page 211
Cambridge International AS and A Level Business Studies 9707	Paper 32, Section A, Q5(a)&(b)	June 2010	Chapter 36, Page 218
Cambridge International AS and A Level Business Studies 9707	Paper 31, Section B, Q7	June 2011	Chapter 37, Page 225
Cambridge International AS and A Level Business Studies 9707	Paper 32, Section B, Q7	June 2011	Chapter 37, Page 225

Enterprise

1

Revision Objectives

After you have studied this chapter, you should be able to:

☞ Understand what business activity involves
☞ Understand what 'adding value' means
☞ Recognise what makes a successful entrepreneur

☞ Assess why enterprise is important to a country
☞ Recognise what social enterprises are and how they differ from other businesses.

1.1 Business activity

Businesses aim to meet the needs of customers by using resources to make goods and services that they will buy. These products can be either for final consumers or capital and intermediate goods for business customers. Which resources (factors of production) do businesses need?

✓ Labour: human effort to produce goods or provide services to customers
✓ Capital: equipment and machinery
✓ Land: a location to operate the business from
✓ Enterprise: risk taking and decision making undertaken by an entrepreneur.

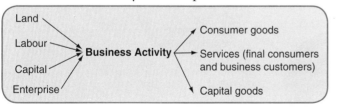

Key terms

Consumer products (goods and services): bought by 'final' consumers who will benefit from them and not use them to produce other products
Capital and intermediate goods: goods bought by industry to be used in the production of other products

1.2 Adding value

Key term

Added value: the difference between the cost of purchasing raw materials and the price of the finished good

Business activity aims to increase added value. Increasing 'added value' has many benefits – the key one being that it could lead to higher profits for the owners of the business.

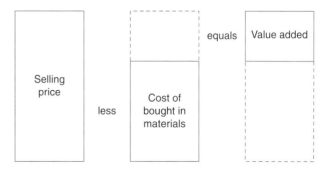

Ways of adding more value to raw materials include:
1. Raising the selling price but keeping the raw material costs constant *but* will customers still buy?

2. Purchasing cheaper raw materials but keeping selling prices the same *but* will customers notice a reduction in quality?
3. Using raw materials more efficiently so the cost per item falls *but* this might need more accurate machines or more highly trained staff.

Progress Check A

1. What capital equipment would a hairdressing business need?
2. Where is an entrepreneur likely to locate a new shop selling mobile (cell) phones?
3. What types of workers would an entrepreneur operating a road transport business most probably need to employ?
4. A business making clothes has managed to use 10 per cent less material on each item of clothing by using a new cutting machine. Explain what will happen to the 'value added' by this business.
5. Explain how a computer could either be sold as a 'consumer good' or a 'capital good'.

1.3 The role and characteristics of successful entrepreneurs

Key term

Entrepreneur: someone who takes the financial risk of starting and managing a new business venture

Entrepreneurs are people who are determined to create their own business – not work as an employee for another firm. This means they must have:

✓ a business idea
✓ some savings to invest
✓ willingness to take risks and accept responsibilities.

(See diagram below)

1.4 Why some new enterprises fail

These are the most common reasons for new enterprises not succeeding:

1. Lack of finance or working capital – often difficult to encourage people or banks to invest in new business ideas

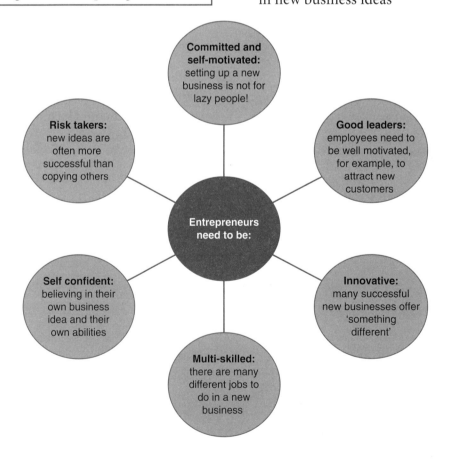

Entrepreneurs need to be:

Committed and self-motivated: setting up a new business is not for lazy people!

Good leaders: employees need to be well motivated, for example, to attract new customers

Innovative: many successful new businesses offer 'something different'

Multi-skilled: there are many different jobs to do in a new business

Self confident: believing in their own business idea and their own abilities

Risk takers: new ideas are often more successful than copying others

2. Lack of record keeping – not having sufficient information to operate the business
3. Poor management skills – even the hardest working and most enthusiastic entrepreneur needs basic management skills for example, communication and leadership skills
4. Competition – most new enterprises are small and compete against larger rivals who may try to 'squeeze them out of business'
5. Changes in the business environment – economic or technological changes can be a serious problem for new small businesses as they often do not have the resources to deal with them.

Progress Check B

1. Why are leadership skills important to an entrepreneur?
2. Why is it often important for an entrepreneur to be prepared to be a 'risk taker'?
3. Why might an 'entrepreneur's innovation' be important for the success of a new business?
4. Explain why a new business might fail even though the entrepreneur who set it up has all of the 'key characteristics' listed above.

1.5 Enterprise – benefits for the country

New businesses created by entrepreneurs can lead to important economic benefits for a country:

- ✓ Reduce unemployment
- ✓ Increase output – which might be exported
- ✓ Create additional competition for existing firms
- ✓ Increase government tax revenue
- ✓ Innovate and accept technological change
- ✓ May develop and expand into huge corporations!

1.6 Social enterprises

Key term

Social enterprise: business with mainly social objectives that reinvests most of its profits into benefiting society rather than maximising returns to owners

It is wrong to assume that 'all businesses want is to make profits'. This is too simple – as Chapter 4 shows. Good examples of business organisations that try to achieve non-profit based objectives are 'social enterprises'. Many co-operative organisations are operated as social enterprises (see Chapter 2).

The 'triple bottom line' of social enterprises means that they aim to achieve:

1. Economic objectives – making profits to reinvest
2. Social objectives – supporting disadvantaged groups such as providing work for disabled workers or providing support for refugee groups
3. Environmental objectives – managing the business in an environmentally sustainable way.

Progress Check C

1. Explain *two* reasons why most countries' governments are trying to increase the number of new enterprises in the economy.
2. Why might a social enterprise find it easy to recruit well motivated staff?
3. Does a social enterprise need profits?
4. What other objectives might a social enterprise have apart from making a financial return?

4 Enterprise

1. Which one of the following best explains business activity?
    (i) Using resources to make goods and services that workers need
    (ii) Using factors of production to supply resources for customers
    (iii) Using resources to make products that meet customer needs
    (iv) Making factors of production to satisfy customer requirements

2. Which of the following is *not* a factor of production?
    (i) Labour
    (ii) Customer
    (iii) Capital
    (iv) Land

3. A business could 'add value' by:
    (i) making higher profits
    (ii) employing more workers
    (iii) using more expensive materials and keeping the selling price low
    (iv) using materials more efficiently

4. Which of the following is a common characteristic of successful entrepreneurs?
    (i) Committed
    (ii) Unskilled
    (iii) Shy
    (iv) Cautious

5. Which one of the following is a common problem faced by most entrepreneurs?
    (i) Too many different sources of finance to choose from
    (ii) A large number of customers to serve from the day the business is set up
    (iii) Premises that are too near the city centre
    (iv) Inadequate finance to buy capital equipment

6. In which *one* of the following business activities would you *most* expect a *new* entrepreneur to be successful in today's business world?
    (i) Aircraft manufacturing
    (ii) Banking
    (iii) Taxi services
    (iv) Oil exploration

Exam-style Question

1. (a) Explain the importance of business activity to a country. [8]
    (b) Discuss the characteristics an entrepreneur needs to set up a successful new retail business. [12]

Student's answer to 1 (b)

An entrepreneur is a person who is prepared to take risks in setting up and managing a business, often with their own savings or capital.

Such a person needs to have several personal characteristics if they are going to set up a successful business. They will have to be prepared to work hard as there will be so much to do. Plans will have to be made, a location needs to be arranged, stock bought and, if the shop is going to be big enough, workers will have to be employed. If an entrepreneur was lazy the retail business is unlikely to succeed.

The entrepreneur will need to be good at making decisions. As there are already so many shops the entrepreneur will need to make the new retail store 'stand out'. Perhaps unusual products will be sold to attract customers or the location of the shop might be really important. If it was a shop selling sandwiches and drinks then locating it near where many people work would be a good idea. If the entrepreneur was not good at making decisions, the shop will fail.

The entrepreneur will need people skills too. This means they will need to be able to get on well with customers and workers. If they are bad leaders and shout at workers in front of customers in the shop then this will lead to customers leaving. If they cannot talk to customers to find out what they really want then the shop may end up selling the wrong products.

Perhaps the most important characteristic that the entrepreneur must have is to be multi-skilled. They will have to be good at numbers to do the accounting and check the stock. They need to know about the product they are selling. They will need to know about displays and presentation. As the business is new and small the owner will not be able to afford to employ people to do all of these things which is why multi-skilling is so important.

So, a successful entrepreneur must have many characteristics to succeed in retailing. However, even all of these might not be enough to make sure the business is successful if there is a recession or if customer tastes change quickly.

Authors' Comments

This is an excellent answer. It demonstrates knowledge as entrepreneur is defined and good awareness of personal characteristics is shown. Can you also see that the answer is applied to retailing? This is very important – the student tries to make points that are particularly relevant to setting up and running a shop. The points made are well explained or analysed and there is good judgement or evaluation. The evaluation is strong in two ways. The student suggests and justifies the 'most important characteristic' and also looks briefly at other factors, apart from the entrepreneur, that could affect the success of a shop.

Revision checklist – tick when done and understood!

Topic	Textbook read	Revision complete
What businesses do		
Adding value (see also Chapter 14)		
What businesses need		
The role of entrepreneurs and the characteristics they need		
Why new businesses can fail		
Enterprise and benefits to the country		
Social enterprises		

Business Structure

2

Revision Objectives

After you have studied this chapter, you should be able to:

☞ understand the different levels of economic activity

☞ know the difference between the private sector and public sector

☞ understand legal forms of business organisation

☞ assess the factors that influence the most suitable form of business organisation

☞ understand the arguments for and against privatisation

☞ evaluate the reasons for growth of multinational companies and their impact.

2.1 Economic activity

It is common to divide economic activity into three sectors. The relative importance (as % of total national output) of these varies greatly between countries. Generally it is true that in high income developed economies the tertiary sector is the most important. In middle income emerging economies such as Brazil and China, the secondary sector tends to be the most important. In low income developing economies the primary sector is often the most significant. This helps to explain the low average incomes in these countries – the value added of the primary sector is usually much lower than that of the other two.

Key terms

Primary sector: businesses involved in farming, fishing and extracting natural resources

Secondary sector: businesses involved in manufacturing products from primary goods

Tertiary sector: businesses involved in providing services to consumers and other businesses

2.2 Private sector and public sector

Private sector businesses are often operated with the objective of earning profits. Public sector organisations – such as police force, schools, universities and hospitals – have other objectives. These could include social aims, such as caring for the elderly, or keeping law and order.

Nearly all economies have a 'mixture' of these two sectors and are referred to as mixed economies. If there was no public sector activity it would be called a free-market economy. If there was no private sector, it would be called a command or a planned economy.

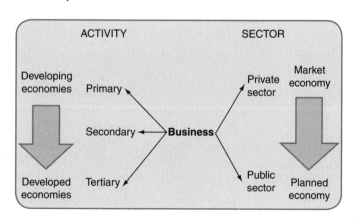

Progress Check A

1. Research (using the Internet) the share of the total economy accounted for by the private sector in any two countries of your choice.
2. Would you classify a business that roasts and grinds coffee beans as being in the primary or secondary sector of industry?
3. Explain one reason why the tertiary sector is often much more important in developed economies than in developing economies.
4. Is the private sector more or less important than the public sector in your economy?
   Use employment or output data to help you answer.

2.3 Forms of business organisation (private sector)

Table 2.1

	Sole Trader	Partnership	Private Limited Company	Public Limited Company
	A business owned and controlled by one person	A business owned by two or more people sharing investment and responsibilities	A business owned by shareholders, often family members, which cannot sell shares to general public	A business, owned by shareholders, which has the right to sell shares to general public
Ownership	One person	Shared between partners	Shareholders (but shares not available publicly)	Shareholders (general public or investment/pension funds)
Senior managers	The owner	One or more of the partners	Usually one of the main shareholders but can be a professional manager	Professional directors elected by shareholders – CEO appointed by Board of Directors
Financial liability	The owner	Shared by the partners – except in case of limited partnership	Limited to the amount invested by shareholders	Limited to the amount invested by shareholders
Main capital sources	Owner's savings Bank loans	Partners' savings Bank loans	Capital from sale of shares Retained profits Bank loans	Capital from sale of shares Retained profits Bank loans
Common problems	Lack of management skills Lack of capital for expansion Unlimited liability	Some partners may be more competent or harder working than others Unlimited liability Profits shared	Some loss of control/ownership when the original owner sells shares to friends/business contacts Cannot sell shares to general public Legal formalities Some disclosure of accounts	Further loss of control/ownership by original owners Divorce between ownership and control Full disclosure of accounts as legally required
Common benefits	Owner keeps all profits Owner takes all decisions – no need to consult with others which can be time consuming	More capital invested by partners Sharing of responsibilities Often partners have different skills and experience	Limited liability for shareholders Less disclosure of accounts than public limited company Continuity	Limited liability for shareholders – this makes it easier to attract new shareholders who can now include the general public Access to more capital through sale of shares via Stock Market Continuity

Top tip

There is no one correct or appropriate form of business organisation – it depends on the size and nature of the business and the objectives of the owners.

2.4 Other important types of business organisation

Cooperatives

All members can contribute to the running of the organisation and profits are shared between them.

Franchise

A business that uses the name, logo and trading systems of an existing business. An entrepreneur might decide to take out a franchise of an existing successful business to reduce risks, to receive advice and training, to gain a reliable source of supplies and benefit from a well-established brand. However, this business model will reduce the entrepreneur's independence and there will be franchise fees to pay plus, probably, a share of the sales or profits to the franchisor.

Joint venture

Two or more businesses agreeing to work together on a particular project. This allows risk and costs to be shared although it might lead to disputes over leadership. This structure is particularly common when expanding abroad as local knowledge can be gained through a joint venture with a firm based in the country.

Holding company

A business owns and controls a number of separate businesses but does not unite them into one overall company.

Progress Check B

1. List two types of business organisations that do not give their owners limited liability.
2. Why is 'shareholders limited liability' important to a public limited company when it advertises its shares for sale?

3. Why might a sole trader decide **not** to take a partner into the business?
4. Why might the directors of a private limited company decide **not** to convert the business into a public limited company?
5. Differentiate between a joint venture and a franchise.
6. Explain why the managers of a retailing business might choose to expand the business through franchising.
7. Explain why a business planning to operate in a foreign country for the first time might decide to establish a joint venture there.
8. Why is limited liability important to someone planning to invest in a business?

2.5 Privatisation

Key term

Privatisation: selling state owned organisations to investors in the private sector

This process has become increasingly widespread in recent years. The reasons for this include:

- raises finance for government
- businesses can now operate without political control/interference
- private owners will expect profits from their investment so the business will have to be operated efficiently
- without government financial support the business will be subject to market forces – to be successful it will have to produce what customers are prepared to pay for
- it could lead to increased competition as other businesses enter the industry.

Some economists and politicians are opposed to privatisation claiming that:

- some important public services will now be cut back if they are not profitable
- job losses are inevitable when the private owners attempt to improve efficiency to increase profits

- some industries are too important to be operated by private investors
- if a state controlled monopoly is replaced by a private owned monopoly then customers may be exploited with higher prices.

2.6 The growth of multinational companies and the impact they can have on an economy

> **Key term**
>
> **Multinational company (or corporation):** businesses with headquarters in one country but with operating branches or factories in other countries

The recent growth of multinational companies can be explained by:

✓ increased free trade and reduction in barriers makes it easier for businesses to start up operations in other countries
✓ cost savings might be made by operating in a low cost country
✓ the businesses foreign operations might be closer to important markets
✓ gaining access to local resources that might not be available in 'home' country.

Top tip

Be prepared to examine the impact of the growth of multinational corporations on your country's economy.

The impact of multinationals

The issues to be considered include:

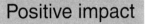

Positive impact	Negative impact
Local jobs created	High income jobs go to foreign workers
National output increases	Profits back to 'home country'
May increase exports May increase tax revenues	Local competition squeezed out Large scale production could damage environment
Skills of local workers increased	Less cultural diversity

> **Progress Check C**
>
> 1. What factors are important in deciding whether the water supply industry in your country should operate in the public sector or the private sector?
> 2. Name four multinational businesses operating in your country.
> 3. Suggest reasons why each of these multinationals is operating in your country.
> 4. Discuss whether your country should encourage more multinationals to become established.

Multiple Choice Questions

1. Which one of the following statements is most likely to be correct?
   (i) Primary sector activity includes food packing and freezing businesses
   (ii) Tertiary sector activity includes small scale farming operations
   (iii) Secondary sector activity includes using materials such as wood, clay bricks and sand to construct a house
   (iv) The secondary sector is gaining in importance compared to the tertiary sector in most high income developed countries

2. A typical example of public sector organisations is:
   (i) fee paying schools
   (ii) army
   (iii) public limited companies
   (iv) sports clubs open to the public

3. Which of the following is *not* a reason for a sole trader taking partners into the business?
   (i) To increase the capital available for expansion
   (ii) To gain limited liability for all owners
   (iii) To increase the expertise available to the business
   (iv) To share management functions

4. One of the reasons why some private limited companies convert to public limited company status is:
   (i) to gain limited liability for all shareholders
   (ii) to avoid having to disclose important accounting results
   (iii) to share the management tasks with other shareholders
   (iv) to obtain finance for expansion which has no interest charges

5. A potential benefit of a cooperative organisation is:
   (i) the shareholders will be able to keep all of the profit
   (ii) customers will always benefit from lower prices compared to other private sector businesses
   (iii) the members tend to be highly motivated as they will benefit from any surplus made
   (iv) as they are state owned and controlled the workers can never lose their jobs

6. Privatisation of a state owned business is likely to lead to which one of the following?
   (i) Increased job opportunities as the new owners will want to reduce unemployment
   (ii) Cost cutting decisions by managers as the profit incentive will be strong
   (iii) Lower prices to help consumers on low incomes
   (iv) Increased government spending to invest in new factories for the business

Exam-style Question

1. "I do not see how we are going to compete with ROC Incorporated" said Joe Sainz, the managing director and main shareholder of Spanish Minerals Ltd. This is a private limited company that extracts minerals from three quarries in Spain. "As one of the largest multinational mineral producing and exporting companies in the world, ROC Inc's decision to start up operations in Spain by opening a huge new quarry will force us out of business!"

   "We have capital saved from retained profits and we could consider conversion to a public limited company" said the other main shareholder of Spanish Minerals, Pablo Massa. "With the capital raised we could aim to become a highly mechanised and efficient supplier of high grade minerals. If the sale of shares was successful, we could also become very rich!"

   Joe replied, "Perhaps we could aim to provide specialist knowledge and materials to ROC Inc rather than try to compete with them head-on".

   (a) Differentiate between a private limited company and a public limited company. [4]
   (b) Evaluate whether Joe and Pablo should convert Spanish Minerals Ltd. into a public limited company. [10]
   (c) To what extent does a county's economy benefit from increased operations of multinational corporations? Use the case study and knowledge of your own country in your answer. [14]

Student's plan for 1 (c)

Define multinational

Benefits: Use ROC example and others from own country such as: ROC will create jobs; add to national output; output may be exported; may force local firms to become more efficient, for example, Spanish Minerals Ltd investing to become more efficient.

Drawbacks: May lead to closure of local firms – will Spanish Minerals be able to compete? Profits may be taken out of Spain (refer to own country's experience too).

Evaluation: Overall effect depends on how many local jobs are created compared to jobs lost; how much tax government is able to raise from company; whether output is exported. Perhaps in the long term the benefits will exceed the drawbacks if the government controls ROC's operations to limit damage to the environment.

Authors' Comments

Good structure; balance of positive and negative points (will student actually use own country examples though?); excellent ideas for final evaluation. Should be possible to write excellent answer based on this plan in time available.

Final revision checklist – tick when done and understood!

Topic	Textbook read	Revision complete
Sectors of industry		
Different types of economic systems		
Advantages and disadvantages of different legal business structures		
Privatisation		
The impact of multinational corporations		

Size of Business

3

After you have studied this chapter, you should be able to:

☞ understand ways of measuring business size

☞ recognise benefits of small firms for an economy

☞ understand the advantages and disadvantages of small and large businesses

☞ differentiate between internal and external growth

☞ evaluate the impact of different types of business integration

☞ understand how problems of rapid growth can be tackled.

☞ recognise benefits and limitations of family businesses.

3.1 Measuring business size

Why is it important to know 'how big' a business is or 'how many' small businesses there are in a country? Business managers and governments are interested in measuring business size. For example:

✓ managers want to know if their business is becoming relatively larger than others in the industry

✓ governments want to know if national businesses are becoming larger compared to those of other countries – and whether the number of small businesses is increasing.

None of the measures of business size is perfect. In some cases they can give rather misleading indications of business size – which is why it is common to use more than one measure to make comparisons between businesses.

Some of the problems include:

- **market capitalisation** would exclude IKEA, Virgin and other large private limited companies. The market capitalisation values can also change greatly with a Stock Market 'boom' or 'slump'

- **employment:** this would make a nuclear power company – with relatively few employees but huge capital investments – appear quite small

- **capital employed:** this would make a labour intensive industry – such as a postal service – appear quite small compared to the large number of people it employs

- **sales value:** although useful for making comparisons between firms in the same industry, it is of limited value in making inter-industry comparisons

- **market share:** useful for making comparisons between the relative importance of firms in the same industry, it is of no use in making size comparisons between firms in completely different industries.

Measuring business size

Progress Check A

1. Company *A* is a construction business employing 100 part-time workers who, on average, work 20 hours per week. Company *B* is a construction business employing 30 full time workers (40 hours per week, on average). Which company is larger (using the employment measure)?
2. Why would it be misleading to compare the size of an electricity generating business with that of an office cleaning business using the 'capital employed' measure?
3. Why would it be impossible to compare the size of two sole trader businesses by using the 'market capitalisation' measure?
4. Explain whether 'sales value' is a good way of measuring the size of two car manufacturing businesses.

Top tip
All measures of size have shortcomings.

It is best to use a measure in the context of an industry/sector and over time.

The level of profit made by a business is ***not*** a good measure of size.

It may be a useful indicator of performance/effectiveness but not size.

3.2 Small firms can benefit an economy

Most governments are willing to offer special support for small businesses because of the economic benefits they offer.

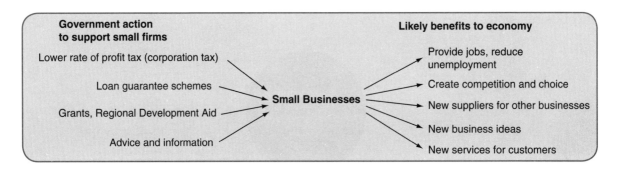

3.3 Common strengths and weaknesses of family businesses

Businesses owned and managed by a family often have strengths and weaknesses.

Table 3.1

Feature	Common Strengths	Common Weaknesses
Structure	Informal, flexible, entrepreneurial, innovative	Resistant to change, lack of management development, no organisation charts–unclear structure
Roles	Family members often play multiple roles, flexible, quick decision making	Role confusion, jobs don't get done, family favouritism can lead to unqualified family members in jobs
Leadership	Creative, ambitious, informal authority, entrepreneurial	Autocratic, resistant to new ideas, avoids delegation
Employees including family members	Employees often committed and loyal, shared values and culture	Can't keep family issues out of business, inability to balance family's and business's needs, inward looking, can't separate work and family, family rivalries
Succession	Training successors can begin early, can choose when to leave	Family issues get in way, unwillingness to let go, unwilling to choose a successor
Ownership/Control	Closely held, family owned, high degree of control, earnings are motivators	May sacrifice growth for control, often no outside Directors, need for privacy
Culture	Innovative, informal, flexible, creative, adaptable, common language, efficient communications	Founder's role can stifle innovation, inefficient, emotional, resistant to change, high risk of conflicts

3.4 The relative advantages of small and large businesses

Figure 3.1 shows the relative advantages of small and large businesses.

Progress Check B

1. Research the support given by the government in your country to small businesses.
2. Explain two problems often faced by small businesses.
3. Explain two problems that often result from managing a large business.

3.5 How businesses grow

Many owners and managers of businesses want their firm to expand. Some do not – and the reasons for different business objectives are considered in Chapter 4.

Business expansion can take place in two ways:

✓ internal or organic growth through expanding existing operations and opening new ones
✓ external growth through integration with another business.

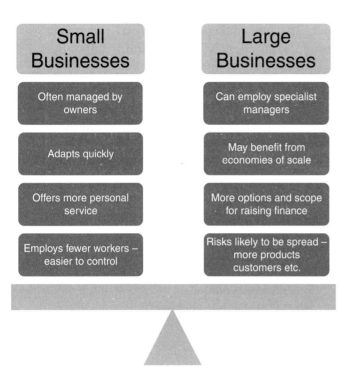

Key terms

Internal growth: expansion of a business by means of opening new branches, shops or factories – also known as organic growth

External growth: expansion achieved through integration – by a business merging with or taking over another business. This can be from either the same or a different industry.

Top tip Remember that internal growth is often easier to manage than sudden external growth.

Figure 3.1 Comparing small and large businesses

External growth

A

3.6 Business integration – do all stakeholders benefit?

A merger of two businesses or a takeover of one by another is a good example of a business decision that can cause 'stakeholder conflict'. This means, some stakeholders will benefit more than others – and some, in fact, may lose out.

Table 3.2

Type of integration	Possible impact on business	Stakeholders might gain or lose
Horizontal	• Higher market share • More control over market, for example, in setting prices • Opportunities for economies of scale • Opportunities for cost cutting e.g. rationalising production onto one site • Greater bargaining power over suppliers • Greater influence on government policy	• Customers – prices could be reduced because the larger business can cut unit costs **but** less choice and prices could rise as the business now has more market share/power. • Suppliers – able to supply higher quantities to the larger business **but** forced to cut cost of supplies as the larger business puts more pressure on suppliers • Workers – more opportunities for promotion within larger business **but** some jobs lost through rationalisation
Vertical forward	• Control over next stage of production • Control over marketing strategy, for example, if manufacturer takes over chain of shops • Obtains a secure outlet for the firm's products	• Customers – retailers dedicated to selling just one manufacturers' products **but** less product choice in the manufacturer's own shops • Senior managers – may have problems controlling a business in another sector of industry **but** workers and managers have opportunities to gain experience in different part of industry
Vertical backward	• Control over supplier • Able to monitor quality of supplies more easily • Able to control costs of supplies • Joint research into improved materials or components more likely	• Customers – product quality may improve as firm now has control over suppliers **but** the expanded business may refuse to supply materials or components to other manufacturers, limiting product choice • Senior managers – may have problems controlling a business in another sector of industry **but** workers and managers have opportunities to gain experience in different part of industry
Conglomerate	• Diversification of risks by moving into different products and markets • These products/markets may offer opportunities for faster growth	• Managers and workers – greater career opportunities **but** business may lack focus and sense of direction which may reduce motivation

Top tip Discussing stakeholder conflict can be an effective way of showing evaluation when judging the impact of a merger or takeover.

The overall benefits of integration depend on the level of synergy that results from the merger or takeover.

There are several reasons why integration might fail to achieve the benefits claimed for it – in other words, the synergy gains are less than expected. These reasons include:

✓ clash of management styles and cultures between the two businesses

✓ the motivation of the combined workforce may fall if redundancies are planned to save costs

✓ the problems of managing a much bigger business outweigh the potential cost savings

✓ customers seek alternative suppliers as they become concerned about increased market share and power of the expanded business.

3.7 Rapid growth can cause problems as well as bring benefits

Businesses sometimes experience serious problems as a result of expanding too quickly:

✓ Lack of capital – expansion can be expensive. Additional fixed assets may be needed. The cost of a takeover may be very high. Additional stocks might be needed and finance also required to allow more customers credit for sales made. Running short of working capital during rapid expansion is sometimes called 'overtrading'.

✓ Lack of management expertise – if growth is slow and 'manageable' then this problem is less likely to occur. Rapid growth, though, may put strains on existing managers and additional new managers may take time to understand how the business operates.

✓ Marketing and production departments – these may struggle to cope with rapid expansion. Is there sufficient capacity to supply many more customers? Will different marketing strategies be needed to allow for the planned increase in sales – especially in different countries or market segments?

5. Which one is an example of horizontal integration?

6. One of the internal consequences to a business that might result from it expanding quickly is:
   (i) market share will increase rapidly and competitors will be worried about this
   (ii) more managers have to be employed so the original owner has more control than before
   (iii) the need to purchase more stocks and allow customers more credit may lead to a lack of finance
   (iv) the cost of marketing products will not increase, even though sales rise, as the same marketing strategy can always be used

Exam-style Question

A failed takeover

LoCost Clothing merged with Exclusive Fashions two years ago. The managers of the two businesses expected the new firm, called Global Wear, to make much higher sales and profits than the two separate companies. The two original businesses used to sell clothes in different countries and in completely separate market segments. "We will now be able to produce clothes at a lower cost and with a greater variety of designs than before." the two former managing directors said when the news of the merger was first announced. Two years later, with falling profits, higher labour turnover and increasing customer complaints, the directors of Global Wear have decided to split the business into the two original companies.

    (a) Explain the type of integration referred to in the case study. [3]
    (b) Analyse *two* likely benefits to stakeholders that could have resulted from this merger. [6]
    (c) Discuss the likely reasons why this merger did not result in the benefits expected. [10]

Student's answer to (b)

Customers are likely to benefit from this merger. Global Wear will be making a higher output than the two original businesses. This should mean that it gains from economies of scale, like buying in large quantities of material for clothes more cheaply. Lower costs per unit of clothing might mean that the business lowers prices to consumers.

    Global Wear is also likely to increase profits from this merger. If it can reduce costs and sell more clothes it should be able to make higher profits. So the business will benefit too.

Authors' Comments

The first paragraph is good – although 'stakeholders' is not defined, there is an appropriate example which shows understanding. The explanation of how customers might benefit is also explained and applied to the clothing industry.

    Can you see the problem with the second paragraph? The business itself is *not* a stakeholder. If the student had explained the impact on owners/shareholders of higher profits then this would have been acceptable. Perhaps it would have helped the student to have given a definition of stakeholders – groups with a direct interest in business performance – as this would have directed the second paragraph towards a second group such as workers or suppliers.

Final revision checklist – tick when done and understood!

Topic	Textbook read	Revision complete
Measures of business size		
Economic benefits of small businesses		
Strengths and weaknesses of family businesses		
Relative advantages of small/large businesses		
Types of business growth		
Different types of integration		
Impact of integration on stakeholders		
Problems of rapid growth		

Business Objectives

4

After you have studied this chapter, you should be able to:

☞ understand why it is important for a business to set objectives
☞ recognise the key SMART features of objectives
☞ understand the links between mission statement, objectives and strategy
☞ be able to explain the factors that determine business objectives
☞ recognise potential conflicts between corporate objectives
☞ be able to discuss the importance of ethics when setting business objectives.

4.1 Why should businesses set objectives?

An objective is an aim or target for the future. If businesses do not have objectives then:

- there is no sense of direction or focus
- workers in the organisation do not know what they are aiming to achieve
- there is no way of assessing 'success' or 'failure'
- investors will not be keen to invest in the business as it is unlikely to have a clear future strategy – because there is no clear objective.

4.2 Why should objectives be SMART?

Consider this statement by a company Managing Director:

"Our company should aim to become bigger in the future and dominate the market we sell our products in".

Is this a clear and effective corporate objective?
REMEMBER: Effective objectives should be SMART (see over):

Progress Check A

1. Explain why the objective above: "Our company should aim to become bigger in the future and dominate the market we sell our products in", is not SMART.
2. Explain *two* benefits to an entrepreneur of setting clear objectives for a newly formed business.
3. Give an example of a SMART objective that a large business might set.
4. Explain *two* benefits to this business of the objective being 'measurable'.
5. Explain how the workers in a business might react if the firm had no clear objectives.
6. Give an example of an 'unrealistic objective' for a small shop selling food and drinks.

SMART objectives

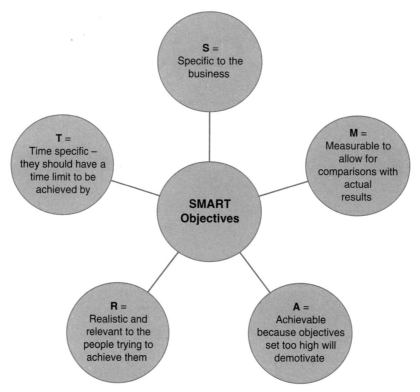

4.3 Linking mission statements, objectives and strategies

Hierarchy of objectives

> **Key terms**
>
> **Corporate aim:** long term goal of the business
> **Corporate objectives:** specific goals set for the business to achieve
> **Mission statement:** statement of the business's core aims and purpose
> **Divisional/Departmental objectives:** the specifc objectives of each division or department of the business, based on the corporate aim and objectives
> **Strategies:** long term plans to achieve objectives

Table 4.1

Advantages and Disadvantages of mission statements	
Advantages	**Disadvantages**
• Tells stakeholders what the business 'is about'	• It can be very general and just 'wishful thinking'
• The process of creating a mission statement can help bring managers together	• It does not provide SMART objectives for use within the business
• It provides a sense of purpose to managers and workers	• It may need to be revised frequently if the nature of the business changes

Further points:

1. Once a corporate objective(s) has been established the senior management of a business will then focus on developing strategies to achieve this objective.

Top tip Remember, without a clear objective, developing effective plans of action or taking strategic decisions will become almost impossible.

2. Corporate objectives should not be 'set in stone'. They may need to be adapted or changed completely over time. For example, once a newly established firm has 'survived' the first crucial few months of operation the owner may seek to expand the business or aim to achieve high profits.

3. Management by Objectives (MBO) is the process of involving all departments, teams and individuals within a business in meeting of objectives. It is an excellent way of communicating objectives to everyone in the organisation. MBO means that everyone in the organisation should be focused on achieving the same overall corporate objective.

> **Key term**
>
> **Management by Objectives:** a method of coordinating and motivating all staff within an organisation by dividing the overall aim into specific targets of each department, manager and employee

Common corporate objectives

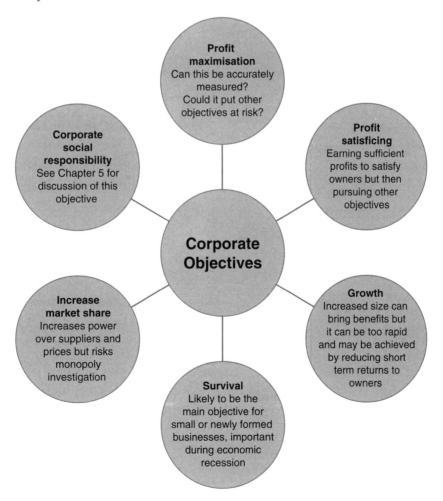

Top tip

Never confuse an objective with a strategy in your answer. An objective is what a business is trying to achieve – a strategy is the means used to achieve it.

For example, expanding the company into another country might be the strategy used to meet the objective of higher shareholder returns in the long run.

Progress Check B

1. "We intend to make our products the best known computers in the world". Do you think this is an objective or a mission statement? Explain your answer.
2. Explain why the objectives set for the marketing and finance departments of a car manufacturing business should be based on the company's overall objectives.
3. Would you advise an entrepreneur to spend time on developing a well thought out mission statement? Explain your answer.
4. Explain one reason why a business might change its objectives over time.
5. Explain one benefit to a business of adopting Management by Objectives.

4.4 Factors influencing corporate objectives

Business objectives will be influenced by:

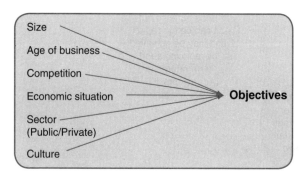

4.5 Potential conflicts between objectives

Conflicts can occur in a number of different ways:
1. maximum sales growth might conflict with a profit objective – selling *more* does not necessarily mean *higher* profits
2. short term objectives with long term objectives – investing capital for long term expansion may conflict with short term profit objectives
3. stakeholders objectives often conflict – see Chapter 5.

4.6 Ethics – should business objectives reflect ethical standards?

Key terms

Ethics: moral guidelines that influence decision making
Ethical code: a document detailing the rules and guidelines on staff behaviour that must be followed by all employees of an organisation

Should business decisions be influenced by just profit calculations – or should moral issues be considered too? This is one of the big debates in global business today. Should managers be allowed to:

- advertise directly to children?
- employ very young workers?
- pay workers as little as possible?
- pollute the environment if it is not illegal to do so?
- pay bribes to gain extra orders?

The arguments for and against ethical decisions are:
For
✓ May give business positive publicity
✓ Attracts customers who are ethically minded
✓ Attracts employees who want to work for an ethical business
✓ Avoids breaking laws and the consequences of this.

Against

X   May add to business costs, for example, paying workers above 'poverty wages'

X   May make the business uncompetitive if other firms in the industry are not acting ethically

X   Sales may be lost if bribes are not paid

X   Most customers want low prices and are not worried about how products are made or how workers are treated.

Most businesses have an ethical code. This can be used as a guide to all employees as to what behaviour is and is not acceptable in that business. However, if workers or managers are paid large bonuses for 'outstanding sales or profits', might they be tempted to break the ethical code to try to cut costs or increase sales?

Top tip

When discussing a question about ethical issues do not just state your opinion without explaining the business arguments for and against a particular decision.

Progress Check C

1.   Explain why the objectives of a business might change if it was a private limited company but is converted to a public limited company.
2.   Explain how the economic cycle of boom and recession might influence business objectives.
3.   Explain why some business analysts think that advertising products directly to children is unethical.
4.   Suggest three statements that might be included in the ethical code of a large oil company.

Multiple Choice Questions

1.   Which one of the following is the best reason for setting business objectives?
     (i)   A clear business objective guarantees that a business will achieve success in future
     (ii) It helps competitors set their own objectives and strategies for the future
     (iii) Managers will be able to decide on future strategies aimed at reaching these objectives
     (iv) Governments often make it a legal requirement for businesses to state clear objectives

2.   A business mission statement:
     (i)   sets out clearly what each individual worker should be aiming to achieve
     (ii) contains SMART objectives for the business to aim for
     (iii) is a statement of the strategies that a business intends to adopt
     (iv) communicates the central purpose of the business to stakeholders

3.   An example of a departmental or functional objective is:
     (i)   to increase sales of Product X by at least 5% in each area of the country this year
     (ii) to increase company profitability by 15%
     (iii) to encourage each worker in the organisation to reduce paper usage
     (iv) to reduce company costs by 10% over the next 2 years

4.   Which one of the following is not likely to be a suitable corporate objective for a business in the private sector?

     (i)   Increase market share in all major markets within 2 years
     (ii) Raise returns to shareholders by 15% within 3 years
     (iii) Increase employment in business divisions that are making a loss
     (iv) Develop a reputation for social responsibility while maintaining profitability

5.   The culture of senior management is likely to influence business objectives because:
     (i)   the views and beliefs of senior managers will be reflected in aims they have for the business
     (ii) shareholders will not expect senior managers to put profits before principles
     (iii) senior managers never have to consider the aims of the owners of the business when setting objectives
     (iv) the divorce between ownership and control in very large businesses means that shareholders set the main objectives

6.   An example of an ethical influence on a business decision is:
     (i)   an economic recession leads to a business closing a factory
     (ii) a supplier offers a bribe to a manager if he gives a contract to the supplier
     (iii) a manager refuses to purchase materials from a supplier using child labour
     (iv) a business increases short term profits by disposing of waste in a river

(a) Analyse how the objectives of a social enterprise are likely to differ from those of a privately owned manufacturing
company.   [8]
(b) Evaluate the extent to which setting clear business objectives will ensure that a book retailing business is successful.   [12]

Student answer to (a)

An objective is an aim to work towards. Social enterprises are managed by people who want to do good for society and help
the environment. For example they might want to operate a bus service for disabled people. This would help people who
would find it difficult to travel. Bus services are more environmentally friendly than other forms of transport. However,
social enterprises cannot operate without some income or profit so they also aim to make a financial surplus. So disabled
people might be charged for the bus service – or government might provide a payment for each person transported by bus.
Usually, any profit made by social enterprises is put back into the organisation to improve services in the future. Profit, people,
environment – this is sometimes called the 'triple bottom line' meaning there is more than one objective for social enterprises.

Privately owned companies are only interested in profit. They have not got any social or environmental aims so the only
'bottom line' they are interested in is making money for the owners. So a manufacturing business will produce in ways that
damage the environment in order to make higher profits for owners. These are the main differences in the objectives of these
two types of organisations.

Authors' Comments

This answer starts off really well. Objectives are defined. There is a very good understanding of social enterprises and their
objectives.

The weakness of the answer is the extreme view of the objectives of 'privately owned manufacturing businesses'.
Although profits are likely to be a higher priority than for social enterprises it is wrong to assume that this is all they are
aiming to achieve. These businesses often **do** have objectives other than just maximising profit. Growth, market share,
maintaining ethical and environmental standards are all possible alternatives to the 'profit is everything' view taken
by the student.

Final revision checklist – tick when done and understood!

Topic	Textbook read	Revision complete
Advantages of setting SMART objectives		
Mission statements, business aims, corporate objectives		
Examples of corporate objectives		
Factors influencing corporate objectives		
Conflicts between objectives		
Ethical influences on objectives and decisions		

Stakeholders 5

5.1 Stakeholders and the stakeholder concept

Key terms

Stakeholder: people or groups of people who can be affected by, and therefore have an interest in, any action by an organisation

Stakeholder concept: the idea that businesses and their managers have responsibilities to many groups not just shareholders (business owners)

Top tip

Careful! Shareholders own shares in limited companies but the term 'stakeholders' has a much wider meaning.

Do not confuse these two terms – and do not forget that shareholders are just one of the many stakeholder groups.

Most organisations accept, in some degree, the stakeholder concept and have moved away from the view that all business decisions must be taken with only shareholders interests in mind. Why this change?

✓ Stricter legal controls over business decisions, for example, pollution levels, wage levels, product standards
✓ Increasing recognition that business activity should operate in wider interests of society
✓ Extensive negative publicity for companies and senior managers who are seen not to be acting in society's interests – and the impact this can have on long run profitability too.

5.2 How stakeholders are affected by business actions

Businesses have responsibilities to stakeholders. For example:

✓ customers – good value, safe products, fair competition
✓ workers – fair pay, job security, safe working conditions
✓ suppliers – payment on time
✓ local community – pollution kept to minimum, support for local groups.

An example of an important strategic business decision that affected many stakeholders was the decision by Burberry clothing to relocate some production from the UK to factories in China. How were stakeholder groups affected? Did Burberry meet stakeholders' objectives?

Impact on stakeholder groups of Burberry's decision

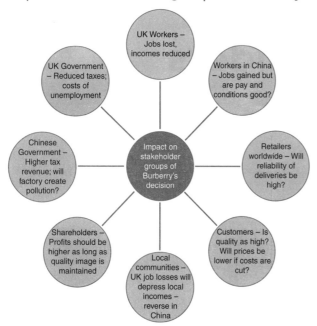

5.3 Rights and responsibilities of stakeholders

Table 5.1

Stakeholder group	Rights	Commonly accepted responsibilities
Customers	• Receive goods and services that meet national legal standards • To be offered replacements, repairs, compensation in the event of failure of the product or service	• To be honest – to pay for goods bought or services received when requested. • Not to steal • Not to make false claims about poor service, under performing goods or failed items
Suppliers	• To be paid on time – as laid down either by law or by the service agreement agreed between the business and suppliers. • To be treated fairly by the purchasing business, for example, not to be threatened with losing big contracts from much more powerful customer businesses	• Supply goods and services ordered by the business in the time and condition as laid down by the purchase contract or 'suppliers service agreements'
Employees	• To be paid at least the national minimum wage • To be given an employment contract with reasonable terms and conditions • In most countries, to be allowed to join a trade union if desired • Increasingly, workers expect to be involved in business activities and to be given opportunities to participate	• To be honest • Meet the conditions and requirements of the employment contract • To cooperate with management in all reasonable requests
Local community	• To be consulted about major changes that affect it, for example, expansion or rationalisation (closure) plans • Not have lives of local residents very badly affected by the businesses activities, for example, pollution or excessive truck movements	• To cooperate with the business, where reasonable to do so, on expansion and other plans • To meet reasonable requests from business for local services such as public transport (for example, to allow staff to get to work) and waste disposal

(Continued)

Table 5.1 (*Continued*)

Stakeholder group	Rights	Commonly accepted responsibilities
Government	• Businesses have the duty to government to meet all legal constraints such as producing only legal goods, and to pay taxes on time	• Treat businesses equally under the law • Prevent unfair competition which could damage business survival chances • Establish good trading links with other countries to allow international trade

5.4 Corporate social responsibility

Key term

Corporate Social Responsibility (CSR): the concept that business should consider the interests of society in its activities and decisions, over and above its legal responsibilities

CSR can be demonstrated in a number of different ways. These are just some examples:

✓ paying higher than legal minimum wages
✓ improving working conditions
✓ improving product safety standards beyond legal minimum
✓ cutting waste and pollution
✓ delaying redundancies or production cutbacks to support workers' job security.

Top tip
Don't forget to explain that just meeting legal obligations is not necessarily being 'socially responsible'. Many CSR policies go beyond the legal minimum requirements of business activity.

Table 5.2

Advantages of CSR	Disadvantages of CSR
• Customer loyalty • Employee loyalty and improved motivation • Increased sales to socially aware and concerned customers • Government contracts – if governments want to be seen to be doing business with such companies • Less risk of legal challenges • Good publicity, for example, from supporting local charities or good customer service • Local community more likely to accept expansion plans • Can result in higher long term profits due to above benefits	• May increase costs: higher pay; better working conditions; more quality checks; better pollution controls • May receive negative publicity if it is perceived as being 'window dressing' or 'greenwash' • Shareholders may sell shares if they consider that short term profits are being cut to pay for CSR policies • Some customers prefer lowest possible prices – less worried about 'how' a product is made • Profit maximisation *is* socially responsible – many stakeholder groups can benefit from this increased profitability

Most large companies – and many smaller businesses – produce an annual social audit (which often includes an environmental audit).

These can have both benefits and drawbacks to businesses that produce them (see figure on next page).

Benefits	**Limitations**
Identifies how well a business is meeting its social objectives	May not be independently audited
Outlines the social objectives to be met in future	It can be expensive in time and money to produce such audits – are they worthwhile?
A well publicised social audit can improve a businesses public image and this might have a marketing benefit	Not legally required – why ... bother them? Consumers might just prefer cheap products
Local community may be more likely to accept business plans, for example, for expansion	The business may exaggerate its social achievements – a form of window dressing or 'greenwash'

Figure 5.1 Social audits

Key term

Social audit: a report on the impact the activities of a business have had on society – for example, pollution; health and safety record; energy use; waste created

Progress Check B

1. Suggest two other examples of data that might be included in a social audit, other than those referred to above.
2. How might increasing company profits benefit any *two* stakeholder groups, other than shareholders?
3. How might a business benefit from treating its workers well?
4. Why might it be important for a successful business to have excellent relations with the local community?
5. Explain why a government is interested in the activities of businesses within its country.

5.5 Conflicting stakeholder objectives

Shareholders' objectives often conflict. It is often impossible for a business to satisfy all stakeholders all of the time. A few examples are given in Table 5.3.

Table 5.3

Decision	Groups that benefit	Groups that lose
Supermarket – expand the business operation by building a new warehouse	**Workers** – more jobs **Customers** – more reliable deliveries and wider choice of stock **Government** – increased economic activity and tax revenues **Suppliers** – likely to be more orders	**Local community** – additional transport of goods, for example, more trucks on roads **Environmental groups** – building of warehouse uses 'greenfield' site and extra truck movements create more pollution
Café chain: purchase more coffee supplies from 'fair trade' producers, paying above market prices	**Suppliers** – offered 'fair trade' prices above the market price **Local community (of suppliers) –** higher local incomes will increase spending	**Customers** – prices might rise to pay for the higher cost of 'ethical' supplies **Non fair trade suppliers and their workers** – fewer orders may lead to going out of business

All important businesses decisions must involve some stakeholders gaining and some losing and therefore a compromise might be necessary. Business managers will have to prioritise – which stakeholder groups are more important in this decision – and which ones might have to accept a negative impact? Can the business do anything to reduce the size of this negative impact? For example:

- ✓ pay substantial redundancy payments to workers who are losing their jobs
- ✓ support local community groups if some residents have to move for a new coal mine
- ✓ plant many trees to support an environmental group to counteract the carbon emissions of a new factory.

Top tip

If you are asked to write about CSR you may want to question why many businesses adopt this concept.

Multiple Choice Questions

1. Which of the following is the best definition of 'stakeholders'?
    (i) Any group that buys goods from or sells goods to a business
    (ii) Any group that owns a business
    (iii) Any group with an interest in the activities of a business
    (iv) Any other business with a stake in the organisation

2. One of the most likely reasons why businesses increasingly adopt the 'stakeholder concept' is:
    (i) it reduces business costs such as wages and suppliers costs
    (ii) it reduces the taxes paid to government
    (iii) satisfying stakeholder objectives can lead to good publicity
    (iv) most large companies are no longer owned by shareholders

3. One of the benefits of accepting responsibilities to employees is:
    (i) it will allow lower wages to be paid
    (ii) it will reduce the need for job enrichment
    (iii) labour turnover could increase
    (iv) easier to recruit effective workers

4. One of the arguments against a business aiming to be socially responsible is:
    (i) no one takes any notice of corporate social responsibility

    (ii) businesses should aim to maximise profits
    (iii) being socially responsible will always increase sales but it always leads to lower profits
    (iv) there are no costs involved if a business breaks the law on pollution or waste disposal

5. When discussing corporate social responsibility, the term 'window dressing' means:
    (i) ensuring that the business always acts responsibly even if this is not reported on
    (ii) producing a social audit so that all stakeholders can read about the company's CSR policies
    (iii) only using ethically sourced clothing and other products in shop window displays
    (iv) appearing to act in a socially responsible way to cover up the negative impact of a company's activities

6. One possible reason why Shell created its Foundation and other charitable funds have been set up by big businesses is:
    (i) it is a legal requirement for businesses to support some charities
    (ii) the funds can be used to balance out some of the negative stakeholder impacts of business activities
    (iii) the people supported by the funds are usually the biggest customers for these businesses
    (iv) finance used to support the funds does not in any way reduce the returns payable to shareholders

Exam-style Question

"The opening of the new open cast copper mine in this country will benefit all stakeholder groups."

This was a recent headline in a company's internal newspaper. The NMR Mining Group is suggesting that its investment in Country *A*, a developing country, would be for the good of everyone. The company plan was to use a large area for open-cast copper mining. Few people live in this area. A new road would be built from the capital city to transport the copper. The world price of copper is very high. It is needed by electronics industries in industrialised countries.

(a) Identify TWO stakeholder groups likely to be adversely affected by this decision. [2]

(b) Explain how both stakeholder groups might be adversely affected. [4]

(c) Evaluate the extent to which business decisions lead to a conflict of stakeholder objectives. [10]

Student's answer to (a) and (b)

(a) Local community; competitors

(b) Although the local community might benefit from increased job vacancies, it could also be affected by dust, noise and pollution from the mine. This could affect local peoples' health. The water supply might be polluted from waste from the mine workings. The new road would mean trucks and other vehicle movements – creating further air and noise pollution.

    Competitors might be affected by lower prices for copper. As the new mine increases total supply, this might cause a fall in the world price of copper, reducing competitor's profits.

Authors' Comments

Very good answers

    Will this student now be able to show the same level of analytical skills in answering question (c)? Also, judgement is required when answering (c). If the student is able to refer to several business examples and assess the degree of conflict between stakeholder objectives – and whether this can be reduced by business taking 'corrective' action – then evaluation will have been demonstrated.

Revision checklist – tick when done and understood!

Topic	Textbook read	Revision complete
Examples of stakeholder groups		
The stakeholder concept		
The responsibilities of business to stakeholders		
The responsibilities of stakeholders to business		
Corporate social responsibility and social audits		
Conflicting stakeholder objectives		

External Influences on Business Activity

6

Revision Objectives

After you have studied this chapter, you should be able to:

☞ know how laws impact on business activity – positively and negatively

☞ understand the threats and opportunities from technological change

☞ recognise how changes in society can affect business activity

☞ understand the increasing influence which environmental considerations are having on business decisions

☞ recognise the value and limitations of environmental audits.

6.1 Legal influences on business activity

Laws which affect business activity include:

Table 6.1

Types of laws	Common requirements	Costs to business	Benefits to business
Consumer laws	• Product safety • Consumer rights for refund or replacement • Weights and Measures • Advertising accuracy	• Higher product development costs • Higher quality/safer material costs • Cost of refunds/replacements	• Consumers more confident about product safety • Consumer loyalty from improved products and services • Consumer confidence in promotional and advertising campaigns
Employment laws	• Minimum wage level • Health and safety at work • Employment conditions, for example, holidays/pensions • Employment contracts • Anti-discrimination in employment/recruitment • Trade Union rights	• Higher wage costs, may lead to relocation to low wage country • Costs of improved safety equipment • Costs of meeting legal requirements on conditions of employment • Costs of monitoring employment/ and recruitment practices to avoid discrimination	• More motivated staff • Fewer accidents at work • Less risk of bad publicity, for example, resulting from discrimination of workers • More likely to sell products to ethical 'customers'
Competition laws	• Not engaging in monopolistic and anti-competitive practices	• Not able to 'fix' prices or engage in uncompetitive actions • Limits to mergers and takeovers as monopolies may be illegal or investigated	• Customers will prefer to deal with businesses that are thought to be competing fairly • Less risk of smaller firms being forced out of business by dominant firms

(Continued)

Table 6.1 (*Continued*)

Types of laws	Common requirements	Costs to business	Benefits to business
Planning and environmental laws	• Restrictions on location of industry, for example, in towns/cities or in areas of natural beauty • Control business developments that damage the environment	• Cheapest sites may not be available for construction • Additional costs of meeting planning laws, for example, waste disposal methods • Applications for planning take time	• Less risk of businesses being accused of damaging residents' health or damaging the environment • Can promote the business as being 'environmentally friendly'

Top tip

Do not be too negative about legal constraints on business activity. They help to provide a framework in which responsible businesses can operate profitably whilst not exploiting workers, consumers or the environment.

Progress Check A

1. Would you advise a restaurant owner to try to cut costs by reducing the frequency of cleaning the kitchens? Explain your answer.
2. Explain *one* benefit to employees and *one* benefit to employers of having a formal contract of employment.
3. How might small businesses risk being forced out of business by anti-competitive practices of larger firms in the industry?
4. If some consumers are happy to pay very low prices for potentially dangerous products, why does the government prevent this with consumer laws?
5. Explain how a business might be affected by an increase in the country's minimum wage level.

Top tip

Be prepared to discuss the impact of laws in your own country on business activity – you will not be expected to have specific knowledge of laws in any other country.

6.2 Technological change – the opportunities and threats

Benefits

Problems

New product development
Example: iPad
Improved efficiency
Example: CAM quicker
design (CAD)

Costs:
• Capital
• Maintenance/Updating
• Training

More effective communication.
Example: emails

Reliability/Security

New marketing methods.
Example: online selling

Need for adaptable workforce
Effective management of change needed

Efficient data processing
Smarter
market knoweldge

Data protection issues

Technological change – the opportunities and threats

Key terms

Information technology: the use of electronic technology to gather, store, process and communicate information

Computer Aided Design (CAD): using computers and IT to assist in the designing of products

Computer Aided Manufacturing (CAM): using computers and computer controlled machinery to speed up production processes and make them more flexible

Note: See chapter 21 for CAD/CAM

Top tip

Nearly all businesses use modern technology to some degree. **But** remember that new technology does not solve all business problems of inefficiency or poor communication. It can create problems too – especially if not well implemented.

Remember, too, employment issues are not necessarily negative, for example, if workers learn new skills that make them more flexible and motivated.

Progress Check B

1. A furniture making business adopts new computer controlled production methods. Explain which business costs might increase and which might reduce as a result of this decision.
2. Explain *two* uses of IT in a typical business office.
3. Explain *two* possible uses of IT by a marketing department of a business.
4. Explain *three* important stages in the successful implementation of a new technology production system.
5. Suggest one type of business that might employ very little IT.
6. Explain the importance of new technology product developments to a business of your choice.

6.3 Impact of social changes on business activity

In most countries there are significant changes occurring in the structure of society. The main ones are given in Table 6.2.

Table 6.2

Social change	Potential positive business impact	Potential negative business impact
Rapidly increasing population	• Increased potential market • Increased potential workforce	• Increased demand for available land for expansion
Ageing population	• Increased demand for 'old-age related' products • Older workers often more loyal and experienced	• Increased taxation as government has increased pension and other costs • More difficult to recruit younger workers • Older workers may be more resistant to change
Increased numbers of women in workforce	• Greater potential workforce • Higher family incomes created • Potential for increased demand for some products	• Increased levels of maternity leave/pay
Increased multi-culturalism, for example, through migration	• Increased demand potential for culturally specific products • Potential workforce increases if there is net immigration • Foreign workers may be prepared to accept lower wages • New ideas, new products	• Existing products may need to be adapted to suit cultural differences • Cultural differences may need to be reflected in HR policy, for example, different religious holidays may require careful staff planning • Possible friction with existing workers if foreign workers accept lower pay

A

6.4 Influences on environmental policies of business

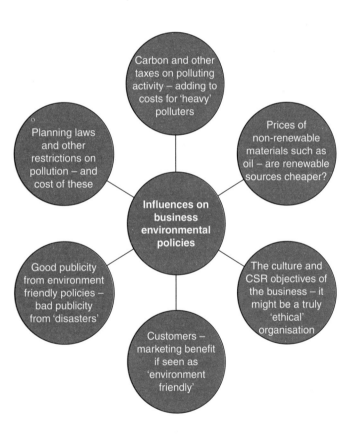

Environmental audits

Environmental audits are part of a businesses Corporate Social Responsibility report.

Benefits

✓ Highlights the efforts made by the business to reduce negative environmental impact, for example, using less energy, producing less waste, reducing 'carbon footprint', using renewable resources.

✓ Informs stakeholders of the progress the business is making to reduce negative environmental impact. This could reduce pressure group activity.

✓ Gives future targets for improvements in environmental impact.

Limitations

✗ Not a legal requirement in most countries – should time and resources be spent on producing it?

✗ It will contain details of current energy use and waste production levels. Even if these are improving, many companies will still be huge users of energy or of non-renewable resources. This might increase pressure group activity.

✗ It must reflect a truthful record of what the company is doing – if there is evidence of 'window dressing' or 'greenwash' then much bad publicity will result.

> **Key term**
>
> **Environmental audit:** report assessing the impact of a business's activities on the environment

Pressure groups

The power of pressure groups increases when:

✓ they have many members and can organise an effective consumer boycott

✓ they have influence over government through lobbying and having popular objectives

✓ they are well organised and well financed, for example, to pay for media campaigns

✓ the company the pressure group is targeting is short of resources, for example, cash; wants to avoid bad publicity and will lose profits quickly from consumer boycotts or other direct action.

> **Key term**
>
> **Pressure group:** organisations created by people with a common interest or aim which put pressure on businesses and governments to change policies to reach a pressure group objective

Top tip

Remember that in the short term a business might cut costs and increase profits by using environmentally damaging methods.

For example, dumping waste cheaply in a river.

You might be asked to consider whether this could damage its long term reputation and profitability.

Other businesses may seem to use 'environmentally friendly' tactics as part of marketing and you might be asked to consider the ethics of this.

Progress Check D

1. Explain why a business might produce an environmental audit even if the government does not demand it.
2. Why might an increase in the price of oil encourage a business to become more 'environmentally friendly'?
3. Explain the marketing benefits that might result from introducing systems and machinery that cause little damage to the environment.
4. Should a business in a competitive industry produce in a less developed country with few environmental controls? Explain your answer.
5. Explain why the impact on profits of a new machine that uses less energy might be difficult to calculate.

Multiple Choice Questions

1. Legal controls over business activity may aim to achieve which one of the following?
   (i) Reduce prices to consumers below the cost of making a product
   (ii) Reduce exploitation of workers by powerful employers
   (iii) Lower business profits so that less investment takes place
   (iv) Reduce number of businesses so that consumer choice becomes easier

2. Which one of the following is a common benefit of Employment Laws?
   (i) Businesses have to employ more workers to reduce unemployment
   (ii) Workers must be trained by businesses to improve their chances of promotion
   (iii) Workers must be given a written employment contract containing key conditions
   (iv) Businesses have to increase workers' pay regularly

3. One reason why a business may not introduce Information Technology (IT) could be:
   (i) IT is still under development and most computers are unreliable
   (ii) a multinational business is so large that the purchase of computer systems would be beyond its resources
   (iii) few other business in the world use IT so it would not be possible to communicate with them using IT
   (iv) a sole-trader offers services to consumers that do not require IT to provide them

4. An ageing population could lead to which one of the following possible effects on a business?
   (i) The business increases research into new products for the younger generation
   (ii) The business will increase its total level of employment
   (iii) The business may increase the age at which its workers can retire
   (iv) The business will continue to make the same products that it developed many years ago

5. One claimed benefit of producing an environmental audit as part of a firm's Corporate Social Responsibility report is:
   (i) it will reduce the costs of the business
   (ii) the printing of the environmental audit will improve the environment
   (iii) it proves to stakeholders that the businesses operations will now have no negative impact on the environment
   (iv) it indicates to stakeholders how the business is attempting to reduce its environmental impact

6. One of the reasons why pressure groups are sometimes successful in changing the decisions of business is:
   (i) a consumer boycott of a firm's products could result in lower profits
   (ii) the business has large cash reserves
   (iii) the business sells products to other business customers not directly to consumers
   (iv) the business has a large promotion budget spent on TV and newspaper advertising

Exam-style Question

AMG manufactures cars that are sold at low prices. It is profitable but the profit margin on cars is falling. The cars have a reputation for reliability but they are not very attractively designed and they use old fashioned engines. They are painted in a very limited range of colours. Due to the equipment and production methods not having changed for 20 years, the cars are standard models with very few variations allowed for customer needs.

The cars have much less safety equipment than models produced by other manufacturers. Some consumers do not worry about this as they just want cheap cars. Some sales have been lost, however, because of the safety issues – some potential buyers lack confidence in AMG cars. The government is planning a new consumer law to make it illegal to produce cars without the latest safety equipment.

AMG workers perform boring, repetitive flow line production jobs. They are paid production bonuses but most of them earn just enough to buy food and other essentials for their families. Some workers want to join a trade union but AMG management are opposed to this. Most workers are told that if they do not work hard they could be sacked yet few of them have written employment contracts – it is not yet a legal requirement in the country in which AMG operates. Productivity levels are low by international standards.

(a) Analyse how changes in consumer protection laws and employees' rights laws could affect AMG. [10]
(b) Evaluate the extent to which AMG might increase its profits from adopting production methods using new technology. [16]

Student's plan for (b)

Explain 'technology' and give examples such as CAD/CAM.
CAD could help businesses design/develop new products quickly.
CAM new technology can increase efficiency and reduce unit variable costs.
Can make production system more flexible – wider range of products – this could increase demand and revenue in long term.
Quality of product could become more consistent.
BUT: higher fixed costs of capital equipment, training etc. In short term, unreliable technology could increase costs too.
So, if increased revenue and lower unit costs outweigh the capital costs – profits should increase.

Authors' Comments

Can you identify the strengths and weaknesses of this plan? It is strong on knowledge and analysis – there are key advantages and disadvantages of technology that the student seems able to fully explain. The last point suggests scope for evaluation too.

BUT – where is the *application to AMG*? The student makes no attempt to consider how the product/productivity problems of AMG might be solved by new technology. A mass market producer of cars such as AMG is likely to benefit greatly from the reduced unit variable costs that technology can offer – probably leading to higher profit margins on cars.
CAD could help design new cars offering better product safety; CAM could increase productivity and make production system more flexible – scope for more colours and more variants of car models.

However, with falling profit margins can AMG afford new technology? Will workers be prepared to accept it and the training needed without being offered secure employment? Will company be able to shed the old image its cars have? Will benefits and cost savings for AMG outweigh the fixed costs?

Specific application to the business in the case – with clear and applied evaluation – will be needed.

Revision checklist – tick when done and understood!

Topic	Textbook read	Revision complete
Laws and their impact on business activity		
Technological changes and their impact on businesses		
Social changes and their impact on businesses		
Environmental constraints – how business can respond to these		

External Economic Influences

7

Revision Objectives

After you have studied this chapter, you should be able to:

☞ know the main economic objectives of governments and how they might conflict

☞ understand why economic growth is important and know the swings in the business cycle

☞ recognise and assess the different strategies that businesses might pursue in different stages of the business cycle

☞ understand and assess how business activity and decisions can be affected by changes in inflation, unemployment and government economic decisions

☞ know how exchange rate movements impact on business activity.

7.1 Government economic objectives

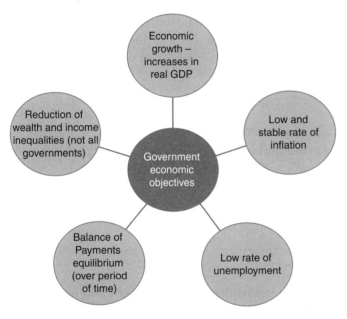

In practice, achieving all objectives at the same time is difficult. There are conflicts.

For example:

✓ rapid economic growth can help to reduce unemployment – but inflation might rise

✓ economic growth, by increasing peoples' living standards and their ability to buy imports, often leads to a Balance of Payments (Current account) deficit.

7.2 Economic growth and the business cycle – impact on business strategy

This is a typical business cycle.

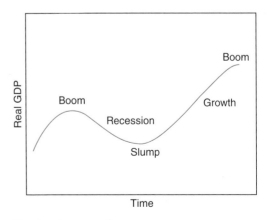

The business cycle

Key terms

Economic growth: an increase in a country's productive potential measured by an increase in real GDP

Gross Domestic Product (GDP): the total value of goods and services produced in a country in one year – real GDP has been adjusted for the effects of inflation

Business cycle: regular swings in economic activity, measured by real GDP, that occurs in economies varying from boom conditions to recession

Recession: a period of six months or more of declining real GDP

Income elasticity of demand: measures the responsiveness of demand for a product after a change in consumer incomes

How can businesses respond to these swings in the economic or business cycle?

Stage of business cycle	Possible business strategies
Economic growth Average consumer incomes should be increasing	• Increase prices to take advantage of higher consumer demand **but** will demand fall? • Develop new products that appeal to consumers with higher incomes – income elastic products. **but** this could be an expensive strategy.
Recession Average consumer incomes likely to fall	• Lower prices as consumers have less to spend – **but** will perceived quality be lower? • Develop new products (perhaps 'inferior' goods) that appeal to consumers with lower incomes – **but** will this damage the brand image and existing consumer loyalty?

Progress Check A

1. What does 'an increase in real GDP' mean?
2. What is likely to happen to average incomes – or living standards – during a period of economic growth?
3. Why might you expect the demand for an inferior product to increase during a recession?

4. Explain an important feature of the 'boom' stage of the business cycle.
5. What would you expect to happen to the level of unemployment during a recession and why?

7.3 Inflation and unemployment – how business activity can be affected

Key terms

Inflation: an increase in the average price level

Unemployment: exists when members of the working population are willing and able to work but are unable to find a job

Causes of inflation

Inflation has two major causes

  ✓   Demand pull inflation: caused by too much demand for available supply of products

Businesses may be able to increase prices without demand falling – but this will depend on price elasticity

  ✓   Cost push inflation: caused by increased costs of production

Businesses may be forced to increase selling prices to avoid making a loss – but the impact on sales and revenue will depend on price elasticity.

Causes of unemployment

Unemployment has several causes.

Key terms

Cyclical unemployment: caused by low demand for products during recession stage of the business cycle

Structural unemployment: caused by decline in important industries

Frictional unemployment: caused by workers losing/leaving jobs and taking a long time to find others – perhaps because they have the 'wrong' skills

Impact of unemployment on business

Unemployment can impact on businesses both negatively and positively.

Negative impact

- ✗ Reduces incomes of those unemployed – less to spend on products
- ✗ May lead to increased taxes to pay welfare benefits – reducing retained profits (if corporation tax increased) or reducing consumer demand (if income tax increased)
- ✗ Unemployed workers lose skills and work incentives – reduces the quality of the labour force.

Positive impact

- ✓ May encourage work incentive of those in employment to reduce chances of losing jobs
- ✓ Increased supply of available labour may allow firms to offer reduced wages – or not to increase wages
- ✓ Unemployed workers may be prepared to move to regions of country where there is labour shortage.

Progress Check B

1. Explain one reason why some unemployed workers might find it difficult to find a job during a period of economic growth.
2. Will all businesses be able to increase prices, with little impact on demand, during a period of inflation? Explain your answer.
3. Give two possible causes of cost push inflation.
4. Why might a business be able to reduce the average labour cost of production during a period of high unemployment?
5. Why might a business find it easier to retain (keep) staff during a period of high unemployment?

7.4 Government economic policies – how business strategy can adapt

> **Key terms**
>
> **Fiscal policy:** decisions about government spending, taxes and government borrowing
> **Monetary policy:** decisions about the rate of interest and supply of money in the economy

Fiscal policy can be used to:

- ✓ raise revenue for government spending
- ✓ vary government spending levels, for example, on health and education
- ✓ boost spending on goods and services in the economy by using expansionary fiscal policy, for example, during a recession
- ✓ cut spending on goods and services if inflation is a major problem
- ✓ cut the government's budget deficit if this is becoming too large

Expansionary fiscal policy operates in the following way:

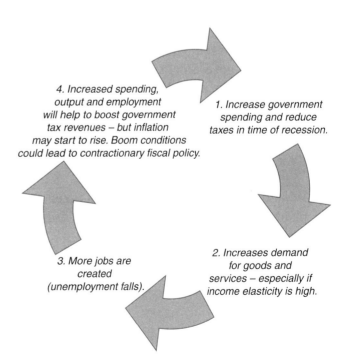

1. Increase government spending and reduce taxes in time of recession.

2. Increases demand for goods and services – especially if income elasticity is high.

3. More jobs are created (unemployment falls).

4. Increased spending, output and employment will help to boost government tax revenues – but inflation may start to rise. Boom conditions could lead to contractionary fiscal policy.

Monetary policy and interest rates are controlled in most countries by the Central Bank. This bank will have the objective of keeping low inflation. If inflation is too high the Central Bank may increase interest rates:

4. Inflation rate should fall – to the central bank target rate. If not, interest rates may have to be increased again.

1. Interest rates increased to try to reduce rate of inflation.

2. Consumers increase saving, reduce spending, businesses spend less on investment. Borrowing by consumers & businesses falls. Currency appreciates.

3. Demand for goods and services falls. Export demand falls. Import demand increases. Less demand pull pressure. Businesses less likely to increase prices

Top tip You will not be asked technical questions about fiscal and monetary policy – but you will need to know how government policy decisions are likely to affect different businesses.

Progress Check C

1. What decisions might a government take if it planned to introduce an 'expansionary fiscal policy'?
2. Why might the demand for some businesses products be little affected by a reduction in income tax?

3. How might an increase in a country's rate of corporation tax (on profits) affect a multinational company's plans to invest in the country?
4. Which business is likely to be more affected by an increase in interest rates: petrol retailing business or house construction business? Explain your answer.
5. Under what economic circumstances is a central bank likely to increase interest rates?

7.5 Exchange rates – how business activity can be affected

Key terms

Exchange rate: price of a currency in terms of another
Exchange rate appreciation: rise in the value of a currency relative to other currencies
Exchange rate depreciation: fall in the value of a currency relative to other currencies

Impact of exchange rate appreciation

- Costs of imports fall – business may decide to import more materials/components from foreign suppliers; consumers may buy cheaper imported goods rather than those made domestically
- Export prices increase – this makes exports less competitive and foreign demand may fall
- It would now be cheaper – than before the appreciation – for a domestically based business to locate in a foreign country.

Impact of exchange rate depreciation

- Cost of imports rise – domestically produced goods appear better value and demand for them might increase

- Export prices fall – demand for exports might increase. Businesses may now be more likely to expand into foreign markets
- It would now be cheaper – than before the depreciation – for foreign businesses to locate in the domestic country, creating more competition for local businesses.

Top tip

Many students get the effects of currency appreciation or depreciation the 'wrong way round'! Avoid this!

Progress Check D

1. Give a numerical example of an exchange rate appreciation of your own country's currency.
2. Give a numerical example of an exchange rate depreciation of your own country's currency.
3. Explain why a business importing components and exporting completed products would **lose** and **gain** from a currency appreciation.
4. Why might a business be encouraged to begin exporting following a depreciation of the currency?

Multiple Choice Questions

1. Which of the following is **not** an economic objective of most governments?
   (i) Keep the rate of inflation low
   (ii) Achieve a steady rate of economic growth
   (iii) Maintain a low level of unemployment
   (iv) Reduce the level of employment

2. One of the common features of an economic 'boom' is:
   (i) a reduction in the rate of inflation
   (ii) a reduction in the rate of employment in the economy
   (iii) an increase in demand for income elastic products
   (iv) a reduction in land and property prices

3. During a long period of economic growth, which of the following statements is likely to be correct?
   (i) Manufacturers of essential products may try to develop a range of income elastic goods
   (ii) Retailers will often reduce the price of products to try to reverse falling consumer demand
   (iii) Manufacturers of income elastic products will cut back on production
   (iv) The number of entrepreneurs setting up new businesses is likely to fall

4. Which of the following is the most likely cause of cost-push inflation?
   (i) An increase in consumer demand
   (ii) An increase in demand for a country's exports
   (iii) A rise in demand for essential commodities such as oil
   (iv) An increase in government subsidies to industry

5. A reduction in the rate of interest set by a country's Central Bank is likely to lead to:
   (i) house construction businesses cutting back on output
   (ii) a fall in the value of a country's currency exchange rate
   (iii) an increase in demand for inferior goods
   (iv) a fall in expansion investment decisions by industry

6. An appreciation of a country's currency exchange rate is most likely to lead to businesses in that country:
   (i) importing more raw materials and increasing prices in export markets
   (ii) reducing imports of raw materials and reducing prices in export markets
   (iii) reducing outsourcing from firms in other countries
   (iv) increasing prices in the domestic market to be more competitive against imports

Exam-style Question

TeenPrint

Ahmed set up TeenPrint with some friends. They each invested $5000. The business, located in Country A, publishes a magazine for teenagers called 'TeenMag'. It is printed on imported paper as this is cheaper than that produced in Country A. The magazine sold so well in the first few months that expanded production facilities were opened using old but cheap printing machines. Production levels increased but print and picture quality was poor.

The owners TeenPrint were approached by a venture capital business called Novak. The proposal was to convert TeenPrint to a private limited company in which Novak would have a 50% stake for an investment of $40 000. Ahmed and the other owners agreed to this as they realised that the capital injected could be used to purchase new computer-controlled printing machines and pay development costs for an online version of TeenMag.

These developments have proven to be successful. Production quality is now much improved and the online magazine is very popular. A new magazine is planned. It could be aimed at either older people – say 56–70 year olds – or at 20–35 year olds. Market research results suggest that the older group buy more magazines than 20–35 year olds but their incomes do not rise with inflation. In contrast, the incomes of the 20–35 year olds usually increase faster than inflation. Ahmed thought that the economic forecasts shown in Table 1 would be useful when making this decision.

Some printing workers within TeenPrint are worried about job security and the way in which they are managed at work. The sales of the printed TeenMag magazine have declined as the success of the online version has grown. Ahmed has tried to reassure them that a new magazine will help to secure their jobs. He is not prepared to change the ways he pays the print workers though – by piece rate – or change the structured and authoritarian way in which they are managed.

Table 1

Economic forecasts for Country A			
	2013	2014	2015
Real GDP growth rate (%)	4	2	1
Inflation rate (%)	6	7	9
Interest rate (%)	5	7	8
Exchange rate index (2012 = 100)	100	90	85
Unemployment rate (%)	10	13	15

Evaluate the extent to which external economic change will be the most important factor determining TeenPrint's future profitability. Refer to data in Table 1 in your answer. [20]

Adapted from Cambridge 9707 Paper 31 June 2010

Student's plan

Explain three of the economic forecasts (haven't got time for all five).

Analyse how each forecast might impact on TeenPrint's profits, for example, lower rate of economic growth – this could reduce the growth of consumers incomes. This could limit the future demand increase for magazines and reduce profits. **But** how income elastic is demand for magazines?

Higher inflation will reduce consumers' real incomes (after inflation). Impact greater on older readers. Higher costs of production (reducing profits) – could TeenPrint increase prices? **Depends** on price elasticity.

Depreciating exchange rate – raises prices of imported paper. Adds to TeenPrints costs and reduces profit margin. **but** how important is paper cost out of total costs?

Final evaluation: Many factors influence TeenPrints profits – not just economic data. For example, whether the HR problem with workers can be solved; choice of second magazine could be very important for profits too. Perhaps most important factor is Ahmed's decision making skills – can he deal with a changing external environment?

Authors' Comments

This is a very detailed essay plan (you would not have time for one this detailed in the examination!). The student has selected 3 pieces of data to discuss – this is a good strategy. No need to comment on **all** data presented.

It is a very good plan as it has clear structure; useful references to the case; good opportunities for analysis and a number of evaluative points to be developed.

This plan should be the basis of a good answer.

Revision checklist – tick when done and understood!

Topic	Textbook read	Revision complete
Stages of the business cycle		
How business strategy might change during economic growth and recession		
How inflation and unemployment can affect business		
Different government economic policies and how business strategies are affected		
Exchange rate changes and their impact on businesses		

Management and Leadership

8.1 Functions of management

Managers of a business perform many important functions:

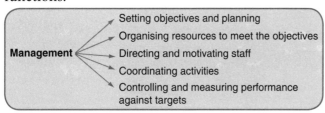

Management →
- Setting objectives and planning
- Organising resources to meet the objectives
- Directing and motivating staff
- Coordinating activities
- Controlling and measuring performance against targets

Key term

Manager: responsible for setting objectives, organising resources and motivating staff so that the organisations aims are met

Progress Check A

1. Give three examples of how businesses could be badly managed.
2. Why are objectives important for managers?
3. Give examples of how a manager of a supermarket could undertake each of the five functions of management.

8.2 Mintzberg's management roles

To carry out these functions, managers have to undertake many different roles.

Mintzberg's managerial roles		
Interpersonal	Figurehead	Symbolic leader, for example, meeting important visitors to the business
	Leader	Motivator, selector, for example, explaining his/her vision for the business
	Liaison	Internal, external, for example, leading or 'chairing' meetings
Informational	Monitor	Collector, for example, attending conferences and gaining information about the industry
	Disseminator	Making information available, for example, communicating with key staff
	Spokesperson	Communicating externally, for example, appearing on TV news programmes
Decisional	Entrepreneur	New ideas/opportunities, for example, encouraging workers and managers to develop new ideas
	Disturbances	Responding to change, for example, developing strategies to deal with competitive threats
	Resource allocator	Deciding on spending, for example, approving budgets for the business and its departments
	Negotiator	Representing the organisation, for example, meeting government ministers to influence policy.

8.3 Qualities of leaders

Not everyone can become an effective leader. Successful leaders often have all or most of the following personal qualities.

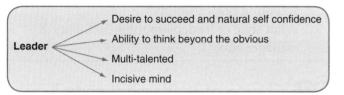

Leader
- Desire to succeed and natural self confidence
- Ability to think beyond the obvious
- Multi-talented
- Incisive mind

Key term

Leadership: the art of motivating a group of people towards achieving a common objective

Progress Check B

1. Give two features of a poor leader.
2. Give four features of a good leader and explain why each one is important.
3. Explain two problems a business might experience from poor leadership.

8.4 Important leadership positions

In nearly all businesses there will be people who are given important formal leadership positions. The chart (Figure 8.1) shows some of the common ones in a limited company.

Key term

Workers' representative: elected by workforce to represent the workforce

Progress Check C

1. In a public limited company, which two types of leaders could be elected?
2. Give examples of activities corresponding to Mintzberg's leadership role of 'Disturbance Handler'.
3. What factors could influence the leadership style of a supermarket manager?

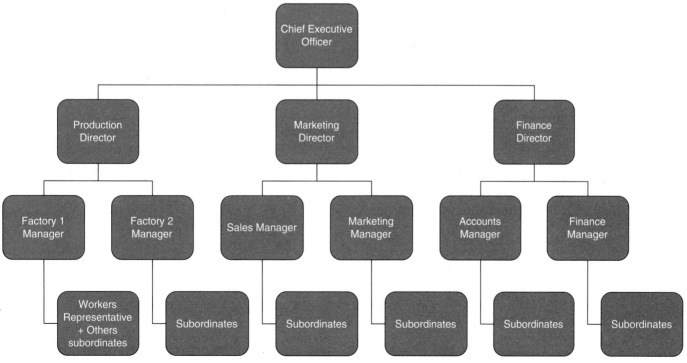

Figure 8.1 Typical leadership position

8.5 Styles of leadership

Leadership styles vary greatly. It is important to remember that there is never just one leadership style that is the best one to use in all business situations.

> **Key terms**
>
> **Leadership style:** the way in which managers take decisions and communicate with their staff
>
> **Autocratic leadership:** a style of leadership that keeps all decision making at the centre of the organisation
>
> **Laissez-faire leadership:** a leadership style that leaves much of the business decision making to the work-force – a 'hands off' approach and the reverse of autocratic
>
> **Democratic leadership:** a leadership style that promotes the active participation of workers in taking decisions

> **Progress Check D**
>
> 1. List three situations in which autocratic leadership might be appropriate.
> 2. Which leadership style might be appropriate in a research institution?
> 3. List two drawbacks of democratic leadership.
> 4. Which leadership style encourages staff involvement?
> 5. Why might the most suitable leadership style change in different situations?

8.6 McGregor's Theory X and Y

McGregor's famous Theory X and Theory Y did not claim that there are two different types of workers – but that there were two extreme management views about workers.

> **Key terms**
>
> **Theory X managers:** managers view workers as lazy, workers dislike work
>
> **Theory Y managers:** managers view workers as enjoying work, workers prepared to accept responsibility

> **Progress Check E**
>
> 1. Is it true that McGregor claimed there are two types of worker?
> 2. Which theory, X or Y, attributes workers with accepting responsibility?
> 3. What style of leadership might a Theory X manager adopt?

8.7 Choice of leadership style

In 8.5 we explained that there is no one 'right' leadership style. The most effective leadership style depends on the following factors.

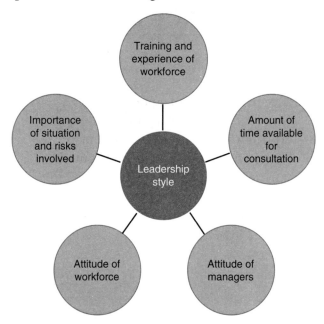

> **Progress Check F**
>
> 1. Why is there no one right choice of leadership style?
> 2. If a decision is needed quickly, which leadership style might be adopted?
> 3. How might workers' attitudes to change be influenced by leadership style?

8.8 Informal leadership

So far we have only considered 'formal leaders' appointed by the business. They have formal authority over subordinates.

In many situations, such as a business, there are often informal leaders who also have influence over others.

> ## Key term
>
> **Informal leader:** a person who has no formal authority but has the respect of colleagues and some power over them

Progress Check G

1. Do informal leaders have formal authority? Explain your answer.
2. List three abilities that an informal leader might have.

8.9 Emotional Intelligence (EI)

Goleman has suggested that effective leadership depends not just on the personal qualities we identified in 8.3 but also on whether people have 'emotional intelligence'.

> ## Key term
>
> **Emotional Intelligence (EI):** the ability of managers to understand their own emotions, and those of the people they work with, to achieve better business performance

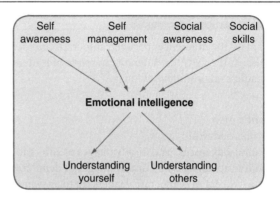

Progress Check H

1. Give three possible weaknesses of a manager who lacks high EI.
2. Explain three benefits of a leader having high EI.

Multiple Choice Questions

1. Which function of management involves leading staff?
   (i) Organising resources
   (ii) Directing and motivating
   (iii) Controlling and measuring
   (iv) Coordinating activities

2. Organising resources involves:
   (i) ensuring a business is structured appropriately
   (ii) ensuring a business has appropriate objectives
   (iii) ensuring managers are trained effectively
   (iv) ensuring staff have sufficient resources to carry out their duties

3. According to Mintzberg 'Negotiator' is an example of:
   (i) informational role
   (ii) interpersonal role
   (iii) decisional role
   (iv) management role

4. Which of the following is *not* a characteristic of a good leader?
   (i) Desire to succeed
   (ii) Incisive mind able to analyse new situations quickly
   (iii) Needs to be liked by everybody
   (iv) Strong personality to be able to influence others

5. Which of the following is *not* an advantage of autocratic leadership?
   (i) Workers do not like unstructured organisations
   (ii) Consultations can be time consuming
   (iii) It involves staff in decisons
   (iv) It suits workers who do not like responsibility

6. McGregor's Theory is related to:
   (i) different types of worker
   (ii) different types of manager
   (iii) different attitudes of managers
   (iv) different roles of managers

7. Which is the most accurate statement about the choice of leadership style?
    (i) There is no single right or wrong way of leading people
    (ii) Lazy workers deserve Theory X leaders
    (iii) Clever workers do not need leadership
    (iv) Theory Y leaders are better managers

Exam-style Question

(a) Explain the differences between autocratic and democratic leadership. [8]

(b) Discuss the view that a democratic style of leadership is the most effective leadership style for a business in the competitive business environment of today. [12]

Cambridge 9707 Paper 11 Section B Q5 November 2010

Student's plan

(a) Define leadership

Outline advantages and disadvantages of autocratic leadership

Outline advantages and disadvantages of democratic leadership

(b) Link concept of democratic leadership to answer in (a)

Discuss the leadership needs of 'today's competitive environment'

    ✓ The need to manage and lead change using actual examples

    ✓ The global nature of markets and increased competition using actual examples

    ✓ Increased expectations of workers, for example, the need to be involved or consulted at work

Link these needs with the importance for leaders to respond to different situations. Develop the idea that leadership style should adjust to a given situation (using actual examples). Respond rapidly to change brought about by a competitor or market (autocratic?)

    ✓ Introduction of new working practices (democratic?)

    ✓ Dealing with people of different cultures etc. (autocratic unlikely to be best here?)

Draw these arguments together and conclude that it is not possible to support the view in the question in all circumstances.

Authors' Comments

The student showed a ***limited approach*** to part (a) of the question. While there was clear understanding of both autocratic and democratic leadership styles there was no attempt to compare and contrast them. 8 mark questions on Paper 1 require the demonstration of analytical skills as well as application of the concepts to realistic situations. The student could have achieved this, for example, by identifying and analysing situations in which autocratic leadership might be appropriate and then analysing why democratic leadership might not work.

The plan for part (b) would allow a good answer. Not only are there opportunities for clear analysis and evaluation of leadership styles, these are related to the context of today's competitive environment. The conclusion pulls together the previous discussion in an evaluative fashion (the student will make a supported judgement on the view).

Revision checklist – tick when done and understood!

Topic	Textbook read	Revision complete
Functions of management		
Mintzberg's managerial role		
Leadership qualities		
Leadership styles		
McGregor's theory X and Y		
Informal leadership		
Emotional intelligence		

Motivation

9

Revision Objectives

After you have studied this chapter, you should be able to:

☞ explain what motivation means
☞ compare and evaluate the main motivational theories
☞ assess the main financial methods of motivation
☞ assess the main non-financial methods of motivation.

9.1 Motivation

Key term

Motivation: the internal and external factors that stimulate people to take actions that lead to achieving a goal

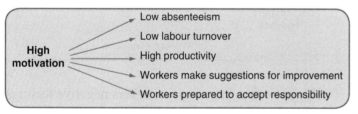

Progress Check A

1. Give three examples of poor motivation in a business.
2. Why is a motivated workforce important for managers?
3. How might a supermarket benefit from a well-motivated workforce?

9.2 Taylor's scientific approach

The theory of Economic Man

Man is driven by money alone.

Taylor's work has had impact on:

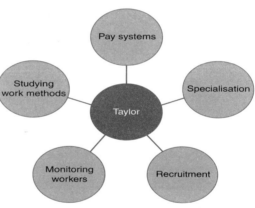

Taylor applied the scientific approach to management:

Select ⇨ Observe ⇨ Record ⇨ Identify quickest method ⇨

Train ⇨ Supervise ⇨ Pay by results

Progress Check B

1. Why did workers mistrust Taylor?
2. How did Taylor have an impact on recruitment methods?
3. Why is the Economic Man principle considered simplistic?

9.3 Mayo

Motivation improved by:

- ✓ consulting workers
- ✓ working in teams
- ✓ workers making decisions that affect themselves
- ✓ establishing targets.

Less affected by:

- ✓ working conditions.

Progress Check C

1. How might a manager of a factory use the ideas of Mayo to improve productivity?
2. How does Mayo differ from Taylor in his views on money as a motivator?
3. How does workers' welfare fit into Mayo's ideas?

9.4 Maslow

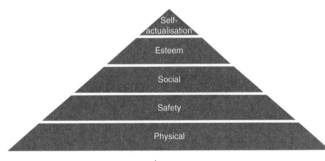

Start at lowest level ⇨ Achieved: move to next levels

- ✓ Self actualisation is not reached by many people
- ✓ Once a need is met it ceases motivating
- ✓ It's possible to go down as well as up (reversion).

But

- Not everyone has same needs
- When is a need met?
- Money may be needed to meet several needs
- Self-actualisation is never permanently achieved.

Key term

self-actualisation: a sense of self-fulfilment reached by feeling enriched and developed by what one has learned and achieved

---

Progress Check D

1. Why is it difficult to achieve self-actualisation?
2. What might cause a reversion down the hierarchy?
3. Why do some managers think it is important to try to satisfy workers' needs?
4. Give examples of business conditions which allow for each type of need to be met.

9.5 Herzberg

Herzberg's motivation theory is based on two factors:

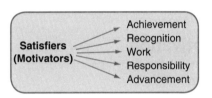

Motivators give workers positive feelings about their jobs and hence motivate.

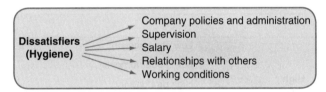

Hygiene factors can give workers negative feelings about jobs when they are absent, so can demotivate. Improving them could prevent dissatisfaction but may not motivate.

For example, improving pay and working condition removes dissatisfaction and may encourage work but not motivation where as job enrichment is a motivator and improves motivation.

Progress Check E

1. List three of Herzberg's motivators.
2. How might pay demotivate workers?
3. Which leadership style encourages staff motivation?
4. Why might leadership style be a hygiene factor?

Key terms

Job enrichment: aims to use the full capabilities of workers by giving them the opportunity to do more challenging and fulfilling work

Hygiene factors: aspects of a worker's job that have the potential to cause dissatisfaction, such as pay, working conditions, status and over-supervision by managers

Motivating factors (motivators): aspects of a worker's job that can lead to positive job satisfaction, such as achievement, recognition, meaningful and interesting work and advancement at work

Progress Check F

1. Do leaders need a strong sense of affiliation?
2. Why do successful enterpreneurs need acheivement motivators?
3. Explain the main difference between McClelland and Maslow.

9.7 Process theories

Vroom

Effort ⇨ Performance ⇨ Reward ⇨

Satisfy need ⇨ Effort worthwhile

9.6 McClelland

McClelland said that there are three types of motivational need, the mix should depend on the characteristics of the workers/managers.

Achievement	Authority/ Power	Affiliation
A strong motivational need to achieve. Need for feedback and sense of accomplishment.	A person with dominant need. Desire to control and make an impact.	Need for friendly relationships and interaction with others. Need to be liked.
Attitude of successful business people and entrepreneurs.	Strong leadership instinct.	Good team members.

Key terms

Valence: depth of want of employee
Expectancy: degree to which people believe reward leads to performance
Instrumentality: confidence that employees will get what they require

Top tip
When there is a question about motivation try to use the theories rather than list their main findings – applying their ideas is more important than showing just knowledge.

9.8 Motivation in practice – Financial methods

Piece rate and Commission	• Encourages effort • Unit costs known, helps setting prices	• Needs measurable output/sales • May lead to falling quality/'bad' sales • Workers may only want to achieve target pay • Provides little security • Workers discouraged from change
Salary	• Should depend on experience, progress • Security of income • Linked to status • Helps costing • Suitable for where output is not measurable • Suitable for management (unpredictable hours)	• Income not directly related to effort/productivity • May lead to complacency • Regular appraisal essential, time consuming

(Continued)

Performance related pay	• Staff motivated to improve performance • Target setting important • Appraisal may be of benefit	• Will not motivate if staff not driven by financial rewards • Team spirit can be damaged • Could be subject to claims of manager favouritism • May push conformity rather than innovation
Profit sharing	• Potential conflicts between owners and workers • Should lead to greater effort/cost reduction • Attract better recruits • Does not add to costs • Could lead to increased profitability	• Reward may not be related to individual effort • Can be costly to operate • Small profits may de-motivate • Reduced shareholder dividends initially • Reduced retained profits may reduce investments • Could dilute value of existing shares
Fringe benefits (Perks)	• Provides benefits that employees might not otherwise have • May be low cost method	• Unlikely to be as important as other methods of financial reward • May have tax implications

Key terms

Hourly wage rate: payment to a worker for each hour worked

Piece rate: payment to a worker for each unit produced

Salary: annual income that is usually paid on a monthly basis

Commission: a payment to a sales person for each sale made

Performance-related pay: a bonus scheme to reward staff for above average work performance

Profit sharing: a bonus for staff based on the profits of the business – usually paid as a proportion of basic salary

Progress Check G

1. Why might piece rate pay be unsuitable for lorry drivers?
2. Give three examples of perks (fringe benefits).
3. What is the main difference between profit sharing and performance related pay?

9.9 Motivation in practice – Non-financial methods

Job rotation	• Gives workers new skills	• Increased workload • Organisational problems
Job enrichment	• Less supervision • Workers have complete jobs • Workers have more responsibility • Challenging	• Not easy to apply in practice • Workers may not respond well • May be seen as threatening jobs • More work for same pay?
Job redesign	• Linked to job enrichment • Can lead to improved recognition • Allows introduction of team working • More skills, better promotion chances	• Difficult to implement • May be seen as a threat
Quality circles	• Good for finding solutions • Involves participation	• Time consuming • Costly • Needs support of management and employees
Worker participation	• Participation in decisions • Job enrichment • More responsibility	• Time consuming • Not suited to some styles of management

(Continued)

Team working	• Better motivation • Makes better use of talents • Can reduce costs • Complete tasks can be allocated	• Time consuming • Not everyone good in teams • Training costs • Time costs
Target setting	• Related to Management by Objectives • Motivating	• Bureaucratic
Delegation and empowerment	See Chapter 12	See Chapter 12

Key terms

Job rotation: increasing the flexibility of the workforce and the variety of work they do by switching from one job to another

Job enlargement: attempting to increase the scope of a job by broadening or deepening the tasks undertaken

Job enrichment: involves the principle of organising work so that employees are encouraged and allowed to use their full abilities – not just physical effort

Job redesign: involves the restructuring of a job – usually with employees' involvement and agreement – to make work more interesting, satisfying and challenging

Quality circles: they are voluntary groups of workers who meet regularly to discuss work-related problems and issues

Worker participation: workers are actively encouraged to become involved in decision making within the organisation

Team working: production is organised so that groups of workers undertake complete units of work

Progress Check H

1. Give three examples of non-financial motivators.
2. Explain the difference between piece rate and performance related pay.

Top tip

You should be able to do more than just describe/explain different methods of motivation.

You should be able to recommend which might be most suitable in particular situations and why.

Multiple Choice Questions

1. What does high absenteeism indicate?
   (i) Workers are motivated by money
   (ii) Workers are not well motivated
   (iii) There is a high rate of labour turnover
   (iv) There is an autocratic leadership

2. Taylor said:
   (i) workers are motivated by money
   (ii) workers do not behave rationally
   (iii) workers expect good management
   (iv) workers expect good conditions of service

3. Hygiene factors mean:
   (i) a clean work place
   (ii) positive factors that motivate

   (iii) factors that de-motivate when absent
   (iv) none of the above

4. Which theorist is associated with self-actualisation?
   (i) McClelland
   (ii) Taylor
   (iii) McGregor
   (iv) Maslow

5. Under Herzberg's two factor theory which of the following is not a motivator?
   (i) Self-actualisation
   (ii) Achievement
   (iii) More recognition
   (iv) More responsibility

6. An advantage of job enrichment is:
  (i) higher pay
  (ii) more work
  (iii) more instructions
  (iv) more responsibility

7. Which of the following is most likely to be used to increase sales in a shoe shop?
  (i) Commission
  (ii) Salary
  (iii) Profit related pay
  (iv) Overtime

Exam-style Question

Discuss why a school might use non-financial rewards to motivate its workers. [12]

Student's plan

  ✓ Explain the meaning of non-financial rewards giving examples
  ✓ Discuss the need for motivation in a school: teachers/other staff (school's objectives)
  ✓ Relate non-financial rewards to motivation theories
  ✓ Apply these ideas to teachers/other staff
  ✓ Briefly mention the possible appropriateness of financial motivators
  ✓ Analyse suitable methods (limit to two)
  ✓ Conclusion that discusses the extent to which non-financial rewards might meet the schools objectives – likely to be partial.

Authors' Comments

The plan clearly aims for the answer to be contextual and focuses on the theory (non-financial motivators). There are indications that the student recognizes the need for analysis and identifies an opportunity for evaluation. This promises to be a very good answer.

Final revision checklist – tick when done and understood!

Topic	Textbook read	Revision complete
Motivation		
Motivation theories		
Financial methods		
Non-financial methods		

Human Resource Management

10.1 Purpose and role of HRM

A business depends on the effficiency and motivation of some of its most important assets – the people who work for it. HRM is the tool to achieve the best from the workforce.

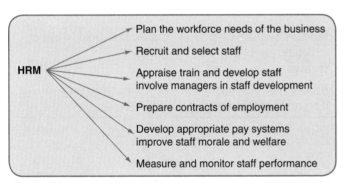

HRM:
- Plan the workforce needs of the business
- Recruit and select staff
- Appraise train and develop staff involve managers in staff development
- Prepare contracts of employment
- Develop appropriate pay systems improve staff morale and welfare
- Measure and monitor staff performance

Table 10.1

Hard HRM	Soft HRM
Cutting costs	Developing staff
Increasing flexibility	Motivating through fulfilment
People treated like materials, equipment	People related
Strategy related	Maslow, Mayo, Herzberg
Taylor	

Top tip Small/Medium firms may not have or need HRM Department. The functions are often carried out within other functional departments.

Key terms

Human Resource Management: the strategic approach to the effective management of an organisations's workers so that they help the business gain a competitive advantage

Hard HRM: an approach to managing staff that focuses on cutting costs, for example, temporary and partime employment contracts, offering maximum flexibility but with minimum training costs

Soft HRM: an approach to managing staff that focuses on developing staff so that they reach self-fulfilment and are motivated to work hard and stay with the business

Progress Check A

1. Why is training and development important?
2. Why is HRM different from a personnel department?
3. Why would a supermarket want an effective HRM department?

10.2 Strategic workforce planning

Having the wrong number of workers or workers with the wrong skills could be disastrous for a business.

Workforce planning process

Workforce audit ⟹ Knowledge about skills and qualifications of existing workforce

Demand for firm's product ⟍
Productivity levels ⟶ **Number of staff** ⟵ Technological change
Objectives of business ⟶ **Skills needed** ⟵ Flexibility and training
Laws about employment ⟋
Labour turnover/absenteeism ⟋

Key terms

Workforce planning: analysing and forecasting the numbers of workers and the skills of those workers that will be required by the organisation to achieve its objectives

Workforce audit: a check on the skills and qualifications of all existing workers/managers

Top tip

Workforce planning should be closely linked with a firm's long term objectives and with external factors influencing the firm.

Progress Check B

1. Why should a business undertake a workforce plan if a global downturn is predicted?
2. Why would a car manufacturer about to open a new factory need a workforce plan?
3. Explain the possible consequences of not having a workforce plan.

10.3 Recruiting and selecting staff

Businesses want the best workforce possible within the constraints on it. A workforce with the wrong people would reduce the chances of meeting objectives.

Internal versus external recruitment

Table 10.3

Internal advantages (External disadvantages)	External advantages (Internal disadvantages)
Known to business	New ideas and practices
Candidate knows business and its culture	Wider choice of potential applicants
Quicker and cheaper	Avoids problems with staff not promoted
Workers have career structure, promotion chances	Candidates could be better qualified
Known style of management if recruiting for senior post	No further internal positions to fill

Process of recruiting and selecting

Table 10.2

Establish nature of the job	What sort of person?	Attract applicants	Shortlist	Select
• Job Description	• Person specification	• Job advertisement	• Chosen from applications/ CV/References	• Selection criteria • Achievements, intelligence, skills, interest, personal manner, physical appearance, personal circumstances
• Job Title • Tasks to be performed • Place in hierarchy • Working conditions • Assessment/ measurement	• Person profile in terms of qualities and skills needed	• In business premises • Newspapers • Agencies • Job Centres • Online	• A small number to interview selected	• Interviews • Aptitude tests • Psychometric tests • Tasks • Problem solving

Key terms

Recruitment: the process of identifying the need for a new employee, defining the job to be filled and the type of person needed to fill it, attracting suitable candidates for the job and selecting the best one

Job description: a detailed list of the key points about the job to be filled – stating all its key tasks and responsibilities

Person specification: a detailed list of the qualities, skills and qualifications that a successful applicant will need to have

 Top tip Do not confuse job description and person specification.

Progress Check C

1. Why might a software business seek to recruit product developers externally?
2. What are the benefits of a bank recruiting for senior positions internally?
3. What are the differences between a job description and person specification?

10.4 Staff development

The costs of **not** developing/training staff are high as workers will be less productive and less motivated.

Development should be integrated into business activities with managers as well as HRM department involved.

Key terms

Training: work related education to increase workforce skills and efficiency

On-the-job training: instruction at the place of work on how a job should be carried out

Off-the-job training: all training undertaken away from the business, for example, work related college courses

Induction training: introductory training programme to familiarise new recruits with the systems used in the business and the layout of the business site

Staff appraisal: the process of assessing the effectiveness of an employee judged against pre-set criteria

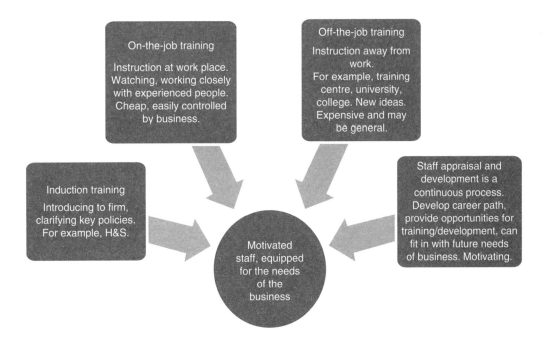

Top tip

One reason commonly given by firms for *not* training their staff is that these well trained staff will then be 'poached' by other firms.

Perhaps they should focus on motivating their staff to stay.

Progress Check D

1. Why might training help a car manufacturer introduce flexible working?
2. How does staff development fit in with the ideas of Herzberg?
3. What are the main differences between induction training and off-the-job training?
4. Why is it important to involve managers in staff development?
5. What sort of training would be best if a business was going to upgrade all of its computers?

10.5 Contracts of employment

Key terms

Dismissal: being dismissed or sacked from a job due to incompetence or breach of discipline

Unfair dismissal: ending a worker's employment contract for a reason that the law regards as unfair

Redundancy: when a job is no longer required, so the employee doing this job becomes redundant (loses the job) through no fault of his or her own

Top tip

The precise legal requirements of employment contracts are likely to vary slightly between different countries. It would be useful to research what these legal requirements are in your own country– but you will not be examined directly on them.

10.6 Expanding the workforce

There are several ways a business can expand its workforce:

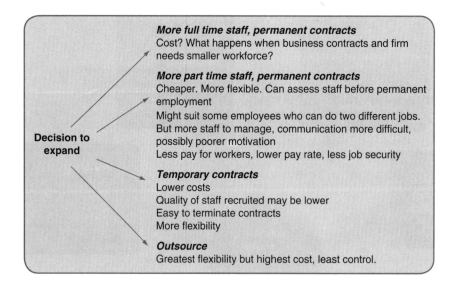

Decision to expand

More full time staff, permanent contracts
Cost? What happens when business contracts and firm needs smaller workforce?

More part time staff, permanent contracts
Cheaper. More flexible. Can assess staff before permanent employment
Might suit some employees who can do two different jobs. But more staff to manage, communication more difficult, possibly poorer motivation
Less pay for workers, lower pay rate, less job security

Temporary contracts
Lower costs
Quality of staff recruited may be lower
Easy to terminate contracts
More flexibility

Outsource
Greatest flexibility but highest cost, least control.

Handy's Shamrock organisation

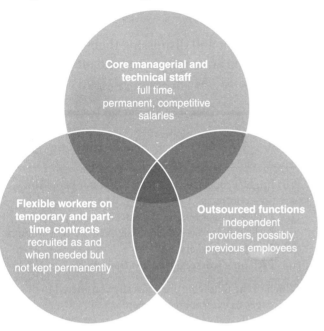

Core managerial and technical staff
full time, permanent, competitive salaries

Flexible workers on temporary and part-time contracts
recruited as and when needed but not kept permanently

Outsourced functions
independent providers, possibly previous employees

New workers will require (legal requirement in most countries) a contract of employment which usually contains:

Responsibilities + Working hours + Rate of pay + Holidays + Days notice to leave (employer and employee)

Reducing work force

Circumstances may require business to reduce number of workers or individual workers may need to be fired. Businesses have to go about solving these problems the right way.

Redundancy and Dismissal

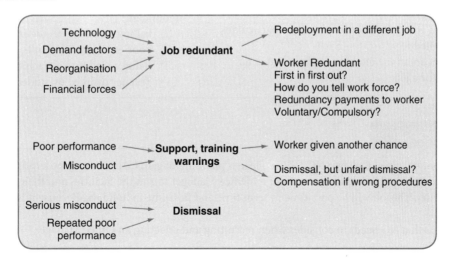

Technology
Demand factors → **Job redundant**
Reorganisation
Financial forces

→ Redeployment in a different job

→ Worker Redundant
First in first out?
How do you tell work force?
Redundancy payments to worker
Voluntary/Compulsory?

Poor performance → **Support, training warnings**
Misconduct

→ Worker given another chance

→ Dismissal, but unfair dismissal?
Compensation if wrong procedures

Serious misconduct → **Dismissal**
Repeated poor performance

Progress Check E

1. Why might a global downturn lead to redundancies at a fashion shop?
2. What are the main differences between making someone redundant and dismissing them?
3. Why is it important to follow the correct procedures when making an employee redundant?
4. Give *three* reasons why redeployment is better than redundancy.
5. Give *two* reasons why a worker might legally be dismissed.

Multiple Choice Questions

1. HRM functions exist to:
   - (i) ensure the business does not break the law
   - (ii) represent workers' opinions
   - (iii) ensure human resources are used effectively
   - (iv) ensure managers do not have too much power

2. The most important consequence of a business failing to produce a workforce plan is:
   - (i) saving money
   - (ii) paying workers too much
   - (iii) not having the right people to meet future needs of the business
   - (iv) ensuring business aims are met

3. Which of the following is likely to cause an increase in the future number of staff required by a firm?
   - (i) A decrease in the demand for the firm's products
   - (ii) A decrease in labour turnover
   - (iii) A decrease in the firm's productivity
   - (iv) An increase in the minimum wage

4. A job specification is:
   - (i) a statement about the type of person required for a particular job
   - (ii) a statement about the work involved in a production process
   - (iii) a statement about the tasks involved in a particular job to be filled
   - (iv) a statement about the questions to be asked at an interview for a job

5. Why might a supermarket prefer to employ people on part-time contracts?
   - (i) Part-time workers want a career in supermarkets
   - (ii) Part-time workers have less skills than full-time workers
   - (iii) Part-time workers cost less
   - (iv) Part-time workers need less training

6. Which of the following are generally considered to be advantages to external recruitment?
   - (i) Usually quicker than internal recruitment
   - (ii) Access to a wider range of candidate
   - (iii) Less expensive
   - (iv) External candidates are always better trained

7. Off the job training is most likely to be useful for:
   - (i) coping with new people starting at a business
   - (ii) telling workers about standard procedures at a business
   - (iii) assessing workers' performance
   - (iv) developing new IT skills

8. An employee can be immediately dismissed for:
   - (i) being late
   - (ii) stealing
   - (iii) making sexist comments
   - (iv) being inefficient

9. In what circumstances might a college make a teacher redundant?
   - (i) Falling numbers of students attending the college
   - (ii) Poor examination results
   - (iii) Being a leader in a teaching union
   - (iv) Teacher disliked by students

Exam-style Question

The case study is about Newton College (NC). The college is planning to gain extra revenue by letting out facilities during school holidays. The Principal would like to appoint an Office Manager to run the facilities and their letting as well as marketing the facilities. The job will be part-time in term time and full-time in holidays. Because it is a college the salary is likely to be limited.

Discuss the factors that NC needs to consider when recruiting and selecting an Office Manager.   [10]

Adapted from Cambridge 9707 Paper 21 Q2(d) November 2010

Student's answer

Explain the recruitment/selection process in general terms

Discuss advantages and disadvantages of interviews, tests and tasks as selection methods

Conclude that since the job is at a college it would be a good idea to include teachers and students

Discuss the issues that because the salary is likely to be low it might not attract the best candidates

Assert that the most important experience the candidate should have is experience letting facilities

Conclude that it is very important to recruit the right person for the job.

Authors' Comments

The student showed depth of knowledge about the recruitment process and at times showed analytical skills – for example in the discussion about involving staff and students in the selection process. The answer was also partly contextual – the student picked up points about low salary, the need for administration skills, issues specifically relating to a college and letting facilities. However, there were important aspects of context that were overlooked – it is going to be difficult to find someone who wants the specified mix of part-time and full time employment, and also someone with marketing skills who would work for a low salary.

Although the student made evaluative comments (a recommendation for the best selection method, a statement about the most important factor and a suitable conclusion) the comments needed to be supported by the earlier discussion/analysis, but this was absent from the answer. A better answer might have developed the salary issue further by developing the likely consequences of not being able to recruit the right person for the job. This discussion should have enabled the student to put the factor of salary into proper perspective with regard to the recruitment process.

Revision checklist – tick when done and understood!

Topic	Textbook read	Revision complete
Role of HRM		
Workforce planning		
Recruitment and selection		
Training		
Dismissal/Redundancy		

Further Human Resource Management

11

Revision Objectives

After you have studied this chapter, you should be able to:

☞ understand and apply the methods of measuring human performance
☞ interpret actual measures of performance
☞ recommend methods of improving performance
☞ explain the role of trade unions
☞ discuss trade unions from the perspective of employers and employees
☞ recommend methods of reducing/resolving industrial disputes
☞ discuss the importance of conciliation and arbitration.

11.1 Measuring human performance

The consequences of poor workforce performance can be damaging to a business. It is important to be able to measure workforce performance and take measures to improve it.

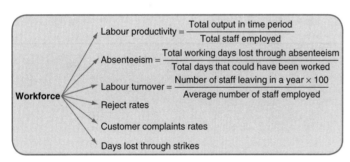

Top tip

There are other measures of employee performance. However, you will not be asked to calculate reject rates, customer complaints rates, days lost through strikes but you should be able to comment on data that you are given in a question.

Progress Check A

1. Why is improving employee performance important to a business?
2. Give one way labour productivity could be measured in a fashion clothing shop.
3. Give three reasons that may reduce labour productivity in a fashion clothing shop.
4. Why would high labour turnover be a problem at your school?

11.2 Improving employee performance

✓ Performance appraisal – targets set and monitored
✓ Training – stretch and challenge workers
✓ Quality circles – identify and solve problems
✓ Cell production/Autonomous groups – multi-skilling and team work
✓ Financial incentives – give workers a stake in the business.

For more detail on these measures see Chapter 9.

Top tip

Low productivity may not be due to poor workforce performance. It could be due to poor machinery or supply disruptions such as strikes. High labour turnover may not be an indication of poor motivation. For example, businesses that employ students (for example, supermarkets) will always have high labour turnover.

Progress Check B

1. Explain how training could improve employee performance in a hotel.
2. How could teamwork reduce absenteeism?
3. Why might giving workers a stake in an airline business improve labour productivity?

11.3 Management By Objectives (MBO)

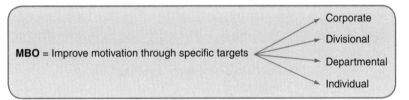

MBO = Improve motivation through specific targets
- Corporate
- Divisional
- Departmental
- Individual

Advantages
1. Feature of job enrichment
2. Everyone knows what to do
3. All working to same overall targets
4. Managers able to monitor success/failure

Disadvantages
1. Can be time consuming
2. Objectives can be outdated quickly
3. Targets do not guarantee success

Progress Check C

1. A school plans to introduce MBO. Give two possible objectives that a business studies teacher might agree with management.
2. Identify one possible problem with each of these objectives.
3. Why might targets not guarantee success?

11.4 Industrial relations legislation

In addition to laws governing labour, for example, Health and Safety, Equal Opportunities (see Chapter 6) the government influences relationships between it and trade unions.

The government
- Industrial relations laws, for example, laws governing strike action
- Agencies to improve industrial relations, for example, arbitration councils
- Government policies towards its own employees

Top tip

You will not be examined on the precise details of labour laws in any country – but you are advised to research the industrial relations laws in your own country.

Progress Check D

1. Why would your government make laws regarding industrial relations?
2. Why might the requirement for 'secret ballots' in union votes be necessary?

11.5 Relationship between workforce and management

Workers, managers and owners may not share the same objectives so there is scope for *conflict*.

For example,

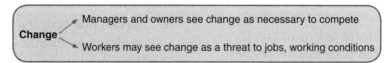

Approaches to labour management relations

Table 11.1

Management style	Advantages	Disadvantages
Autocratic management style – 'take it or leave it' attitude to workers	• Low labour costs • Quick, easy to make decisions	• No security, poor motivation • Often no training • No common objectives • No job enrichment, participation
Collective bargaining at industry level (powerful unions negotiate with major employees/associations)	• Reduces needs for individual negotiations • National agreements	• Not suitable for small businesses • Strikes likely – loss of output/sales • Unions tend to resists essential changes • May affect national competitiveness
Co-operation at local level	• Fewer strikes • Involves participation, so better motivation • Working towards common goals • Local decisions	• More complex, time consuming decisions

Progress Check E

1. Explain why good labour relations are important to employers.
2. State two benefits to an employee of collective bargaining with employers.
3. A fast food business has 200 restaurants. Why would co-operation and negotiations between workers and management at a local level be difficult?

11.6 Trade unions

Key term

Trade union: an organisation of working people with the objective of improving pay and working conditions of their members and providing them with support such as legal services

Trade unions achieve:

For workers

✓ Power through solidarity
✓ Greater likelihood of success through action
✓ Protection for members (legal support)
✓ Pressure on employers to meet legal standards (for example, health and safety).

For employers

✓ Negotiating with one body rather than many people
✓ Useful channel of communication
✓ Unions impose discipline on members
✓ Responsible partnerships between unions and employers can bring benefits to a business.

Employers' attitude to unions

In many countries it is not a legal requirement to recognise trade unions. Employers can:

✓ recognise unions – may have benefits to employers
✓ have single-union agreements – makes negotiating easier, reduce inter-union disputes but union might be stronger, may not represent everyone
✓ require no-strike agreements – can lead to better relationship with employer and the general public

Key terms

Trade union recognition: when an employer formally agrees to conduct negotiations on pay and working conditions with a trade union(s) rather than bargain individually with each worker

Single union agreement: an employer recognises just one union for the purpose of collective bargaining

No-strike agreement: unions agree to sort problems out without resorting to strikes

Industrial action: measures taken by the workforce or trade union to put pressure on management to settle an industrial dispute in favour of employees

Balance of negotiating power

Table 11.2

Likely success of union/business interaction		
Possible union activities	Increased likelihood of conflict	Possible employer activities
Negotiations		Negotiations/Arbitration
Arbitration		Public relations
Go Slow		Threat of redundancies
Work to rule		Changes of contract
Overtime ban		Closure
Strike action		Lockouts

11.7 Conciliation and arbitration

Key terms

Conciliation: the use of a third party in industrial disputes to encourage both employer and union to discuss an acceptable compromise solution

Arbitration: resolving an industrial dispute by using an independent third party to judge and recommend an appropriate solution

Employer/Employee problem

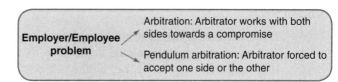

Progress Check F

1. How could a teacher benefit from joining a teaching union?
2. Why would a 'no strike' deal be important for the police service?
3. In your country there is a dispute over working conditions between the major airline and its cabin crew. Discuss the factors that will influence the outcome of the dispute.
4. A car manufacturer wants a single union deal. Why would the unions object to this idea to begin with?

Progress Check G

1. Why would the government want fire-fighters to go to arbitration in a pay dispute?
2. Would you advise a business in a highly competitive market to agree to pendulum arbitration in an industrial pay dispute?

A Multiple Choice Questions

1. Which one of the following will not lead to an increase in labour productivity?
   (i) Better staff training
   (ii) New markets
   (iii) New equipment
   (iv) The introduction of quality circles

2. High absenteeism is most likely a result of:
   (i) a motivated workforce
   (ii) a large proportion of workers leaving the business
   (iii) a clear objective for the business
   (iv) a demotivated workforce

3 and 4 are based on the following data:

Company	Average number of employees last year	Number of employees who left last year	Average daily staff absences
A	200	30	5
B	400	20	20
C	600	60	21
D	800	8	8

3. Which one of the following statements is true?
   (i) Company *C* has the worst record for both labour turnover and annual absenteeism
   (ii) Company *C* has the worst record for labour turnover, company *B* has the worst record for annual absenteeism
   (iii) Company *A* has the worst record for labour turnover, company *B* has the worst record for annual absenteeism
   (iv) Company *A* has the worst record for labour turnover, company *C* has the worst record for annual absenteeism

4. Company *C* has high staff turnover. This could be because:
   (i) Company *C* employs a lot of healthy workers
   (ii) Company *C* employs a lot of women
   (iii) Company *C* employs a lot of students
   (iv) Company *C* employs highly trained people

5. Which one of the following statements is *not* true about trade unions?
   (i) All unions organise strikes
   (ii) All unions seek better conditions for employees
   (iii) All unions will represent employees in legal disputes with employers
   (iv) All unions gain power through solidarity

6. In an industrial dispute employers can:
   (i) work to rule
   (ii) go slow
   (iii) create new legislation
   (iv) threaten redundancy

7. A union is likely to be in a strong position in a dispute with employers if:
   (i) the union is right and the employers are wrong
   (ii) there is public support for the union
   (iii) the business's profits are falling
   (iv) labour costs in the business are high

Exam-style Question

To what extent would an airline, operating in a highly competitive market, be helped or constrained by the trade union membership of its workers?

Student's plan

✓ The importance of staff in an airline – pilots, cabin crew, ground staff
✓ The impact of competition on the airline
✓ How customers might chose their airline
✓ Possible role of the union: conditions of service, pay, representing staff
✓ The attitude of the airline
✓ Situations in which workers' union membership might help the business
✓ Situations in which it might hinder
✓ Conclusion that balances the arguments on the assumption that it behaves responsibly.

Authors' Comments

It is very important that these questions are answered contextually even though the context is often limited. This student clearly recognizes the context of the airline as well as the context of a highly competitive market.

The student also clearly plans to adopt an analytical approach through looking at both 'help' and 'hindrance' factors. Whether or not high analysis marks can be awarded will depend on the depth in which such issues are discussed but the plan looks very promising.

The student has also thought through how evaluation marks are going to be achieved – by balancing the arguments to make a conclusion. Particularly impressive is the way the answer is to be framed within the assumption of 'reasonable behaviour' on the part of the union. This will be even more convincing if the assumption is based on the highly competitive nature of the industry.

The plan suggests the student will achieve a very good mark if the plan is fulfilled with respect to depth of analysis/evaluation.

Revision checklist – tick when done and understood!

Topic	Textbook read	Revision complete
Measuring employee performance		
Improving employee performance		
Management by Objectives		
Labour legislation		
Workforce conflict		
Trade unions		
Conciliation and arbitration		

Organisation Structure 12

Revision Objectives

After you have studied this chapter, you should be able to:

☞ understand the needs for organisational structure
☞ discuss advantages and disadvantages of hierarchical structures
☞ discuss advantages and disadvantages of matrix structures

☞ discuss the usefulness of delegation
☞ discuss the factors influencing the choice of organisational structure
☞ recommend a structure in a given situation
☞ recognise consequences of choosing a particular structure.

12.1 Need for structures

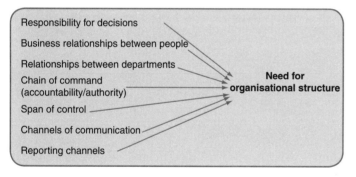

Responsibility for decisions
Business relationships between people
Relationships between departments
Chain of command (accountability/authority)
Span of control
Channels of communication
Reporting channels

Need for organisational structure

Key terms

Level of hierarchy: a stage within an organisation structure at which the personnel on it have equal status and authority
Chain of command: this is the route through which authority is passed down an organisation – from the chief executive and the board of directors
Span of control: the number of subordinates reporting directly to a manager

Progress Check A

1. Why do organisations need a formal structure?
2. Why might a small organisation have a different structure to a large one?
3. How might an organisation structure be used by an employee looking for information?

12.2 Hierarchical structure

Different layers, with authority/responsibility increasing the higher up the organisation.

Chief executive
Directors
Middle managers
Supervisors
Line workers

A typical hierarchical pyramid

The advantages and disadvantages of a hierarchical structure are shown here.

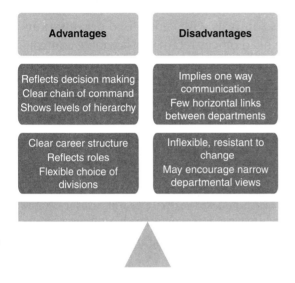

12.3 Matrix structure

> **Key term**
>
> **Matrix structure:** an organisational structure that creates project teams with team members from different functional areas

The advantages and disadvantages of a matrix organisational structure are shown in the following figure.

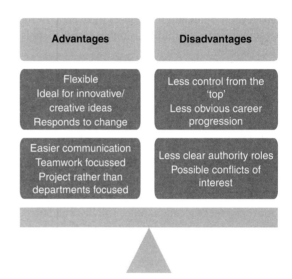

The matrix structure (Figure 12.1) is ideal for situations in which the business is task or project focused.

Progress Check B

1. Give three disadvantages of a hierarchical structure.
2. Why might employees like a clear career structure in their organisation?
3. Why is it important for businesses in your country to be able to respond quickly to change?

	Finance Department	Production Department	Marketing Department	Human Resources	Research & Development
Project Team 1					
Project Team 2					

Figure 12.1   A matrix organisational structure

A

Progress Check C

1. Explain two benefits of a matrix structure.
2. How could a matrix structure be used at your school/college?
3. Outline possible problems with a matrix structure for a multinational pharmaceutical company.

12.4 Delegation

In decentralised organisations much of the work is delegated.

This contrasts with centralised organisations where head offices retain considerable control.

Delegation transfers the authority and accountability to undertake particular tasks but the final responsibility remains with the delegator.

Table 12.1

Advantages of centralisation and decentralisation	
Advantages of centralisation	**Advantages of decentralisation**
• A fixed set of rules and procedures in all areas of the firm should lead to rapid decision making – there is little scope for discussion.	• More local decisions can be made that reflect different conditions – the managers who take the decisions will have local knowledge and are likely to have closer contact with consumers.
• The business has consistent policies throughout the organisation. This prevents any conflicts between the divisions and avoids confusion in the minds of consumers.	• More junior managers can develop and this prepares them for more challenging roles.
• Senior managers take decisions in the interest of the whole business – not just one division of it.	• Delegation and empowerment are made easier and these will have positive effects on motivation.
• Central buying should allow for greater economies of scale.	• Decision making in response to changes, for example in local market conditions, should be quicker and more flexible as head office will not have to be involved every time.
• Senior managers at central office will be experienced decision makers.	

Key terms

Delegation: passing authority down the organisational hierarchy

Centralisation: keeping all the important decision-making powers within head office or the centre of the organisation

Decentralisation: decision-making powers are passed down the organisation to empower subordinates and regional/product managers

Progress Check D

1. Outline the importance of delegation in a school/college.
2. Explain why increased delegation might involve increased risk.
3. Distinguish between authority and responsibility.
4. Distinguish between authority and accountability.

Delegation:

Achieves
Motivation
More time for managers to do other tasks
Staff development
Can achieve self-fulfilment

But
Manager retains responsibility
Need for monitoring and control
Can be time consuming
Depends on trust
Clear definition of task needed

12.5 Factors influencing organisational structure

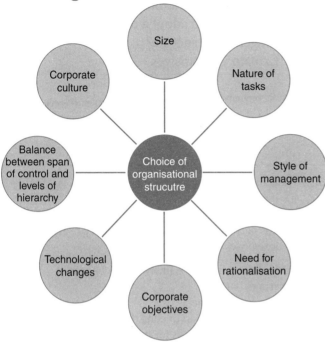

Progress Check E

1. Why might the introduction of email based information flows have an impact on organisational structure?
2. Why is delegation more likely in a school than in a bank?
3. Explain why delegation is more likely in an organisation with a wide span of control.
4. Why would large businesses pay more attention to designing an organisational structure?

12.6 Consequences of organisational structure

More levels ⇨ longer chain of command ⇨ smaller span of control

Tall structure ⇨ communication problems ⇨ slowness to change

Delegation requires trust ⇨ which may increase risk

Organisations and people often confuse accountability with responsibility. Workers need to account for tasks delegated to them, managers retain responsibility.

✓ Role of staff managers as well as line managers
✓ Informal organisations are also important
✓ Current trends to simpler structures and for delayering

Key terms

Line managers: managers who have direct authority over people, decisions and resources within the hierarchy of an organisation

Staff managers: managers who, as specialists, provide support, information and assistance to line managers

Delayering: removal of one or more levels of hierarchy from an organisation structure

Delayering has been a major development in large business as globalisation and competition have forced business to look at their competitiveness.

Table 12.2

Advantages and disadvantages of delayering	
Advantages of delayering	**Disadvantages of delayering**
• Reduces business costs	• Could be 'one-off' costs of making managers redundant, for example redundancy payments
• Shortens the chain of command and should improve communication through the organization	• Increased workloads for managers who remain – this could lead to overwork and stress
• Increases spans of control and opportunities for delegation	• Fear that redundancies might be used to cut costs could reduce the sense of security of the whole workforce – one of Maslow's needs
• May increase workforce motivation due to less remoteness from top management and greater chance of having more responsible work to perform	

A

Progress Check F

1. Explain why delayering has become increasingly more important for businesses that operate in global markets.
2. Why is it likely that businesses with tall organisational structure find it difficult to change?
3. Give examples of roles likely to be fulfilled by staff managers.
4. Would you advise a multinational food manufacturer to adopt a decentralised management structure?
   Explain your answer.

Multiple Choice Questions

1. Which of the following best describes a matrix structure?
   (i) A structure designed around functions
   (ii) A structure designed around geographical areas
   (iii) A structure designed around project (teams)
   (iv) A structure designed around levels of hierarchy

2. Which of the following are disadvantages of a hierarchical structure?
   (i) It does not provide a career structure
   (ii) It can be inflexible
   (iii) There is no clear chain of command
   (iv) It is a new style of structure

3. Which of the following is most likely to result from a narrow span of control in a large organisation?
   (i) Delegation is essential
   (ii) The manager will know all their staff well
   (iii) There will be few levels of hierarchy
   (iv) There will be few managers

4. Delegation is useful for:
   (i) handing over responsibility, authority and accountability
   (ii) handing over accountability but not authority
   (iii) handing over authority but not accountability
   (iv) handing over authority but retaining responsibility

5. An advantage of delegation is that:
   (i) it reduces risk
   (ii) it motivates workers through trust
   (iii) it is part of Taylor's motivation theory
   (iv) it removes the need for training

6. Which of the following is likely to be a benefit of delayering?
   (i) It reduces business costs
   (ii) It reduces the span of control
   (iii) It reduces workloads for managers
   (iv) It reduces opportunities for delegation

7. A good description of a line manager is:
   (i) a manager in charge of a production line
   (ii) a manager in charge of other staff managers
   (iii) a manager who gives professional advice to staff managers
   (iv) a manager who has authority over others in a hierarchical structure

8. A decentralised structure is useful for:
   (i) keeping tight control on an organisation
   (ii) promoting consistent marketing messages
   (iii) a business operating from a single location
   (iv) empowering managers

Exam-style Question

Evaluate the usefulness of a matrix structure for a manufacturer of consumer electronics in a highly competitive market.　[12]

Student plan

Para 1
Outline of main features of matrix structure: flexibility, project oriented, good for ideas; but more difficult to control, maybe leadership problems.

Para 2
Outline of main features of consumer electronics in competition: New product design/launch important, therefore project based; must be quick to respond; technical skills needed as well as assessing market needs.

Para 3
Extent to which matrix meets these needs, on balance 'yes' but may be issue with speed of response.

Para 4
Would hierarchy work better? Loses team spirit, even less responsive, inflexible. But decisiveness might help.

Para 5
Summary concluding on balance advantages outweigh because of critical importance of new, competitive products needed quickly.

Authors' Comments

This approach looks good at the planning stage. Efforts have been made to contextualise the answer and the approach is analytical in that it looks at both advantages and disadvantages.

The student has chosen to evaluate the usefulness by setting up the arguments so that the student demonstrates that it is a better way than the traditional hierarchy.

Provided that the discussion follows the plan and has sufficient depth to convince the reader of the conclusion the answer should get high marks.

Revision checklist – tick when done and understood!

Topic	Textbook read	Revision complete
Need for organisational structure		
Hierarchical structure		
Matrix structure		
Delegation		
Choosing structure		
Consequences of structures		

13.1 Communication process

Effective communication is two-way:

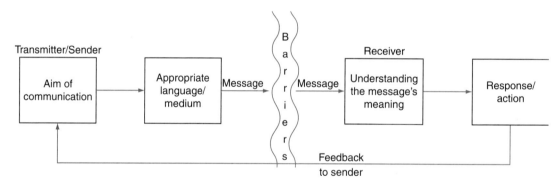

Effective communication – barriers must be reduced or eliminated

Benefits of effective communication:

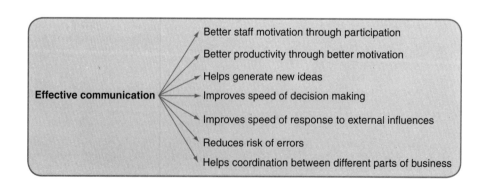

Key terms

Effective communication: the exchange of information between people or groups, with feedback

Communication media: the methods used to communicate a message

Progress Check A

1. Outline two reasons why is effective communications important in your school/college.
2. Define effective communication.
3. How can effective communication reduce the risk of errors in a large shop?

13.2 Choice of communication medium

Table 13.1

Strengths and weaknesses of communication methods		
Method	**Strengths**	**Weaknesses**
Oral	• direct • can be varied to suit needs of receiver • easy to understand • can be questioned quickly	• need to listen carefully • affected by noise • passive • no permanent accurate record • can be quickly forgotten
Written	• recorded – permanent record • more structured • easy to distribute • cannot be distorted • can be referred to again	• often difficult to read • message identical to each receiver • no body language • feedback slower • no immediate response • may be misinterpreted • costly and time consuming
Visual	• more interactive • demands attention • often easier to remember • creates greater interest	• needs close attention • sometimes too fast • not always clear • interpretations by receivers can vary
Electronic	• great speed • interactive • creates interest • encourages response • ignores boundaries • good image for external communication	• cannot always be received • relies on receiver • is expensive in hardware • risk of communication overload • can be intercepted • diminishes personal contact

The choice of communication medium:

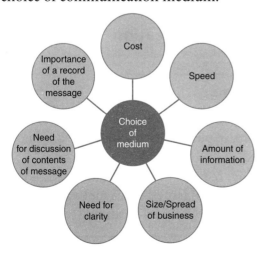

Progress Check B

1. Give three advantages of communicating using an electronic medium.
2. Give one disadvantage of communicating orally.
3. Give two situations in which written communication would be appropriate.
4. Give three examples of the use of visual communication in a supermarket in your country.
5. Outline the factors that influence the decision of communication medium when informing staff of a pay rise.

A

13.3 Barriers to effective communication

> **Key term**
>
> **Communication barriers:** reasons why communication fails

Failure in one of the stages of communication

- Wrong medium
- Channel of communication is too long
- Misleading or incomplete message
- Too much technical language or jargon
- Too much information
- Language/Culture.

Poor attitude of sender/receiver

- Sender not trusted by receiver
- Unmotivated receiver/sender
- Poor intermediaries.

Physical barriers

- Too much noise
- Too much distance between sender/reciever
- Poor equipment/services.

> **Progress Check C**
>
> 1. Give three examples of barriers to effective communication.
> 2. Why might jargon make communication difficult?
> 3. Why might messages get distorted when an intermediary is used?

13.4 Removing barriers to effective communication

Managers should ensure:

- ✓ clear, concise and precise messages
- ✓ as short communication channels as possible
- ✓ channels clear to all involved
- ✓ built in feedback mechanisms
- ✓ trust
- ✓ appropriate physical conditions.

> **Progress Check D**
>
> 1. Explain what is meant by feedback.
> 2. Why might building feedback into a communication system help in preventing errors?
> 3. Why are short communication channels better than long ones?

13.5 Types of communication network

- Chain
- Vertical
- Wheel
- Circle
- Integrated.

> **Progress Check E**
>
> 1. Give one situation in which a vertical network might be appropriate.
> 2. Give two advantages of an integrated network for communicating.

> **Top tip**
>
> When discussing suitable communication methods, try to assess which type of communication network would be most appropraite in the given situation.

13.6 One way or two way communication

> **Key terms**
>
> **One way:** quick, easy to send message to large numbers of people, used where response not needed
>
> **Two way:** reduces misunderstandings, allows development of issues, more motivating through participation but time consuming

The 'Virtuous Circle' of communication

Good communication can be achieved by:

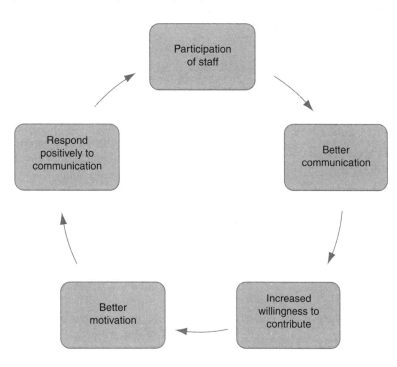

Participation of staff → Better communication → Increased willingness to contribute → Better motivation → Respond positively to communication → Participation of staff

---

Progress Check F

1. Examine two reasons why good communication might motivate workers.
2. Explain how the virtuous circle of communication relates to motivation theories.

Top tip   Try to link communication effectiveness with organisational structure. Traditional structures will tend to use vertical communication; matrix structures will use horizontal communication.

13.7 Other types of communication

Horizontal

Between people of roughly equal status in different parts of an organisation.

Informal

The grapevine.

Natural part of human behaviour – sometimes unwanted but often effective.

Progress Check G

1. Give two reasons why the marketing department of a business might find it difficult communicating with the finance department.
2. Explain how the grapevine could be a positive force in a business.
3. Why do some managers fear informal communications?

Multiple Choice Questions

1. Which of the following is a disadvantage of oral communication?
    (i)   No opportunity for feedback
    (ii) No written record
    (iii) Slow to be effective
    (iv) Relies on equipment that can go wrong

2. Which of the following is not an advantage of electronic communication (email)?
    (i)   It can be quick
    (ii) It ensures a record is kept of the conversation
    (iii) It ensures instant communication
    (iv) It enables communication with many people

3. Which of the following is not a barrier to communication?
    (i)   Technical language
    (ii) Quick feedback
    (iii) Length of channel of communication
    (iv) Wrong choice of medium

4. Which of the following is most likely to have barriers to communication?
    (i)   Where there is a leader at the centre
    (ii) Where a manager communicates with each subordinate individually

    (iii) Where communication starts at the top and is passed downwards
    (iv) Where every individual in a group can communicate directly with everyone else

5. A vertical network is best described as:
    (i)   suitable when there is a small span of control
    (ii) a system allowing full two-way communication between everybody
    (iii) suitable within a hierarchical structure
    (iv) a system that does not allow two-way communication

6. Why might informal communication be important?
    (i)   It can be used to test out management ideas
    (ii) It wastes time
    (iii) It ensures coordination of activities
    (iv) It helps spread rumours

7. A good way to inform a new employee that they are not performing well would be:
    (i)   using a notice board
    (ii) discussing orally with the manager
    (iii) sending a letter
    (iv) Facebook

Exam-style Question

Typical Toys (TT) have recently taken over Junior Games, another toy manufacturer which has factories in several other countries. Discuss the difficulties that TT might have with internal communications in the expanded business.   [14]

Student's response

There are two key issues that need to be discussed. First there is the nature of the communications within the new organisation, and secondly there are issues arising from fusing together two different organisations.

In relation to the different types of communications, TT needs to consider the variety of communications that might be involved. These include day-to-day issues that are routine (such as announcements about holidays etc.), and at the other extreme information about major strategic issues (such as new products). In between are operational issues such as production levels. The extent to which there are likely to be difficulties is likely to be influenced by the complexity of the type of communication and messages. Simple operational issues are likely to be relatively easy to communicate while more complex matters, such as that needed to develop strategic decisions, could prove to be difficult.

A second important issue is the extent to which there are likely to be barriers to communication following the joining together of the two organisations. With factories now in several countries, geographical and time factors may prove to be important although most of these are likely to be overcome by means of electronic communications. Of greater significance are the differing approaches to communication between TT and JG. This may arise through language (factories are now located in several countries), culture (TT may, for example, have a culture of openness, with JG being more select about information flows), and organisational structure (TT could, for example, employ an integrated communication network, while JG could, for example, be more of a chain network). Clearly the communication network chosen is going to affect, to a greater or lesser extent, the effectiveness of communication – it will be difficult, for example, for the organisation with chain network to adapt to a different kind of network.

Some issues are always difficult to communicate, such as that involved in important decisions as there is often a great deal of complex information to communicate. This will only be made more difficult through the involvement of two, possibly completely different, organisations.

Of greatest concern are the organisational differences since these are likely to affect communication at all levels and all degrees of complexity.

Authors' Comments

Although the student has not started off in the traditional way of defining terms, the student clearly understands about communication, barriers to communication and communication networks. In addition, all of the comments made are within the context of a takeover and the likely communication problems arising from that. More could have been made of the multiple locations of the firm. However, the organisational and cultural issues are handled well and are contrasted effectively with problems arising from different types of information.

The student has effectively balanced two types of communication and the conclusion that organisational issues are the most important are evaluative and partially supported the earlier discussion. Better evaluation would have included cultural differences in the weighing up of difficulties.

Revision checklist – tick when done and understood!

Topic	Textbook read	Revision complete
Communication process		
Communication media		
Barriers to communication		
Communication networks		
One-way/Two-way communication		
Informal communication		

What is Marketing?

14.1 The role of marketing

Marketing is one of the important functional departments of all businesses. Marketing is more than just 'selling'. The role of marketing in a profit seeking business is to:

✓ find out what customers are prepared to buy

✓ communicate this to other departments

✓ sell the product (i.e. either a physical good or a service) to customers at a profit.

Businesses can sell products in either consumer markets – to the final users of the products – or to industrial markets where businesses buy the product to be used in further production. This distinction is important because products will be sold in different ways in these markets. For example, trade fairs and industry exhibitions might be used to sell industrial products but most consumer products are sold through retailers or the Internet.

Key terms

Marketing: the management task that links the business to the customers by identifying and meeting the needs of customers profitably

Consumer markets: markets for goods and services bought by the final user of them

Industrial market: markets for goods and services bought by businesses to be used in the production process of other products

14.2 Marketing objectives

Objectives are targets to work towards. An effective marketing department should have clear objectives. These should be aimed at achieving the objectives of the corporation. They should be coordinated with the objectives of other departments to try to ensure that resources are available for meeting the marketing objectives.

> **Key term**
>
> **Marketing objectives:** the goals set for the marketing department to help the business achieve its overall objectives

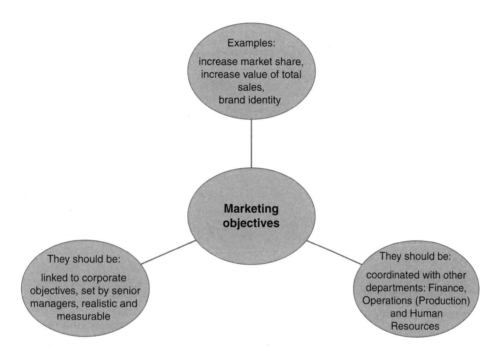

14.3 Distinguish between market orientation and product orientation

These are two contrasting approaches to marketing. A market oriented business (often called 'market led') will put the customer first and use market research to identify needs and potential demand. This information is then used to develop products that will meet this demand. Product oriented (or product led) firms focus on the production process and 'getting the product right' before attempting to sell it to customers. So, market oriented firms put much more focus on market research whilst product oriented firms put the focus on selling a product that has already been developed or produced.

Two other approaches to marketing are:

✓ **asset led marketing** – basing new products on a firms' existing products and strengths such as Apple focusing on consumer electronics – not electric heating!

✓ **societal marketing** – making marketing decisions based not just on consumer wants but 'what is good for society' such as wooden furniture made from sustainably sourced materials.

Market oriented (Market led)	Product oriented (Product led)
Customer first	Product design first
Use market research to find what customers want	Then find market (get the product right)

Key terms

Market orientation: bases product decisions on consumer demand as established by market research

Product orientation: focuses on products that can be made or have been made for a long time and then trying to sell them

Asset led marketing: bases marketing strategies on the firm's strengths and assets instead of purely on what the customer wants

Societal marketing: marketing strategies consider not just the demands of consumers but also the effects on society

Top tip

You should be able to evaluate these different approaches to marketing. For example:

✓ whether market orientation reduces risks;

✓ the extent to which societal marketing will increase in importance in countries where consumers are becoming increasingly worried about the environment.

Progress Check A

1. If a relative of yours tells you that 'they work in marketing' list four typical tasks that they might actually perform in this role.
2. Why do you think it could be important to 'put the customer first' when taking marketing decisions?
3. Give *two* examples of marketing objectives that the Apple Corporation might have.

4. Why would it be important to link these two objectives to:

   ✓ Apple's corporate objectives
   ✓ objectives of other departments within Apple.

5. Explain what this statement means: 'Market led companies use more market research than product led companies – but product led companies might have to spend more money on advertising.'

14.4 Demand, supply and price

In free markets – with no government controls and where many firms operate – prices are determined by the 'forces of demand and supply'. The prices of many world food commodities such as rice increased greatly in 2011 due to supply restrictions (drought in many producing countries) and rising demand (world population growth).

Key terms

Demand: the quantity of a product that consumers are willing and able to buy at a given price in a time period

Supply: the quantity of a product that firms are prepared to supply at a given price in a time period

Equilibrium price: the market price that equates supply and demand

Top tip

Make sure you draw the demand and supply curves correctly!

Factors influencing **demand** include:
- Population
- Advertising
- Prices of competitors or complements
- Fashion/Taste
- Incomes

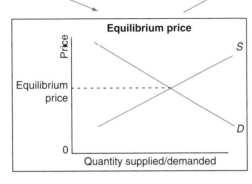

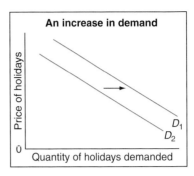

Factors influencing **supply** include:
- Weather
- Indirect taxes
- Subsidies
- Changes in production costs
- Technology changes

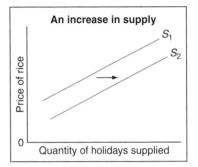

14.5 Market size, market growth and market share

Marketing objectives are often expressed in terms of 'increasing annual sales by 5%' or 'increasing market share by 10%'. A high market share gives a business more influence and power over retailers and suppliers. If a product becomes a brand leader it can use this in its advertising.

Key terms

Market size: the total level (or value) of sales of all producers within a market

Market growth: the percentage change in total market size over a period of time

Market share: the percentage of total market sales in a market sold by one business

Market share % $=\dfrac{\text{Sales of business} \times 100}{\text{Total market sales}}$
(in a time period)

It is therefore very important for a marketing manager to know:

✓ How big is the market in which we sell our products?
✓ Is it getting bigger or smaller?
✓ Are our sales a greater or smaller share of the total market than last year?

It is often easier for a business to increase the sales of a product if the **total** market is growing **but** increasing product sales does not necessarily mean that the market share of the business has increased. Competitors might have increased sales at an even faster rate!

Progress Check B

1. Draw a graph showing a 'typical' demand curve for one brand of television. If consumer incomes increased by 5%, draw a new demand curve on the graph.
2. Draw a graph showing a 'typical' supply curve for crude oil. If there is a major disaster at a large oil field, draw a new supply curve on the graph.

3. In both Q1 and 2, explain what is likely to happen to the equilibrium price of each product after these changes.
4. Calculate the % annual growth in market size if the total value of the mobile (cell) phone market in one Country Z was $90m in Year 1 and $110m in Year 2.
5. Refer to Q4. Company A sells mobile phones in Country Z. In Year 1, its sales value was $30m. In Year 2, its sales increased to $35m. Calculate Company A's market share in both years.
6. If Company B has 15% market share for a product and total market size is $230m, calculate the value of Company B's sales.
7. Explain why it is important to a producer of breakfast cereals to have a high market share.

14.6 Adding value

This links with Chapter 1. Marketing managers have an important role to play in increasing the value added to a product.

Top tip

If a question asks you to explain how a business can add value to its products, make sure your suggestions are based around the products the firm is selling – apply your answer!

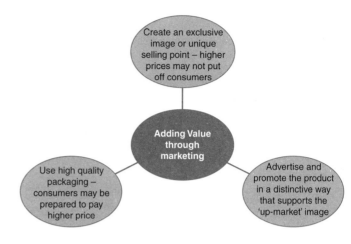

Create an exclusive image or unique selling point – higher prices may not put off consumers

Adding Value through marketing

Use high quality packaging – consumers may be prepared to pay higher price

Advertise and promote the product in a distinctive way that supports the 'up-market' image

14.7 Niche marketing and mass marketing

Key terms

Niche marketing: identifying and exploiting a small segment of a larger market by developing products to suit it

Mass marketing: selling the same products to the whole market with no attempt to target groups within it

	Advantages	Disadvantages
Niche marketing	• Small firms are often able to survive by exploiting niche markets • Allows big business to create separate and exclusive images for products. For example, Lexus owned by Toyota • Unexploited niche markets may allow higher prices to be charged to the business that enters them first	• No economies of scale in terms of production and marketing • Quite a risky strategy if the tastes of niche market consumers change • Total sales – and possibly profits – will be lower than mass marketing • Cost of developing products to suit different niche markets
Mass marketing	• Potential for economies of scale • High sales likely – could be more profitable than niche marketing	• Profit margins could be lower than niche marketing if the mass market is very competitive • Business may have a low image or status if it does not develop any niche market products

Niche marketing is increasingly common because modern production techniques allow much more product flexibility of design and built in features – once you have studied. Operations Management, you should be able to make these links in your answers.

14.8 Market segmentation

This marketing concept is becoming much more important for many consumer products. As consumer incomes rise in most of the world, so expectations change. Many consumers would prefer to buy products that are specifically designed for their needs supported by a marketing strategy that focuses on them and their needs.

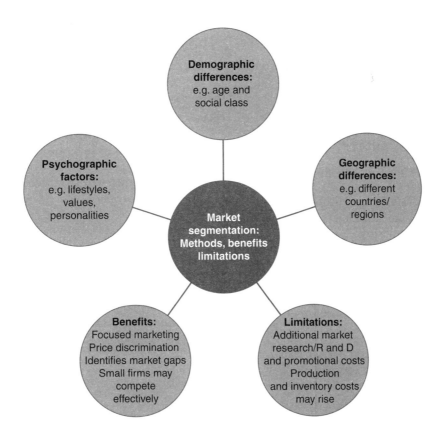

Key terms

Market segmentation: identifying different segments within a market and targeting different products or services to them

Market segment: a sub-group of a whole market in which consumer have similar characteristics (similar consumer profile)

Consumer profile: a quantified picture of consumers of a firm's products showing age groups, income levels, gender and social class

Progress Check C

1. Explain *two* ways in which a supermarket could add value to the fresh produce (for example, meat and vegetables) that it sells.
2. In the global market for computers there are many 'market niches'. Identify *four* of these.
3. Explain the benefits to a computer manufacturer of only focusing on niche marketing.
4. Explain *three* ways in which a large clothing manufacturer could segment its market.

1. Which one of these is the best definition of marketing?
   (i) Selling products that have been produced by advertising and promotion
   (ii) Convincing customers that they really want to buy a firm's products rather than those of a competitor
   (iii) Finding out consumer wants, providing this information to the operations department and then persuading customers to buy products
   (iv) Selling products at the lowest price possible with the aim of increasing sales and market share

2. One of the main reasons why a business sets marketing objectives is to:
   (i) provide a clear focus for the marketing department's strategies
   (ii) encourage consumers to purchase the product
   (iii) make sure that the firm achieves all of its corporate objectives
   (iv) ensure that the firm's cash flow is always positive

3. Which one of the following is an example of a market oriented business decision?
   (i) Selling only products that are environmentally friendly as all consumers are interested in protecting global resources
   (ii) Increasing advertising spending on a product that is becoming less attractive to many consumers
   (iii) Reducing the price of a product that is experiencing increased competition from rivals' new products
   (iv) Basing new product decisions on market research data

4. Which one of the following is most likely to lead to an increase in the equilibrium price of crude oil?

   (i) A huge new oil field is discovered
   (ii) Improved production efficiency reduces the cost of making cars
   (iii) Increasing publicity on the dangers of global warming
   (iv) Improved production efficiency allows much smaller oil fields to be developed

5. A small manufacturing business, Company A, produces high quality leather steering wheels for makers of luxury sports cars. Which one of the following is the most likely effect on Company A of operating in a niche market?
   (i) Sales will be higher than if Company A made steering wheels for family cars
   (ii) Advertising costs will be high as Company A has to advertise the steering wheels to consumers who buy cars
   (iii) Economies of scale will be limited as the production level is likely to be low
   (iv) Selling prices to makers of luxury sports cars will be low as many large manufacturers of steering wheels will be competing in this market

6. Company B produces white T-shirts and sells them in street markets. If the company decided to use market segmentation and developed different styles and colours of T-shirts it would be likely to:
   (i) sell fewer white T-shirts but sell more T-shirts of other designs at higher prices
   (ii) increase prices of white T-shirts as demand would increase
   (iii) reduce total production costs
   (iv) reduce its total sales but increase market share

Exam-style Question

HiQ Fashion sells children's clothing through two out of town retail stores. The business buys in school uniforms, jeans, sport clothes and other children's clothing from some of the lowest cost suppliers. HiQ Fashion stores contain a huge range of items but they are poorly displayed and most of the staff employed operate the tills or fill the shelves. There is very little consumer service provided. The Marketing Director has just reported to the other directors these key points about the company's recent sales:

   ✓ "Our sales increased by 15% last year to $4.6m.
   ✓ The total value of the children's clothing market was $32m last year and $35m this year.
   ✓ Our average prices are 10% lower than competitors".

The Managing Director was pleased with these results but wanted the company to expand further. She said, "I suggest we research the market for adult sports clothing. I think this is a fast growing market which we could move into. Consumer incomes are rising. People are playing more sport and demanding very high quality sports clothing. With our market research results we could then decide which sports to focus on".

(a) Calculate the value of HiQ Fashion sales last year. [3]
(b) Calculate the change in HiQ Fashion's market share between the two years. [4]
(c) Explain why the Managing Director is suggesting a market oriented approach to entering the sport clothing market. [4]
(d) Analyse *two* ways in which the sports clothing market could be segmented. [10]
(e) Would you advise HiQ Fashion to sell adult sports clothing through their existing two stores? Justify your answer. [10]

Student's answer to (c)

A market oriented business uses a lot of market research. It collects information about what consumers want to buy and uses this to decide what to produce. This makes the business less risky as only those things that consumers want are being made.

The Managing Director of HiQ Fashion probably wanted to use market research because his business had not sold adult sport clothing before. People play many different sports and it would be important to know which the most popular ones were. HiQ Fashion could then stock clothes for the most popular sports.

Authors' Comments

This is a very good answer. Brief but to the point. The definition of market orientation shows full understanding. The reasons why HiQ Fashion might use market orientation were well applied.

Revision checklist – tick when done and understood!

Topic	Textbook read	Revision complete
The role of marketing		
Consumer markets and industrial markets		
Marketing objectives		
Market orientation, product orientation, asset led marketing and societal marketing		
Demand, supply and equilibrium price		
Market size, market growth and market share		
Adding value		
Niche marketing and mass marketing		
Market segmentation		

Market Research 15

15.1 Need for market research

Market orientation is explained in Chapter 14. This concept, adopted by most businesses these days, requires market research to be undertaken before product and other key decisions are taken. Market research is often a continuous process. It is helpful not just to decide what to produce and sell but also to keep the business as aware as possible of changing consumer needs or market trends.

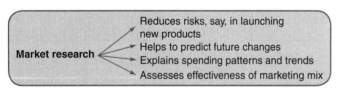

Key term

Market research: the process of collecting, recording and analysing data about customers, competitors and the market

15.2 Market research process

Market research can be an expensive process. It is important to make sure that the time and money

spent on it is geared towards solving clear marketing problems. This can be done by following the market research process.

Progress Check A

1. How can market research improve the effectiveness of business decisions?
2. Why is it important for a business to know about its customers?
3. How does market research support new product development?

Key terms

Primary research: the collection of first-hand data that is directly related to a firm's needs
Secondary research: collection of data from second-hand sources
Qualitative research: non-numerical research into the in-depth motivation behind consumer buying behaviour or opinions
Quantitative research: research that leads to numerical results that can be statistically analysed

PROMBLEM ──────▶	OBJECTIVES ──────▶	SOURCES ──────▶	METHOD
Market size? Falling sales? New market? New competitors?	Set SMART objectives to achieve a solution to the problem through market research. ***Example 1*** How many people are likely to buy our product in Country *X*? (Quantitative data needed)	START with Secondary research • Government • Libraries • Trade organisations • Market intelligence • Newspapers • Company records • The Internet	Desk Research
Which customers to target? Which new products to develop?	***Example 2*** Why do consumers prefer Company *Y*'s products to ours? (Qualitative data needed)	Primary • Qualitative • Quantitative	Field Research • Focus groups • Observations • Test markets • Surveys

Focus group: a group of people who are asked about their attitude towards a product, service, advertisement or new style of packaging

Key term

Sample: the group of people taking part in a market research selected to be representative of the overall target market

Progress Check B

1. List three advantages of primary data over secondary data.
2. Why should secondary data usually be collected first?
3. Under what circumstances will secondary data collection be impossible?
4. Why might qualitative research be useful? Give a business example.

Key terms

Random sample: every member of the target population has an equal chance of being selected

Systematic sample: every *n*th item in the target population is selected

Stratified sampling: this draws a sample from a specified sub-group or segment of the population and uses random sampling to select from each stratum

Quota sampling: when the population has been stratified and the interviewer selects an appropriate number of respondents from each stratum

Cluster sampling: using one or a number of specific groups to draw samples from and not selecting from the whole population, for example, using one town or region

15.3 Sampling methods

In most market research situations it is impossible to ask questions to the whole 'population' or target market. This is because of the cost involved or the distances that would have to be covered by researchers or, perhaps, because the identity of all consumers is not known. In these cases a sample must be selected.

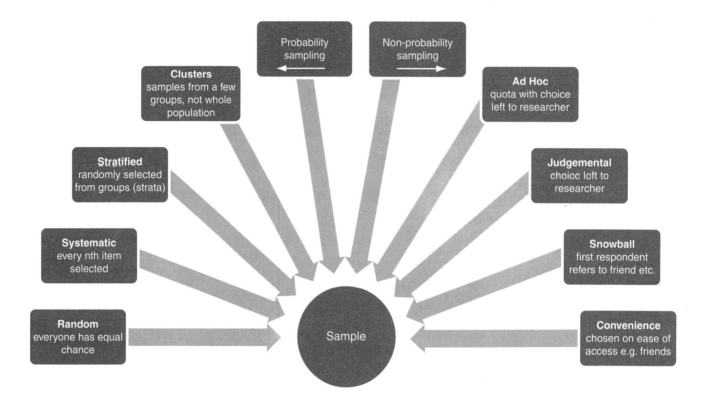

Progress Check C

1. Give four types of non-probability sampling.
2. For each method listed in Q1, outline a business situation in which it might be the best method of sampling.
3. Why use samples during primary data collection?

Questionnaire design should:

✓ be based on clear objectives
✓ be unambiguous
✓ have a logical sequence
✓ avoid leading questions
✓ use easy to understand language
✓ give results that allow analysis.

15.4 Questionnaires

Much primary data collection is gathered by means of questionnaires. These can either be self completed or the questions can be read out during an interview.

Self completed	Direct interview
Response rate often poor	Depends on skill of interviewer
Questions easily misunderstood	Follow up questions can be asked
Cheap	Expensive

Key terms

Open questions: those that invite a wide-ranging or imaginative response – the results will be difficult to collate and present numerically

Closed questions: questions to which a limited number of pre-set answers is offered

15.5 Is primary data always reliable?

The short answer to this is no! Here are some reasons why:

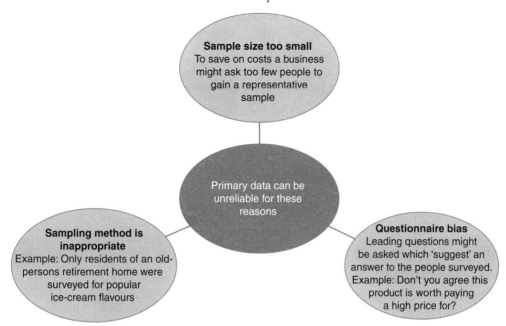

15.6 Presentation of information

This is an important part of the market research process. Effective presentation of results can improve managers' understanding of them.

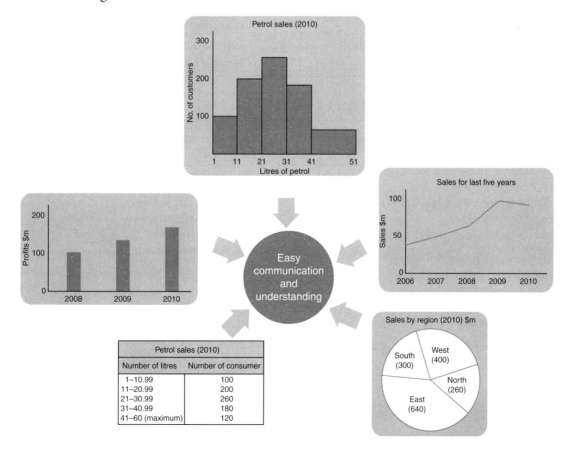

Progress Check D

1. Give one disadvantage to open questions.
2. Give three types of bias.
3. Give one advantage of self-completed questionnaires.
4. An entrepreneur researched the potential market for a new gardening service by surveying ten members of her family. Explain why the results are likely to be unreliable.

Progress Check E

1. What is the difference between a bar chart and a histogram?
2. What are the advantages of graphical presentation of information?
3. When might you use a line graph?
4. Give one disadvantage of a pie chart.

Key terms

Range: the difference between the highest and lowest value
Interquartile range: the range of the middle 50% of the data

15.7 Statistical analysis

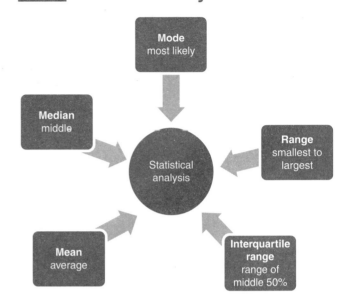

Progress Check F

1. If you were making shoes, which would be the most useful measure of shoe size – mean, median or mode?
2. How can the mean be distorted?
3. Explain the benefits to a clothing manufacturer of calculating the range and inter-quartile range of dress sizes bought by female customers.

Multiple Choice Questions

1. Which of the following is an example of secondary research?
   (i) Collecting information in a focus group
   (ii) Undertaking a survey
   (iii) Collating information from Mintel and the Population Census
   (iv) Observation of customers behaviour

2. Quantitative research is best defined as:
   (i) asking closed questions
   (ii) asking questions that require a measurable response
   (iii) using a focus group
   (iv) asking questions that lead to written results

3. Which of the following is an advantage of primary research?
   (i) Low cost
   (ii) Specific to needs
   (iii) Fast response rate
   (iv) Always reliable

4. An A level student conducts market research by asking students he knows at the college about how many hours television they watch each week. This is an example of:
   (i) probability sampling
   (ii) systematic sampling
   (iii) quota sampling
   (iv) convenience sampling

5. An advantage of a pie chart is that:
   (i) it clearly communicates proportions
   (ii) it shows frequencies
   (iii) it is easy to read totals
   (iv) it shows progressions over time

6. The interquartile range is:
   (i) the difference between the highest and the lowest
   (ii) the range of the middle 50%
   (iii) the difference between the median and the mode
   (iv) the range of the middle 90%

Exam-style Question

Newtown Hospital (NH) is a public sector hospital. The managers are planning to spend money improving facilities. To raise finance for the hospital, these facilities would then be rented out to private sector health organisations who would sell their services to fee paying private patients. The market research the managers will do before improving facilities will collect both qualitative and quantitative data about the market for private health care. One of the managers knows a doctor who works in a private sector hospital. He has offered to ask 5 or 6 other doctors what extra facilities they think NH should provide.

    (a) What is meant by the terms?

      (i) Qualitative data   [3]

      (ii) Quantitative data   [3]

    (b) Analyse methods of market research that NH could use to help set the prices that it might charge private sector health organisations.   [8]

Adapted from Cambridge 9707 Paper 22 Q2(c) November 2010

Student's answer to (b)

NH is a hospital in the public sector. The hospital is planning to provide extra revenue by renting out facilities to private sector health organisations whose patients pay fees for their treatment. Before spending money on improving facilities, the hospital managers should do some market research.

They should undertake secondary research first. This is data that has already been collected. They could find other hospitals that provide similar facilities and try to get information on what these organisations charge. However, the other hospitals may be reluctant to give this information. However, it should be possible to get information on market sales and growth which might provide useful background information. It may be possible to get information on how much the private health organisations charge their patients.

The NH managers should then do primary research. NH managers could visit other hospitals and interview doctors for the information that they need. They could ask the doctors how much they would pay for the facilities. NH could send a questionnaire out to all of the private health providers and ask them how much they would be prepared to pay for NH's new facilities.

Authors' Comments

The student clearly has a grasp of the situation described in the case. They also understand the difference between primary and secondary research as well as the need to undertake secondary research first. The first paragraph does little more than repeat the case.

There are hints of analysis. For example, the student recognises that secondary research is cheaper and might be better. However there is no real discussion of why this might be the case – for example, being a public sector organisation it might have limited finance available for primary research, the primary research may well not lead to the answers it is seeking and so on.

It would be better to take each of primary and secondary research and to discuss their relative merits in context. These should be tied in to the notion of setting prices. This would enable a realistic and justifiable conclusion to be reached as to which was the better.

The student could also have shown suitable skills by looking at various types of primary research and/or sources of secondary information and compared the strengths and weaknesses of these.

Revision checklist – tick when done and understood!

Topic	Textbook read	Revision complete
Need for market research		
Sampling methods		
Questionnaires		
Reliability of primary data		
Presentation of information		
Statistical analysis		

Marketing Mix: Product and Price

16

Revision Objectives

After you have studied this chapter, you should be able to:

☞ understand what the marketing mix is
☞ analyse the importance of customer relationship marketing
☞ assess the importance of product decisions in different business situations
☞ understand the product life cycle and its significance

☞ calculate price elasticity of demand and understand the results
☞ assess different pricing techniques and apply them to business situations
☞ evaluate the importance of pricing as one element of the marketing mix.

16.1 The marketing mix

The traditional marketing mix comprises the '4Ps' but to this list others can also be added such as People and Processes.

> **Key term**
>
> **Marketing mix:** the four key decisions that must be taken in the effective marketing of a product

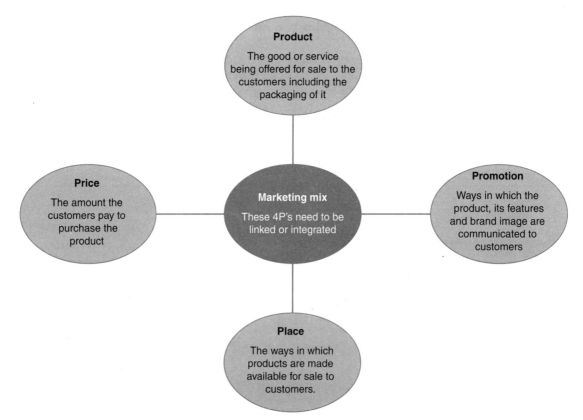

Product
The good or service being offered for sale to the customers including the packaging of it

Price
The amount the customers pay to purchase the product

Marketing mix
These 4P's need to be linked or integrated

Promotion
Ways in which the product, its features and brand image are communicated to customers

Place
The ways in which products are made available for sale to customers.

16.2 Customer Relationship Marketing (CRM) and the 4 Cs

This recent development moves away from the 4P's to focus on how a business can establish a long term relationship with customers. The aim of CRM is to keep existing customers – the focus of the 4Ps is to gain new customers.

> **Key term**
>
> **Customer relationship marketing:** using marketing activities to establish successful customer relationships so that existing customer loyalty can be maintained

Table 16.1

The 4 Cs		
Customer solution	What the business needs to provide to meet the customers' needs and wants	The product and the service provided with it must meet customers' requirements – these requirements have to be monitored by market research and this information may allow for more effective market segmentation
Cost to customer	The total cost of the product including actual price plus guarantee cost, delivery, finance costs	This needs to be maintained at a competitive level
Communication with customer	Promoting the product to customers – but also gaining information back from them	Two way communication will help to improve relationships with customers
Convenience to customer	Providing easy access to both the product (the place where it is sold) and information about it	This may be becoming easier for many customers with increased access to the Internet – but this is not always the most 'convenient' channel for all products

This emphasis on customer loyalty has been encouraged by estimates that suggest it often costs five times more to win a new customer (for example, promotional costs) than to keep an existing one (for example, by offering excellent after-sales service). Recent research suggests that by keeping just 5 per cent more of their existing customers, some companies could increase profits by nearly 100 per cent!

16.3 Product decisions and the product life cycle

A product – any good or service – needs to meet customer expectations if customer loyalty is to be retained. A market map helps to identify the most suitable 'position of new products'. The product life cycle concept can help marketing managers take decisions about products and other elements of the marketing mix.

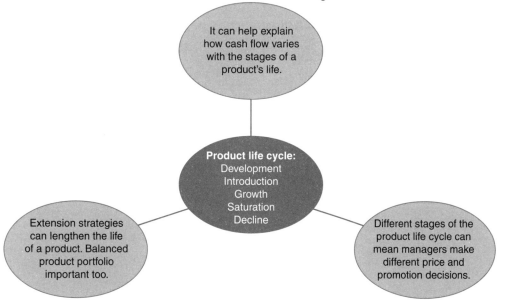

> **Key term**
>
> **Product life cycle:** the pattern of sales recorded by a product from launch to withdrawal from the market

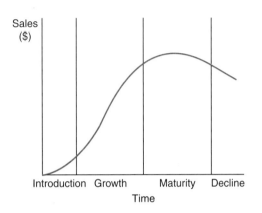

Top tip

The product life cycle is difficult to predict for any new product – and for an existing product it may be difficult to determine which stage it is currently at.

These are possible limitations of this model.

Progress Check A

1. Using any relevant example of a product that you are familiar with, outline the meaning of the '4Ps'.
2. Do you think that 'more advertising' could lead to long term success of any product? Explain your answer.
3. Explain why customer relationship marketing is important for:
   (a) a bank   (b) a car manufacturer
4. Draw and label a typical product life cycle diagram.
5. Give examples of 'extension strategies' for a well known product of your choice and explain the likely impact of them.
6. Explain how the type and level of promotion spending on a product might change as it passes through its life cycle.
7. Explain two limitations of using the product life cycle in decision making.

16.4 Price Elasticity of Demand

This is an important concept as it measures the responsiveness of customers' demand for a product as the price of it is changed.

Price Elasticity of Demand (PED) =

$$\frac{\% \text{ change in quantity demanded}}{\% \text{ change in price}}$$

To calculate a percentage change, use this formula:

$$\frac{\text{Change (in demand or price)}}{\text{Original (demand or price)}} \times 100$$

The PED formula can also be used to answer questions such as these:

If demand increased by 10% and PED is estimated to be −2, what was the change in price?

$$\text{PED} = \frac{\% \text{ change in quantity demanded}}{\% \text{ change in price}}$$

$$-2 = \frac{10}{x}$$

So, $x = \dfrac{10}{-2} = -5\%$

The price was reduced by 5% in order to achieve an increase in sales of 10%.

Progress Check B

1. Copy and complete this table (based on demand per week in units sold).

Original price	New price	Original demand	New demand	PED	Comment
$5	$6	1500	1050	a	Demand is elastic and revenue should fall if the price is increased
$1000	$1050	300	270	b	c
$1	$0.95	5000	6000	d	e
$10000	$11000	20	18	f	g

2. Explain what you understand by the phrase: The demand for product *X* is more price elastic than the demand for product *Y*.

3. A marketing manager estimates that the PED for Product *C* is −0.5 and the PED for Product *D* is −2.3. Explain, with the aid of demand curve diagrams, what would happen to total revenue if the manager increased the prices of both products.

4. State *two* factors that could influence the PED of a product.

Top tip

PED is nearly always a negative result because for most products, when the price is increased the quantity demanded falls – and vice versa with a price reduction.

16.5 Pricing decisions

Setting the price for a product is one of the most important of all marketing decisions. These are some of the factors that influence this decision:

16.6 Pricing methods

There are several different pricing methods or techniques that business can use to determine the actual price to be charged (Table 16.2).

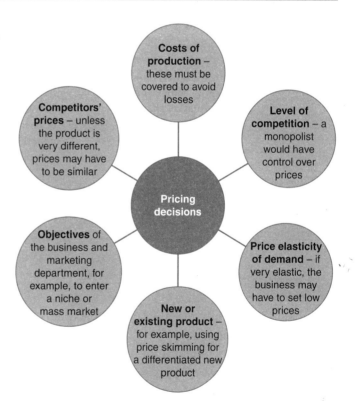

- **Costs of production** – these must be covered to avoid losses
- **Level of competition** – a monopolist would have control over prices
- **Competitors' prices** – unless the product is very different, prices may have to be similar
- **Pricing decisions**
- **Objectives** of the business and marketing department, for example, to enter a niche or mass market
- **Price elasticity of demand** – if very elastic, the business may have to set low prices
- **New or existing product** – for example, using price skimming for a differentiated new product

---

Top tip

It is important, if you are asked to recommend or justify a particular pricing method, to consider the level of competition that exists in the market and the extent to which the product is very 'different from that of competitors' products.

16.7 Why pricing is important

✓ Has major influence on sales and profits of a product
✓ Psychological impact on consumers
✓ Needs to be constantly reviewed especially in fast changing or competitive markets
✓ Essential that the price charged matches and integrates with the rest of the marketing mix.

Table 16.2

Method	Key term	Potential benefits	Potential limitations
Full-cost pricing	Calculating unit cost and adding a fixed profit margin	• Profit will be made if all output sold • Easy to calculate for single product firms	• Difficult to calculate for multi-product firms, for example, may lead to inaccurate allocation of fixed costs • Does not take market conditions into account
Contribution pricing	Prices based on covering variable costs and making a contribution to fixed costs and profit	• Flexible as the price charged can vary considerably with market/ competitive conditions • Variable costs should be covered	• Fixed costs may not be covered (and a loss recorded) if total contribution does not exceed fixed costs
Competitive pricing	Basing price on prices charged by competitors	• Allows the business to remain competitive • Small firms with little market power may have to use this method	• Costs may not be covered – for example, if larger competitors have lower unit costs of production • Price may vary frequently as competition changes
Psychological pricing	Basing price on customers' perceived value of the product	• Customers do not feel they are being charged 'too much' for the product's value • Customers do not feel that a product appears 'too cheap'	• Market research will be necessary to discover customers' perception of value • The psychological price may not cover unit costs
Penetration pricing	Setting a relatively low price in order to achieve high sales volume/market share	• Customers should be attracted to the new (or existing) product as it has a price lower than most competitors	• This price may not cover unit costs • It may be difficult to raise prices later due to customer resistance
Market skimming	Setting a high price for a unique or highly differentiated product	• Should gain high revenue if PED is low • High profit margins	• High prices may attract competitors into the market, reducing sales • Customers may be resistant if prices are lowered later if they consider quality is being reduced too

Progress Check B

1. Use a simple numerical example to explain full cost pricing.
2. Explain how a hotel might use contribution or marginal cost pricing.
3. Under what market conditions would a business be most likely to use competition based pricing.
4. Explain, using a simple example, what price discrimination means.

5. Distinguish between market skimming and market penetration pricing methods.
6. Give one example each of a business situation when
   (a) market skimming and
   (b) market penetration pricing might be used.
7. Give an example of psychological pricing and explain why this method might be used.

Multiple Choice Questions

1. Which of the following is the best definition of 'marketing mix'?
   (i)   All of the factors that influence the success or failure of a product
   (ii) The decisions a firm can make to influence the sales of a product
   (iii) The mix of products produced and sold by any one business
   (iv) The range of products available on the market at any one time

2. The main aim of Customer Relationship Marketing is to:
   (i)   increase sales to new customers
   (ii) encourage customer loyalty
   (iii) increase feedback from customers
   (iv) encourage customers to pay higher prices

3. When a product is in its 'introductory stage' of the product life cycle, which one of the following is most likely to be true?
   (i)   Sales will be high, advertising costs will be low
   (ii) Sales may start low, advertising costs will be low
   (iii) Sales may start low and cash flow may be negative
   (iv) Sales will be falling and cash flow will be positive

4. Which one of the following will tend to lead to the price elasticity of demand for a product being low (inelastic)?
   (i)   Very few close competitors
   (ii) Many competitors
   (iii) Consumers spend a high proportion of income on it
   (iv) Low brand loyalty

5. One of the claimed advantages of using contribution cost (or marginal cost) pricing is that:
   (i)   it ensures that all costs of production are covered by the price charged
   (ii) it makes sure a profit is made on each item sold
   (iii) prices will rise when fixed costs increase
   (iv) as long variable costs are covered, prices can be adapted to market conditions

6. A business is most likely to use market skimming pricing when:
   (i)   an established product is experiencing increasing competition
   (ii) a new product is being launched into a competitive market
   (iii) a new product is launched into an unexploited niche market
   (iv) an established product is reaching the end of its product life cycle

Exam-style Question

Redgate Bakers produces specialist cakes for festivals and birthdays. It has a shop that also sells a large number of loaves of bread of different types but these are all bought in from another bakery.

The costs of producing each specialist cake are:

Materials and labour $15
Weekly fixed costs of cake department $100

Ten cakes are produced and sold each week.

Redgate Bakers has an excellent reputation for its cakes and many customers think they are the best available in town. The market for bread is very competitive. Several large supermarkets also offer a wide range of bread. Some of them sell it as a 'loss leader' and the manager of Redgate Bakers is worried about the effect on his business.

(a) What is meant by the term 'loss leader'?   [3]
(b) Calculate the selling price for each specialist cake if Redgate Bakers use full cost pricing and expect to make a profit of $20 per cake.   [3]
(c) Discuss the pricing methods that the manager of Redgate Bakery could use for the bread sold by the business.   [10]

Student's answer to (c)

There are many pricing methods that Redgate could use. They could use market skimming which means charging a very high price for bread and then, later reducing prices when competitors came into the market. This would mean that the bakery would make a high profit to start with.

Contribution pricing could be used. This means the price would at least cover the variable costs of making the bread and anything extra would be profit.

Full cost pricing could also be used as with the specialist cakes. Each bread sold could have a price fixed on it based on the total cost of making it and adding a profit mark up. This would be the best method for Redgate to use.

Authors' Comments

This is a weak answer. Can you see why? Firstly, the good points are that subject knowledge is shown by stating and explaining three pricing methods – but the student confused contribution with profit when writing about contribution pricing.

Now the weaknesses: The application is very poor because although the name of the business is used in the answer this **is not** application! The student has failed to mention that supermarkets are offering very low prices and this will influence Redgate's decision. Secondly, the answer assumes that bread is made by Redgate – and it isn't, it is bought in from another bakery.

Also, the analytical understanding of the full cost method is weak because the student assumes that the unit cost of each loaf of bread can be calculated accurately – and in practice this is most unlikely. The 'judgement' at the end cannot be rewarded as it shows no understanding of this businesses situation.

Now try to write a better answer!

Revision checklist – tick when done and understood!

Topic	Textbook read	Revision complete
The elements of the marketing mix		
The importance of customer relationship marketing		
Product as an element of the marketing mix		
The significance of the product life cycle		
Factors that determine prices		
Price elasticity of demand		
Pricing methods		
The importance of the pricing decision		

Marketing Mix: Promotion and Place

17

Revision Objectives

After you have studied this chapter, you should be able to:

☞ understand the different forms of promotion

☞ know why objectives for a promotion campaign, such as establishing brand image, are important

☞ analyse factors considered when making promotion decisions and apply these to different business situations

☞ understand why 'place' is an important element of the marketing mix

☞ discuss the suitability of different distribution channels in different business situations

☞ analyse the reasons for and impact of Internet marketing

☞ evaluate the importance of an integrated marketing mix.

17.1 Different forms of promotion

Promotion is about communicating with customers or potential customers – to tell them about a product, to offer special deals on that product and to convince customers that they should buy it.

Key terms

Promotion: the use of advertising, sales promotion, personal selling, direct mail, trade fairs, sponsorship, public relations and viral marketing to inform customers and persuade them to buy

Above the line promotion: promotion (such as advertising) paid for directly by the business

Below the line promotion: promotion that is not a directly paid for means of communication but based on short term incentives to buy

Promotion mix: the combination of promotional techniques that a firm uses to sell a product

Advertising: paid for communication with consumers to inform and persuade, for example, TV and cinema advertising

Sales promotion: incentives such as special offers or special deals directed at consumers or retailers to achieve short-term sales increases and repeat purchases

> **Key term**
>
> **Promotional budget:** the amount of money made available by a business for spending on promotion during a certain time period

17.2 Promotional objectives

Effective decisions about how much to spend on promotion and which methods of promotion to use require a business to establish clear promotional objectives. These could include:

✓ establishing or reinforcing a distinctive brand image for the product to help differentiate it from competitors and to make customers 'ask for the product by brand name'
✓ increase sales by a target %
✓ increase market share to a target %
✓ increase repeat sales to existing customers
✓ attract a target number of new customers.

These promotional objectives should be closely linked in with the overall objectives of the marketing department (which should themselves be linked to the corporate objectives of the business).

How can a business check if these objectives have been achieved?

✓ Consumer feedback, for example, focus groups
✓ Sales before and after the promotion campaign
✓ Response rates to advertisements and sales promotions
✓ Website 'hit' rates.

> **Top tip**
>
> When discussing promotion and how much a business might spend on promotion it is important to refer to: promotional objectives, how to assess whether these have been met, finance resources available and the nature of the market.

Progress Check A

1. Why is promotion important when launching a new product?
2. If a product is already well established in the market why might a business still spend money on promoting it?
3. State three methods of 'below the line' promotion and outline one possible advantage of each one.
4. What is meant by a 'promotional budget'?
5. Should a computer manufacturer that is launching a new model spend as much on advertising 'as its competitors'? Explain your answer.
6. Why is it important for a business to measure the success of a promotion campaign?

17.3 Promotion decisions – the key factors

When marketing managers make decisions about how to promote a product there are a number of key factors that should be considered:

Table 17.1

Key factor	Why important
Product	• Consumer product or industrial product – only one of these is likely to be advertised on television. Which one? • New product or existing product – which one of these is likely to need 'informative' advertising? • Product life cycle – different approaches to promotion are likely to be used at different stages
Target market	• If the product is targeted at the elderly (for example, walking aids) then magazines or news papers with a high proportion of elderly readers might be an effective medium to use • If the product, such as a computer game, is targeted at a young consumers, then viral marketing through social networking sites might be more effective
Cost	• The cost of different promotions needs to be weighed against the potential revenue/profit gains. Would it be worthwhile a local home cleaning service business advertising in national newspapers?

(Continued)

Table 17.1 (*Continued*)

Key factor	Why important
Finance available	• Related to cost. The finance available – promotional/marketing budget – will often limit what forms of promotion can be used
Competitors	• Is it a good idea to copy how competitors advertise and promote their products? Will consumers be attracted to alternative methods?

> **Key term**
>
> **Viral marketing:** use of social networking sites or SMS text messages to 'spread the word' about a brand and to sell products

Top tip

When asked to discuss how a product could be promoted it is not a good idea to just state: the business should spend as much as possible on promotion.

Effective promotion should be well targeted at the people most likely to be effective – it does not have to be expensive.

> **Progress Check B**
>
> 1. Why might viral marketing be an effective form of promotion for launching a new rock band and its music recordings?
> 2. State one product for which TV advertising might be effective – and explain your choice.
> 3. State one product for which 'point of sale' displays could be an effective form of promotion – and explain your choice.
> 4. Explain with examples how the promotion of a product might change as it passes through its life cycle.

Why 'place' is important

When studying the 4Cs, 'convenience to customer' is an important consideration. The **Place** element of the marketing mix is closely related to this. By place, we do not necessarily mean a physical location where a product can be bought – although the position of a shop may well be an important aspect of customer convenience in buying a product. The place element refers to the method or channel of distribution used by the business and how and where the product is to be sold to the customer.

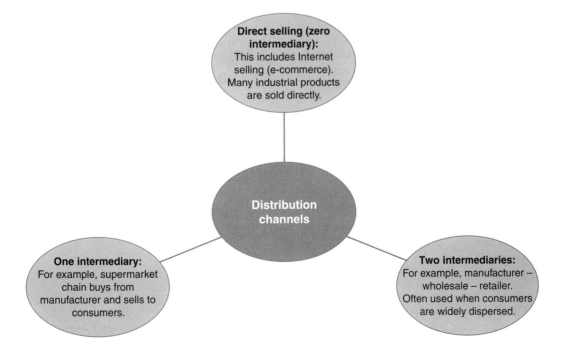

Direct selling (zero intermediary): This includes Internet selling (e-commerce). Many industrial products are sold directly.

Distribution channels

One intermediary: For example, supermarket chain buys from manufacturer and sells to consumers.

Two intermediaries: For example, manufacturer – wholesale – retailer. Often used when consumers are widely dispersed.

17.4 Deciding which distribution channels should be used

Important factors to consider include:

- ✓ need to keep costs low to allow for low prices – intermediaries may add to 'channel cost'
- ✓ importance of product freshness
- ✓ how widely dispersed the market is
- ✓ cost of holding inventories
- ✓ level of service expected by consumers
- ✓ technical complexity of product.

17.5 The impact of the Internet

The rapid growth of Internet marketing has had an impact on most elements of the marketing mix. For example, it is often claimed that *prices* are lower, company websites are a common form of *promotion* and direct selling online means the *place* decision has changed for many products too.

Table 17.2

Internet marketing	
Advantages	**Disadvantages**
Customers can compare prices easily – the business might be the cheapest.	Customers can compare prices easily – the business might **not** be the cheapest!
Global promotion is possible though the website – much cheaper than global TV advertising!	Millions of websites are available – how will customers access yours?
Global selling is possible through a suitably designed website – cutting out intermediaries.	Some customers prefer face to face contact and personal selling – and the ability to 'see and try before they buy'.
Dynamic pricing is possible – charging different prices to different consumers based on information about them.	Customers may object to not always being offered the lowest possible price.
Easy to record web 'hits' and success of online promotions.	Goods need to be delivered (and possibly sent back by customer) at expense of the business.

17.6 Integrating the marketing mix

The four elements of the marketing mix must be integrated with each other. This means that the '4P' decisions cannot be taken in isolation to each other. Consumers need to be given the same 'message' about a product through its design, price level, method of promotion and 'place' of sale.

Top tip

Explaining the importance of an integrated mix to the success of a marketing campaign is a very good conclusion to many examination answers on the marketing mix and marketing strategy.

Progress Check C

1. Explain why expensive jewellery is usually sold through shops with high quality fittings and décor using well trained staff.
2. Why would a computer controlled manufacturing machine usually be sold through 'direct selling'?
3. Why might a furniture manufacture sell most of its products to retailers rather than directly from its factory?
4. Why might a sweet manufacturer use a two intermediary channel of distribution?

Multiple Choice Questions

1. Which one of the following is an example of 'above the line' promotion?
    (i) Delivering 'money-off' tokens to potential customers
    (ii) Using a 'buy one get one free' offer
    (iii) Buying space in a newspaper to inform customers of a new product
    (iv) Using a supplier's new display cabinets to present products more attractively

2. One of the claimed advantages of a supermarket introducing a loyalty card scheme of promotion is that:
    (i) it will not reduce the profit margin on goods bought by customers
    (ii) it will improve the 'quality brand image' of the products sold
    (iii) other firms will not be able to copy the idea
    (iv) it encourages consumers to make repeat purchases from the stores

3. A well established brand image can lead to a reduction in:
    (i) price elasticity of demand for a product
    (ii) consumer loyalty for a product
    (iii) viral marketing of a product
    (iv) the price charged for a product

4. An increase in a firm's promotion budget means that:
    (i) market share will also increase
    (ii) more advertising time on TV could be purchased
    (iii) a different channel of distribution will be used
    (iv) sponsorship of sporting events by the firm will have to be reduced

5. One of the claimed benefits of Internet marketing of books is:
    (i) It might allow reduced prices to be charged as intermediaries will not take a profit margin
    (ii) The business selling the books will not have to dispatch the goods to the consumers
    (iii) The consumers will not be able to send the books back if they are damaged
    (iv) The consumer will receive the books immediately

6. One of the reasons for a business using a wholesaler as part of the channel of distribution for a product is:
    (i) The consumer will be able to buy the product directly from the manufacturer
    (ii) The manufacturer should be able to reduce inventory holding costs
    (iii) The manufacturer will have full control over the marketing of its products
    (iv) The wholesaler should be able to supply retailers with products at lower prices than the manufacturer could have done directly

Exam-style question

(a) Analyse the advantages and disadvantages to a clothing retail business of starting to sell products through the Internet. [8]

(b) Discuss the factors that might influence the marketing mix for a newly launched soft drink. [12]

Student's plan for Question (b)

✓ Define marketing mix

✓ Suggest a marketing objective for the business, for example, to gain 5% market share in first year

✓ The four elements of the mix should aim towards this objective

✓ Product – does it offer anything new, for example, special flavours? This is a very competitive market

✓ Price – competitor based pricing might be necessary especially with well known brands such as Coca Cola as rivals

✓ Promotion – perhaps aimed at children or, if it is an 'energy' drink, at sports people. How big is the budget though? Brand image needs to be built up. TV advertising may be too expensive.

✓ Place – market covers a wide geographical area, low value product – two intermediary channels might be best. As many shops as possible to stock the drinks

✓ Conclusion – will only succeed if it is an integrated mix that convinces consumers to try this product over all of the competing brands. If aimed at children perhaps low prices will be the most important factor.

Authors' Comments

This is an excellent plan. Starting with a definition of a key term in the question is a very good idea. As is the suggested marketing objective.

Do you notice how it makes several references to the soft drinks market? This is very important.

Do you notice how the student is always trying to link the 4Ps together into an integrated mix? This shows good understanding. The conclusion suggests the student is showing signs of evaluating the suggestions made in the answer.

Use this plan to write out your own answer. Try to use 4–5 paragraphs. It should take you no longer than 30 minutes.

Revision checklist – tick when done and understood!

Topic	Textbook read	Revision complete
What promotion is and above/below the line promotion		
Why businesses use promotion – the objectives set for it		
The advantages and disadvantages of different methods of advertising and sales promotion		
Factors that influence the choice of promotional method		
Distribution channels – the different types		
Factors that influence the choice of distribution channel		
Internet marketing – the impact on business and customers		
Integrated marketing mix		

Marketing Planning 18

18.1 Marketing plan

Marketing decisions in large businesses can lead to significant expenditure and can have a huge impact on the future success of the business. These decisions need to be planned for – not taken on the spur of the moment.

> **Key term**
>
> **Marketing plan:** a detailed fully researched report on marketing objectives and the marketing strategies to be used to achieve them

The key contents of a marketing plan are:

✓ purpose of the plan, for example, prepare for launch of new product
✓ background to the business including mission statement (useful for external stakeholders such as potential investors)
✓ situational analysis – SWOT and PEST analysis will help to establish the current strengths of the business and its products, actual and potential competitors, market trends and external problems and opportunities
✓ marketing objectives – to give clear focus and direction to the marketing plan
✓ marketing strategies proposed – the ways in which the business intends to achieve its objectives, for example, developing new markets for existing products or promoting in existing markets to increase market share. The strategy used will have an impact on the 4Ps decisions taken by the business
✓ marketing budget – having a plan but no resources will lead to disaster!
✓ executive summary and time frame for putting the plan into effect.

A

Table 18.1

Evaluation of market planning	
Potential benefits	**Potential limitations**
An important part of a business plan, for example, for a new business or a significant development by an existing business	Detailed plans can be time consuming and costly, for example, external market research may have to be 'bought-in'. Are they justified for small businesses? Are they justified if similar marketing decisions have been taken before?
Encourages integration and close working with other functional departments	Fast changing markets require a flexible approach to planning – a marketing plan that is not adjusted to changing external conditions, for example, would lead to incorrect decisions being taken
Improves the quality of marketing decision making and reduces risks of these decisions failing	Planning cannot guarantee success – effective management of the strategic decision will still be essential

Marketing strategies should be integrated and coordinated:

1. with other departments – to ensure that the necessary finance, people and production capacity are available to put the marketing strategy into operation
2. with all elements of the marketing mix – aiming to support the strategy in a coherent way.

Progress Check A

1. Will marketing planning remove all risks of making strategic decisions? Briefly explain your answer.

2. Explain, with the aid of an example, why marketing objectives should be decided on before making a marketing strategy decision.

18.2 Elasticity

Estimating the following measures of elasticity could be an important part of the situational analysis for a market plan. They are based on the same principle as price elasticity of demand: measuring the relative impact on demand for a product following a change in a variable.

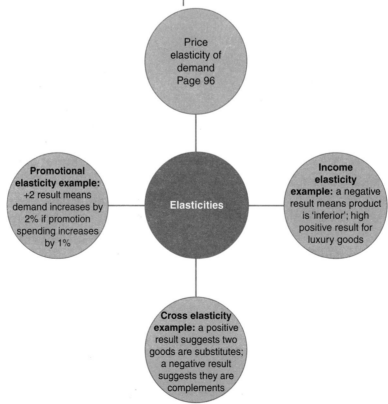

Key formulae

Promotional elasticity of demand

$$= \frac{\text{\% change in demand}}{\text{\% change in promotion spending}}$$

Income elasticity of demand

$$= \frac{\text{\% change in demand}}{\text{\% change in consumer incomes}}$$

Cross elasticity of demand

$$= \frac{\text{\% change in demand of Good A}}{\text{\% change in price of Good B}}$$

Using elasticity results – words of caution!

✓ Often based on estimates
✓ Assumes other factors did not affect sales
✓ May only apply to a certain time period – last year's elasticity estimates may not be accurate for today's market conditions.

Top tip

Elasticity results are not necessarily accurate figures that can be relied upon by marketing managers for future decision making – the results can act as guidelines, no more.

Progress Check B

1. Explain to a marketing manager why the following estimates of income elasticity of demand for three of the company's products are important:

   Product C –2; Product D +0.3; Product E +3.

2. Explain how the demand for the three products in Q1 might be affected by an economic recession.

3. Explain why, other things being equal, a marketing manager might consider switching promotion spending from Product A to Product B using these calculations of promotional elasticity of demand based on last year's data.

   Product A +1; Product B +3

4. In your answer to Q3, why should the marketing manager be cautious about these elasticity results?

5. Explain the possible relationships between the following products if the estimated cross elasticities of demand, following a 10% increase in price of Product P, are:

   Product R + 3; Product S – 2

6. Explain one reason why a product's promotional elasticity result from 2011 might not be relevant this year.

18.3 Promotional models: AIDA and DAGMAR

These models are used to help marketing managers take more effective strategic decisions on promoting products.

Key terms

AIDA (Attention-Interest-Desire-Action): this is the model that explains the successive stages a customer passes through in buying a product
DAGMAR (Defining Advertising Goals for Measured Advertising Results): a process of establishing goals for a promotion campaign to determine whether it has been successful or not

Progress Check C

1. Using an example, explain how the AIDA model can help to explain consumer behaviour.
2. Explain the importance of goals when making decisions about a promotion campaign.

18.4 New product development

Key term

New Product Development (NPD): the design, creation and marketing of new goods and services

A   Stages in NPD

Generate new product ideas
For example, from R and D, employees, adapting existing products.
Idea screening
Is it technically feasible and will it benefit consumers whilst making a profit for the business?
Concept development and testing
What features should the product have? How will consumers react to it?
Business analysis
Assessing costs, likely sales and potential profits.
Product testing
Testing the product in terms of its durability and function; modifying it in response to consumer group feedback.
Test marketing
Small scale market launch to test customer reaction. Is it worthwhile launching nationally?
Commercialisation
Full scale launch of the product.

18.5   Research and Development (R and D)

Top tip
Don't forget that only a small proportion of 'new product ideas' ever reaches the final stage of commercialisation – this is an evaluation of the NPD process.

Key term

Research and Development (R and D): the scientific research and technical development of new products and processes

Top tip
Never confuse research and development with market research!

Evaluation of R and D

Potential benefits	Potential limitations
Creates new products	It is expensive and may take years for new products to lead to higher profits
Develops new production processes, for example, robots to reduce unit costs	Rival firms may be spending more on R and D or using resources to develop even better products and processes
Unique selling point may be created – higher prices may be charged, increasing profit margins	If the new product or process is not differentiated enough to patent it, other companies will copy the development
Can create a progressive and forward looking image for a business	R and D is not guaranteed to lead to successful new developments

Progress Check D

1. State three possible sources of new product ideas.
2. Why is 'idea screening' a necessary stage of the NPD process?
3. Explain the benefits of using a test market for a new product.
4. Why are some industries more focused on R and D than others?

5. Explain how a change in government laws that restricted the use of powerful motor cars might:
   (a) lead some car manufacturers to increase R and D spending and
   (b) make some new car developments less successful?
6. Distinguish between 'offensive' and 'defensive' R and D strategies.

18.6 Sales forecasting

What are the potential benefits to sales forecasting?

- ✓ Preparing marketing plans, for example, are sales forecast to increase faster in some markets than others?
- ✓ Changing marketing strategies, for example, in response to forccasted sales decline
- ✓ Reducing risk of decision making, for example, not launching a new luxury product when a recession is forecast to reduce sales in this market segment
- ✓ Preparing resources in other departments, for example, if sales are forecast to increase.

Sales forecasting methods

Key stages in the moving average method:

- ✓ calculate moving total
- ✓ divide by the number of time periods included to give the moving average (trend)
- ✓ centre the moving average if necessary
- ✓ graph the trend results and extrapolate
- ✓ estimate future trend results
- ✓ adjust by the average seasonal variation.

Top tip Be ready to evaluate any of the methods of sales forecasting – and remember that sales forecasts can never be fully relied on.
The future is not certain!

Progress Check E

1. Using an example, explain what the term 'positive correlation' means.
2. What does 'average seasonal variation' mean?
3. Under what circumstances might market research data be the only possible method of sales forecasting?
4. Calculate the seasonal variations from the following data:

Quarter	Sales $000	Trend (Quarterly moving average) $000	Seasonal variation $000
1	56	63	
2	67	66	
3	80	70	

5. Why might sales for a manufacturer of mobile phones be subject to cyclical variations?
6. Explain two business situations in which sales forecasts could turn out to be very inaccurate.
7. Explain the difference between cyclical variations and seasonal variations.

Multiple Choice Questions

1. One of the reasons often given for marketing planning is:
   (i) It guarantees future sales success
   (ii) It reduces the risk of making bad major strategic marketing decisions
   (iii) It is a legal requirement for public limited companies
   (iv) It is quick and easy to do so all businesses can afford to do it

2. A positive result for a product's promotional elasticity of demand suggests that:
   (i) the product is likely to be an 'inferior' one
   (ii) spending more on promoting the product will always lead to higher profits
   (iii) the sales of the product are likely to rise at a higher rate than promotion spending on it
   (iv) the sales of the product are likely to rise even if less money is spent on promoting it

3. A business sells a product with an estimated income elasticity of demand of −1. Based on this data which one of the following statements is likely to be true?
   (i) The business will increase output of the product when consumer incomes are rising
   (ii) Sales of the product could increase despite an economic recession
   (iii) There is no point in spending any money on promoting this product
   (iv) If the price is reduced by 10%, sales of the product are likely to increase by 10%

4. In which of the following industries is new product development likely to be crucial for success?
   (i) Hairdressing
   (ii) Consumer electronics
   (iii) Furniture making
   (iv) Shoes

5. One of the reasons often given to explain why research and development spending by a business might not lead to higher profits is:
   (i) There are no new possible product developments
   (ii) Consumers are reluctant to buy the latest products
   (iii) Competitors might develop a better product
   (iv) Research and development costs are so low that too many businesses are now developing new products

6. Which one of the following is the best explanation of the moving average method of sales forecasting?
   (i) It uses market research to identify the fastest moving market changes
   (ii) By using qualitative methods, it avoids the need for any calculations
   (iii) By averaging future forecasts it avoids the risk of unforeseen events making the sales predictions inaccurate
   (iv) By averaging past data the predicted trend of future sales is easier to identify

Exam-style Question

Radar manufactures cosmetics, shampoos and creams for women. Increasingly, men are also buying these products too. 80 per cent of Radar's products are sold in country P. The company has transformed its image, mainly through successful research and development. It used to only make products for sale by supermarkets under their 'own brand' label. Recent work by Radar's small research and development team has led to a new range of products sold under the 'Aquaskin' brand name. These were supported by a major advertising campaign that promoted the unique selling point of the products as: 'Aquaskin is an entirely natural product, not tested on animals and guaranteed to make you look younger'. Sales of Aquaskin products were 50 per cent above target in the last two years despite market skimming pricing.

Encouraged by this success and the launch of many new competing products, Radar started to develop other new products. 'Aquaskin Junior' is targeted at young consumers. The Marketing Director told a board meeting, "Young people will be influenced by being told that sports players and music stars use the product. This product is certain to sell well. There is no need for market research as the Aquaskin name is now so well known. We will not even have to spend money on promoting – viral marketing will do that job for us. I don't think there is another product like this on the market".

Despite the Marketing Director's confidence, one year after the launch of Aquaskin Junior, sales were disappointing and the product, despite high prices, was making a very small contribution due to high levels of outdated stock.

(a) Analyse the benefits to Radar of investment in Research and Development. [10]

(b) Evaluate the benefit to Radar of preparing a detailed marketing plan before launching a new product such as 'Aquaskin Junior' cream. [16]

Adapted from Cambridge 9707 Paper 32 Section A Q1&3 November 2010

Student's answer to (a)

Research and development (R and D) is when a business spends money on developing new products for sale and new ways of making products. It can be very expensive. Radar could spend more on R and D to develop new products that could be sold to different markets or market segments. This would increase the company's total sales and profits. Different market segments often have consumers that want to buy products different from everyone else so by producing new goods that appeal to them, Radar would be less dependent on what it already sells.

The company could also discover a completely new product or process that they could patent. This is like a monopoly that no other business could copy. This USP would allow Radar to charge high prices and increase profit margins. This is what Toyota do with their hybrid cars that they have patented the design of.

However, R and D could be a waste of money for Radar if rivals come up with even better ideas. In which case perhaps the money used could have been better spent on promoting existing products.

Authors' Comments

This student knows about R and D – and they have not confused it with market research! So far, so good. The analysis of the benefits of R and D is also impressive. The two points made about extending sales into new market segments and creating a USP are well explained and developed.

There are two weaknesses to this answer. Firstly it is not at all applied to Radar and the products the company produces. Don't forget that just writing the company name is not application! The student could have referred to existing Radar cosmetic products by name and suggested that, perhaps the male market segment was worth developing new products for. The growing number of competitors' products could also have been referred to as a reason why R and D could help to differentiate Radar from its rivals. Absence of specific application, using the material contained in the case study is a real weakness. The second problem is less serious but it shows that the student is not fully aware of the meaning of key examination 'prompt' words. The answer makes some attempts to evaluate R and D spending and this was not what was asked for. The student has wasted time attempting evaluation. Time which could have been better spent on application and analysis – or on evaluating the answer to Question b) – which does need evaluation!

Revision checklist – tick when done and understood!

Topic	Textbook read	Revision complete
Marketing plans		
Elasticities		
AIDA/DAGMAR		
New product development		
Research and Development		
Sales forecasting		

Globalisation and International Markets

19

After you have studied this chapter, you should be able to:

☞ understand what globalisation is and how it affects marketing

☞ explain the relative benefits of different approaches to international marketing

☞ apply and evaluate international marketing strategies.

19.1 Globalisation of markets – and the impact on marketing

The trend towards increased globalisation is being driven by:

✓ less protectionism and freer international trade

✓ expansion of multinational corporations

✓ fewer restrictions on movement of capital and workers

✓ Internet and other technological developments.

Key terms

Globalisation: the growing trend towards world markets in products, capital and labour with less protectionism

Multinational corporations: businesses that have operations in more than one country

Globalisation has both potential benefits and drawbacks for businesses. The benefits include not just increased opportunities for selling in foreign markets but also setting up production operations in other countries and integrating with foreign companies.

The main drawback is one of increased competition – perhaps from lower cost producers in other countries.

Progress Check A

Copy out the following factors in two lists – one with globalisation benefits to businesses and one with globalisation drawbacks to businesses:

(a) New markets open up

(b) More foreign competitors for home market

(c) Costs may be lower in foreign markets

(d) Cultural differences exist in foreign markets

(e) Increased competition can stimulate a business to increase efficiency

(f) Integration with foreign businesses more likely

(g) Takeovers by foreign businesses more likely.

The growth of world trade is creating more opportunities for businesses to sell in foreign markets – international marketing.

Key term

International marketing: selling products in markets other than the home or domestic market

Reasons why businesses market products in other countries:

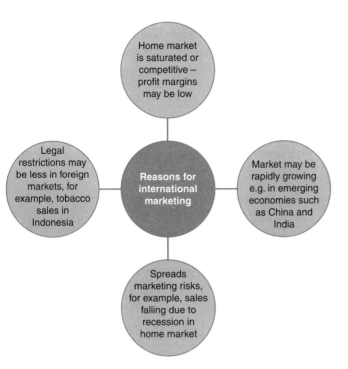

19.3 How to enter foreign markets

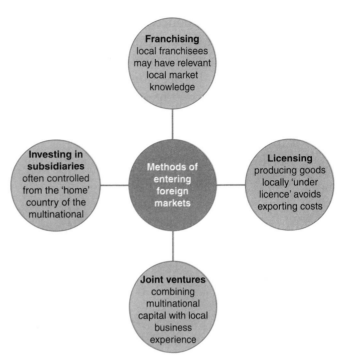

19.2 Differences between 'selling in home markets' and international marketing

✓ Legal differences – for example, laws controlling advertising to children or unethical business practices
✓ Cultural differences – for example, language, religious beliefs relating to whether meat can be eaten and from which animals, role of women in society
✓ Economic and social differences – for example, average income differences, ageing or youthful population
✓ Political differences – for example, some countries are less politically stable than others
✓ Business and market differences – for example, small shops are much more significant (in terms of % of total consumer spending) in India than in the UK
✓ Different approaches to ethical issues.

19.4 International marketing strategies

The two main strategies for selling products in foreign markets are pan-global marketing or global localisation.

> **Key terms**
>
> **Pan-global marketing:** selling the same products in the same way in all international markets
> **Global localisation:** adapting the marketing mix, including differentiated products, to meet national and regional tastes and cultures

The key differences between these two strategies are that 'pan-global' attempts to reduce marketing costs and new product development costs **but** 'global localisation' attempts to satisfy local market conditions – even if this means marketing costs are higher.

Progress Check B

1. Aston Martin, a maker of expensive luxury cars, recently announced it was planning to sell in India for the first time.
   Explain *two* possible reasons why the company took this decision.

2. Apple Corp's latest high tech products are sold in most countries in the world with few, if any adaptations.
   Is this an example of pan global marketing or global localisation marketing?
   Explain your answer.

3. How might the fact that there are different laws in different countries affect a company's international marketing decisions?

4. The average (median) age of Brazil's population was 29.3 years in 2011.
   In Japan the median age was 50 years.
   Explain how these data might influence the marketing strategy of an international clothing retailer operating in both countries.

5. Explain why an international food retailing business might establish a joint venture with a local retailing business when selling in an emerging market country for the first time.

6. Explain two benefits to a soft drink manufacturing business of using pan global marketing rather than global localisation.

Multiple Choice Questions

1. The best explanation of globalisation is:
   (i)   All countries are now part of the same free trade area
   (ii) Countries' economies are now much less dependent on foreign trade than they used to be
   (iii) Companies can sell products abroad and invest abroad more easily than used to be the case
   (iv) Cultural and economic differences between nations are becoming much greater

2. One reason for a company planning to sell its products abroad for the first time is:
   (i)   It will cost less to export products than to sell them in the home market
   (ii) Legal controls over product quality are always much less strict in foreign countries
   (iii) The foreign markets may be saturated
   (iv) Market share could be declining in the home market

3. If Company *A* entered a foreign market by selling a license to a local firm to manufacture products then:
   (i)   quality would certainly improve
   (ii) costs of exporting products would be low
   (iii) profit margins would definitely increase compared to the home market

   (iv) additional capacity in Company *A*'s factory in the home country would be needed

4. One of the claimed advantages of using a global localisation approach to marketing is:
   (i)   Product development costs will be minimised
   (ii) The same product will be recognisable all over the world
   (iii) The same promotional material can be used globally
   (iv) Marketing decisions will be adapted to local conditions

5. One of the claimed advantages of pan-global marketing is:
   (i)   In highly competitive markets the marketing cost benefits it offers could be very important
   (ii) Different adverts in different countries will avoid upsetting local custom and culture
   (iii) Consumers in all countries can be encouraged to buy the same product design even if it is not advertising
   (iv) The product will become so well known that no advertising will be necessary to launch it in a new market

Exam-style Question

Meaty Burgers (MB) is one of the world's best known 'fast food' restaurant chains. It offers cheap meals, quick service and a family friendly atmosphere to millions of consumers all over the world everyday of the year. Recent research suggests that the average age of its customers is 22 years. MB offers six core food products in all countries it sell in – all these products are based around, according to its advertising, 'the largest meat burgers in the world' (burgers are bread rolls filled with grilled meat). MB has many rivals competing for a share of the global fast food market.

Sales at MB restaurants are increasing in all countries except Country B. Country B has an ageing population of 500m people – a huge potential market. Over half the population do not eat meat for religious and cultural reasons. Average incomes are much lower than in most of the countries MB operates in.

Would you recommend that MB changes its pan-global marketing strategy to achieve success in Country B? Justify your answer.   [16]

Student's plan

- ✓ Define 'pan-global marketing'
- ✓ Apply to MB – 'cheap prices, quick service, same core products in all markets' – good example of pan-global marketing
- ✓ Benefits of Pan-global strategy to MB – helps business keep costs down (explain how) and compete in a market with 'many rivals'. MB name may be well known because of its pan-global strategy
- ✓ Drawbacks to MB – does not seem to be working in Country B – explain why not
- ✓ How could global localisation help in Country B? Would the additional revenue benefits outweigh the costs of adapting marketing strategy?
- ✓ Final evaluation: Depends on how important Country B market is; will consumers in other countries start to demand 'differentiated products and marketing too'?

Authors' Comments

This is a logical and well balanced plan. There are very good application points. Can the student develop these and analyse the benefits and drawbacks clearly? Will the evaluation provide the justification required by the question?

If **yes** is the answer to these questions, the student answer should be very good. Try it now!

Revision checklist – tick when done and understood!

Topic	Textbook read	Revision complete
What globalisation is and the key features of it		
How the trend towards globalisation is affecting businesses		
Reasons for international marketing		
Problems of international marketing		
Benefits and drawbacks of pan-global marketing		
Benefits and drawbacks of global localisation		

Revision Objectives

After you have studied this chapter, you should be able to:

☞ understand the production process
☞ use the concept of adding value
☞ discuss ways of increasing value added
☞ explain efficiency

☞ calculate labour productivity and capital productivity
☞ discuss ways of improving productivity.

20.1 Production

Operations management is concerned with the processes involved in converting *inputs* into *outputs* suitable for the customer.

Resources/inputs	Production process	Output
Land	Efficiency	Finished goods
Labour	Quality	Services
Capital	Flexibility	Components for other firms

Top tip

Do not think that Operations Management is only for manufacturing businesses. Businesses such as banks, supermarkets, petrol stations also have to plan to use resources productively and effectively. The term 'production' can refer as much to a business providing a service as to a firm manufacturing a product.

Progress Check A

1. Explain the resources that would be needed to refine crude oil.
2. Who would buy the output from a cement manufacturer?
3. What are the resources used by a shoe shop?
4. Give examples of resources that can be categorised as 'land'.

20.2 The production process

Consumer need ⟹ Suitable product ⟹
Quality method/standards ⟸ Production system ⟸

Progress Check B

1. How might you determine 'consumer need'?
2. Why is quality part of the production process?
3. What aspects of 'banking' can be described as production?

20.3 Adding value

The production process **adds value** – the customer wants the finished products not the raw materials.
   For example, for furniture:

✓ unsawn timber has little value
✓ sawn timber has greater value
✓ furniture made from sawn timber has even greater value
✓ furniture conveniently displayed in the shop for sale has even greater value.

At each stage the value added is the final value of that stage less the costs of the inputs.

A firm sells furniture for $100. Materials (screws, glue etc.) cost $3, the wood costs $30 so the added value is $67.

Progress Check C

1. How does a retail outlet add value?
2. If the leather for handbag costs $10 per handbag and other costs are $20 per handbag, what would customers value the shoes at if the value added is $30 per handbag?

20.4 Increasing added value

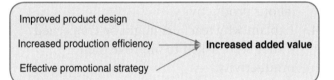

Progress Check D

1. Explain how promotion can increase the value added of a model of car.
2. How could new software add value to a laptop?

Key terms

Added value: the difference between the cost of purchasing raw materials and the price the finished goods are sold for
Production: converting inputs into outputs
Level of production: the number of units produced during a time period

20.5 Increasing efficiency

Productivity measures the efficiency of turning inputs into outputs.

> Better efficiency = Lower unit costs

Key term

Efficiency: producing output at the highest ratio of output to input

Table 20.1

Labour productivity	Capital productivity
Measured by:	Measured by:
$\dfrac{\text{Total output in period}}{\text{Total workers employed}}$	$\dfrac{\text{Output in period}}{\text{Capital employed}}$

Improved by:
- training
- increasing motivation
- better management
- providing better equipment for workers.

Labour intensive	Capital intensive
Production relies heavily on workforce, for example, hand-made furniture	Production relies heavily on capital equipment (for example, machinery) such as car manufacturing

Choice:
- nature of product
- traditions of business and desired image
- relative price of inputs (for example, cheap labour favours labour intensive)
- size of firm and available capital.

Key terms

Productivity: The ratio of outputs to inputs during production, for example, output per worker per time period
Labour intensive: involving a high level of labour input compared with capital equipment
Capital intensive: involving a high quantity of capital equipment compared with labour input

Possible consequences of increased productivity:

✓ only useful if the product remains profitable and production levels remain consistent with consumer demand
✓ workers may want higher wages
✓ workers may fear redundancies
✓ may give the business a competitive advantage.

Top tip

The terms 'production' and 'productivity' can easily be confused. Make sure you use them correctly. Increasing productivity does not necessarily mean increasing production.

It is possible for a business to achieve an increase in labour productivity but to reduce total sales/output too.

If demand for a product is falling, it might be necessary to reduce the size of the workforce – but by a smaller proportion than the reduction in output.

Key term

Effectiveness: meeting the objectives of the enterprise by using inputs productively to meet customers' needs

Top tip

'Efficiency' and 'effectiveness' have different meanings and need to be used correctly.

Progress Check E

1. Explain the difference between efficiency and effectiveness at a school.
2. Outline two ways a soft drinks manufacturer could increase its capital productivity.
3. Outline two ways a college could increase its labour productivity.
4. Explain why teachers might be concerned if they were asked to improve their productivity.
5. A clock manufacturer has decided to change from labour intensive methods of production to capital intensive methods.
   What could be the effects on the workers?

Multiple Choice Questions

1. Which of these statements about production is correct?
   (i) The term production is limited to manufacturing businesses
   (ii) Production is a feature only of the secondary sector
   (iii) All businesses have to plan production activities
   (iv) Production and productivity are the same

2. Added value is:
   (i) the difference between price and value to the customer
   (ii) the difference between value to the customer and the value of the inputs
   (iii) the difference between price before and after tax
   (iv) the mark up made by a retailer

3. Which one of the following is most likely to lead to an increase in labour productivity?
   (i) Decreasing motivation
   (ii) Decreasing labour absenteeism

   (iii) Decreasing pay
   (iv) Employing more unskilled workers

4. Efficiency may be described as:
   (i) the ability of a firm to motivate its workforce
   (ii) the ability of a firm to meet its objectives by using its inputs productively to meet the needs of customers
   (iii) the ability of a firm to buy capital equipment
   (iv) the ability of a firm to turn inputs into outputs

5. Effectiveness can be described as:
   (i) the ability of a firm to motivate its workforce
   (ii) the ability of a firm to meet its objectives by using its inputs productively to meet the needs of customers
   (iii) the ability of a firm to buy capital equipment
   (iv) the ability of a firm to turn inputs into outputs

Questions 6, 7 and 8 are based on the following table which shows two businesses producing the similar products:

	Units produced per month	Full time employees	Wages per day per worker ($)	Capital invested ($m)
Company X	5000	5	20	60
Company Y	4000	8	10	40

6. Which of the following statements about X and Y are true?
  (i) Company Y workers are lazy
  (ii) Labour productivity at Y is higher than X
  (iii) Capital productivity at Y is higher than at X
  (iv) Y is more capital intensive than X

7. Which of the following statements is true about labour productivity?
  (i) X = 1000, Y = 2000 units per worker
  (ii) X = 500, Y = 1000 units per worker

  (iii) X = 5000, Y = 4000 units per worker
  (iv) X = 1000, Y = 500 units per worker

8. Which of the following statements best describes the differences in labour productivity between company X and company Y?
  (i) The difference is because Company X produces more than Company Y
  (ii) Company Y has more employees
  (iii) Company X workers are paid more and so may be more motivated
  (iv) Company X workers like having more machinery

9. In which one of the following situations is the production process most likely to be capital intensive?
  (i) An oil refinery
  (ii) A retail outlet
  (iii) A college
  (iv) A theatre

Exam-style Question

Sam has been examining production data for the two factories owned by Big Sofas, a furniture manufacturer. The data is:

	Factory in country A			Factory in country B		
	2009	2010	2011	2009	2010	2011
Output (sofas)	1000	1200	1400	2000	1800	1600
Workers employed	20	22	24	50	50	50
Machines used	10	9	8	15	15	15

The furniture made in country B is of an old design whereas that made in country A is more modern. Country B has very strict employment laws. The managers in country A have gradually been replacing old machines but falling revenues in country B have not allowed country B's managers to do the same. Workers in country B are paid a salary but country A operates a piece rate pay system.

  (a) Calculate for each year and each factory:
    (i) labour productivity   [3]
    (ii) capital productivity.   [3]
  (b) Briefly analyse the likely reasons for the trends in the productivities you have calculated. [6]
  (c) Suggest ways the managers in country B could improve productivity.   [4]

Student's answer to (a) and(b)

  (a) (i) Factory A: 50, 54.5, 58.3
       Factory B: 40, 36, 32

       (ii) Factory A: 100, 133, 175
       Factory B: 133, 120, 107

  (b) Factory A is benefiting from improving labour productivity and improving capital productivity. More efficient machines are contributing to these improvements. Total output is increasing. Growth in the market has been met by improved productivity, and the piece rate paid to workers has probably helped.

Factory *B* is suffering falling production and productivity. However, there has been no investment in more efficient machines and no retrenchment of workers, probably because of the employment laws.

Authors' Comments

(a) The productivity calculations are correct. Good answer.

(b) The comments are succinct and to the point, and use all of the information provided. Good answer.

Revision checklist – tick when done and understood!

Topic	Textbook read	Revision complete
Production		
Production process		
Adding value		
Increasing added value		
Increasing efficiency		

Operations Planning 21

21.1 Operations planning

Operations planning is about preparing input resources to supply products to meet expected demand.

Forecast demand is the critical factor in this process so it is important for Production and Marketing functions to work together effectively with operational flexibility.

Key terms

Operations planning: preparing input resources to supply products to meet expected demand
Operational flexibility: the ability of a business to vary both the level of production and the range of products following changes in customer demand

21.2 Production methods

Key terms

Job production: producing a one-off item specifically designed for the customer
Batch production: producing a limited number of identical products – each item in the batch passes through one stage of production before passing to the next stage
Flow production: producing items in a continually moving process
Mass customisation: the use of flexible computer-aided production systems to produce items to meet individual customers' requirements at mass-production cost levels
Process innovation: the use of new or much improved production methods or service delivery method

Progress Check A

1. What is meant by operations planning?
2. How might an increase in forecast sales have an impact on operations in a shipbuilding firm?
3. Give three reasons why flexibility in production is important

Top tip

Operations management provides a good example of how business functions need to be integrated.

Main types of production methods

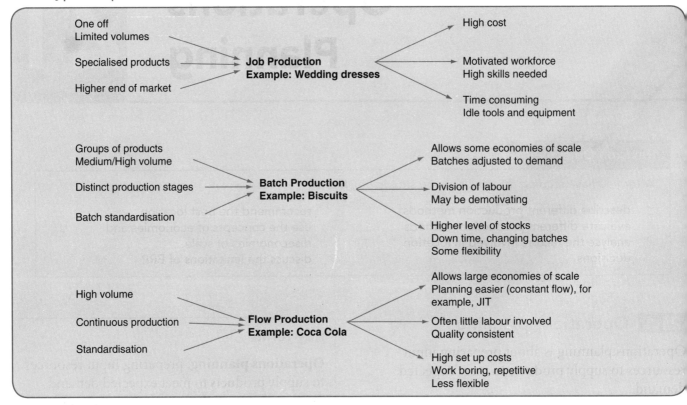

Some products produced in batches, for example, soft drinks are actually produced on continuous production lines so are flow production.

If a question asks you to recommend a method of production in a given situation it is important to weigh up the advantages and disadvantages of each production method in the context of that situation and then justify your decision.

Choice of production system

Choice of production system depends on:

- nature of the product
- size of business
- volume of production
- available technology
- nature of the market
- relative cost of labour and capital
- skills of available work force
- time available
- flexibility required.

Mass customisation

Computer Aided Design (CAD)
Computer Aided Manufacturing (CAM) ➡ Mass customisation
Process innovation

Mass customisation uses the latest technology with multi-skilled workforce to use production lines (usually flow) but with the ability to make a range of products. For example, Dell Computers allows for differentiated marketing.

Progress Check B

1. Give three examples of products likely to be produced using job production.
2. Give three advantages batch production has over job production.
3. Explain why flow production is suited to high volume cars.
4. Analyse how mass customisation can now be applied to high volume cars.
5. Why might mass customisation be chosen for personal computers?

21.3 Location decisions

Decisions involving location require consideration of a number of factors:

Key terms

Optimal location: a business location that gives the best combination of quantitative and qualitative factors

Quantitative factors: these are measurable, in this instance in financial terms, and will have a direct impact on either the costs of a site or the revenue from it and hence its profitability

Qualitative factors: these are non-measurable factors that may influence decisions

Offshoring: the relocation of a business process done in one country to the same or different company in another country

Multinational: a business with operations or production bases in more than one country

Trade barriers: taxes (tariffs) or other limitations (for example, quotas) on the free international movements of goods and services

CAD: using computers and IT when using designing products

CAM: using computers and computer-controlled machinery to manage production processes

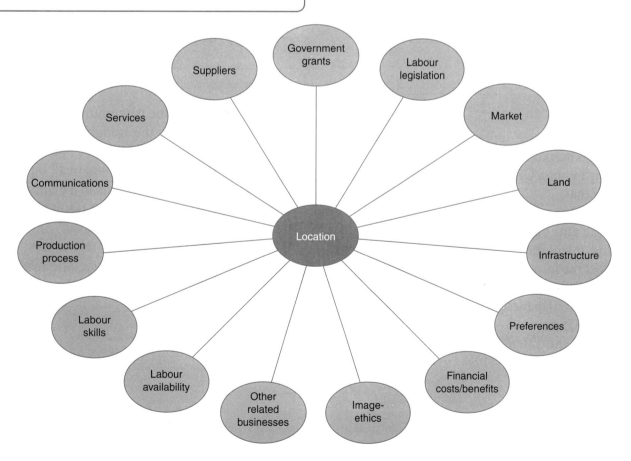

Key location decisions

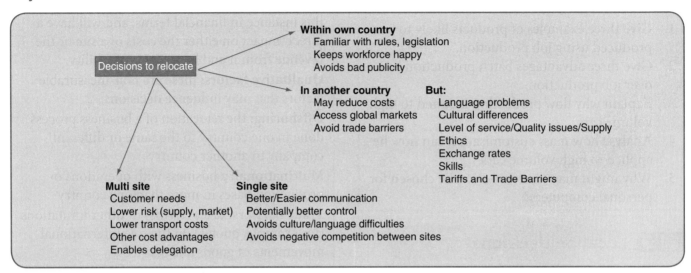

Top tip

Remember that the lowest-cost location may not always be the optimal location – if quality suffers or there is a negative public reaction to products being made by low-paid workers, then low costs may be outweighed by even lower revenues.

Do not confuse 'offshoring' with 'outsourcing' although they may be linked.

Outsourcing is transferring a business functio such as HR, to another company.

It is only offshoring if that company is based i another country.

21.4 Scale of operation

Key terms

Scale of operation: the maximum output that can be achieved using the available inputs (resources) – this scale can only be increased in the long term by employing more of all inputs

Economies of scale: reductions in a firm's unit (average) cost of production that result from an increase in the scale of operations

Diseconomies of scale: factors that cause average costs of production to rise when the scale of the operation is increased

Progress Check C

1. What factors are important for the location of a supermarket?
2. Why might a UK bank relocate its call centre to India?
3. Analyse two ways that the location of theatre might affect its competitiveness.
4. How might the increasing use of the Internet affect the location decisions of a computer manufacturer?
5. Why have Japanese car manufacturers located in the USA?
6. Explain the difference between offshoring and outsourcing.

Impact on unit costs

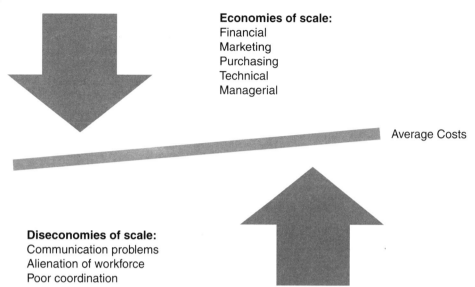

Economies of scale:
Financial
Marketing
Purchasing
Technical
Managerial

Average Costs

Diseconomies of scale:
Communication problems
Alienation of workforce
Poor coordination

Avoiding diseconomies of scale

- ✓ MBO improves coordination
- ✓ Decentralisation – departments behave like smaller businesses
- ✓ Reduce diversification – concentrate on 'core' activities.

Top tip

Economies of scale relate to the *scale* of production and not the level of output of a business. A business working at less than capacity can increase its production (and lower its unit costs) but is benefiting from the level of production not the scale.

When answering questions about economies of scale remember to make sure that your answer is applied to the business specified in the question.

Progress Check D

1. How might a bank benefit from economies of scale?
2. Explain the meaning of managerial economies of scale.

3. Explain how a bus company could benefit from economies of scale.
4. In many countries electricity is supplied by one company. Explain how it might suffer from diseconomies of scale.

21.5 Enterprise resource planning (ERP)

Enterprise resource planning can be used to improve a firm's efficiency.

Key terms

Enterprise resource planning: the use of computer applications to plan the purchase and use of resources in an organisation to improve the efficiency of operation

Supply chain: all of the stages in the production process from obtaining raw materials to selling to the consumer – from point of origin to point of consumption

Limitations of ERP

- ✓ Costs
- ✓ Single system for whole firm may mean change which could cause resentment
- ✓ Takes a long time to implement.

A Impact of ERP

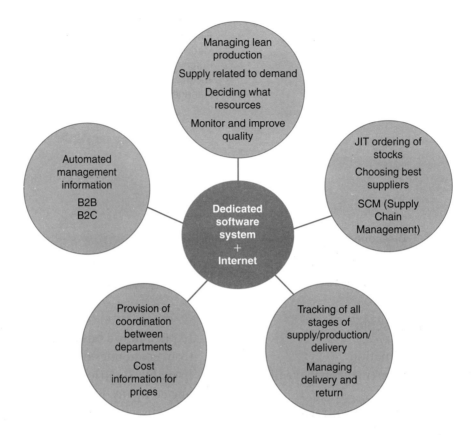

Progress Check E

1. Amazon is an international, online bookshop. Explain why ERP is essential to its operations.
2. Explain how a firm manufacturing car engines will benefit from SCM.
3. Explain the difference between ERP and Lean production.
4. Why is it easier to use JIT stock control when ERP is in operation?

Multiple Choice Questions

1. It is important that the marketing and operations department work together because:
   (i) operations need to know future sales levels
   (ii) all departments have the same objectives
   (iii) marketing needs to know how things are made
   (iv) team work is time consuming

2. Production of computers needs to be flexible because
   (i) demand is price elastic
   (ii) demand is unpredictable
   (iii) there is little competition
   (iv) there is a large market

3. Which one of the following is most likely to need job production?
   (i) Computer game
   (ii) Cell phone
   (iii) Advertising film
   (iv) School furniture

4. Flow production is best for:
   (i) situations where the demand is high but unpredictable
   (ii) situations where the demand is high and consistent
   (iii) situations where there is cheap labour
   (iv) anything liquid

5. Mass customisation is defined as:
  (i) producing a one-off item specially designed for the customer
  (ii) producing items to meet individual customer requirements at high volumes
  (iii) producing a large number of identical products
  (iv) producing items in a continually moving process

6. Which of the following is a quantitative statement?
  (i) Rents are high at location W
  (ii) A large number of similar business are located at X
  (iii) Location Y is preferred by 70% of workers
  (iv) There is a good chance of success at location Z

7. A computer manufacturer is most likely to move to a different country because:
  (i) there is a low skill, low wage workforce in the new country
  (ii) the new country has export restrictions
  (iii) the new country has lower ethical standards
  (iv) the new country has better access to rapidly growing market

8. Which of these is an economy of scale?
  (i) Average costs falling because production is rising
  (ii) Average costs falling because production is falling
  (iii) Average costs falling because productivity is rising
  (iv) Average costs are falling because the factory has an extra production line built

Exam-style Question

Mediquip manufactures equipment for use in hospital operating theatres. It is important that equipment is manufactured to the highest quality and safety hygiene standards. The Directors of the business are considering three possible locations for relocating production. The Managing Director has prepared the following information:

Location – Comments from Managing Director
Our current factory in the centre of town is old and too small. Our products need to be manufactured in a clean, modern environment. The two sites being considered are:

Site	Situation	Rent	Type	Potential	Operating costs	Grants
Southwood	Close to present site	Low rent	Disused car factory needing conversion	No potential for expansion	Low operating costs	Government grants available
Westfield	New site outside of town	High rent	New building	Space for expansion	High operating costs	No grants available

(a) Explain the term 'Director'. [3]
(b) Explain why quality is an important issue for Mediquip. [6]
(c) Recommend which site (Southwood or Westfield) would be best for the relocation of MQ's factory. Justify your choice. [10]

Adapted from Cambridge 9707 Paper 21 Q1(d) November 2009

Student's answer to (c)
Southwood is the best location. It is an important feature of this location that Government grants are available. Businesses involved in the health industry are short of money because hospitals seldom have much money to spend.

The site also has low operating costs and low rents making it ideal. Being an old building, all of the problems will have been sorted out compared with a new building. The closeness to the present site means that transport costs remain about the same which presumably means the business remains close to the hospitals. In today's economic climate, survival is more likely to be important than growth so it is not important that there is little room for expansion.

There seems to be no negative aspects for Southwood, so I recommend this location.

Authors' Comments

The answer, although brief, is clearly contextual. However, it does not directly look at both sides of the argument. A better answer would have analysed the Westfield site. In addition there are key pieces of information overlooked. Would a disused car factory be an ideal site for a business that needs the highest hygiene standards for operating theatres?

Although there is an attempt at a recommendation it is not entirely convincing because of the limitations in the analysis.

Revision checklist – tick when done and understood!

Topic	Textbook read	Revision complete
Link between operations and marketing		
Process innovation		
The main production methods		
Recent innovations in production		
Factors influencing location		
Multi-site locations		
International location decisions		
The types of economy of scale		
ERP		

Inventory (Stock) Management

22

Revision Objectives

After you have studied this chapter, you should be able to:

☞ describe the reasons for holding stock
☞ analyse the costs and benefits of holding stock

☞ interpret stock control diagrams
☞ apply the concept of Just-In-Time stock control.

22.1 Why businesses hold stocks

Top tip

The ideas of stock control apply just as much to retail outlets as they do to manufacturing businesses.

Key term

Inventory (stock): materials and goods required to allow for the production and supply of products to the customer

Stocks are needed

Raw materials and components
So raw materials and components are immediately available

Work-in-progress
Some production may not yet be complete

Finished products
Production is completed and products are waiting to be sent out
Goods held to cope with sudden demand changes
Seasonal goods held ready for demand increases

Top tip

Remember to apply the ideas of stock control to the business in the question. So, for example, a business that sells greetings cards is likely to hold high levels of stocks at festive times. A supermarket will aim to turn stock over as quickly as possible, a furniture shop will hold high levels of stock so that customers are able to look at a range of styles.

Progress Check A

1. Explain why a shoe shop will hold stocks of shoes.
2. Why is a building firm likely to have more work in progress than a fast food outlet?
3. What raw materials would a soup manufacturer require?
4. Give three examples of seasonal goods that may require high stock levels.

22.2 Businesses have to decide stock levels

Amount of stock held is a trade-off between costs and benefits:

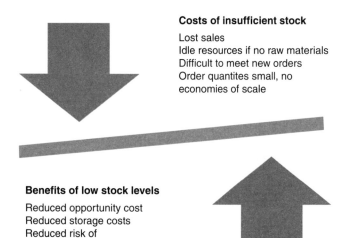

Costs of insufficient stock

Lost sales
Idle resources if no raw materials
Difficult to meet new orders
Order quantites small, no
economies of scale

Benefits of low stock levels

Reduced opportunity cost
Reduced storage costs
Reduced risk of
wastage/obsolescence

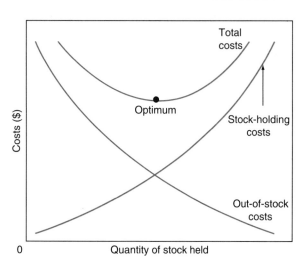

Total stock-holding costs

Stock levels in a firm will be **dynamic** as shown here:

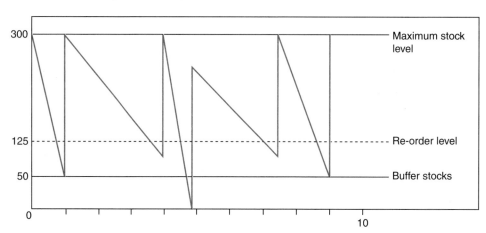

Key terms

Economic order quantity: the optimum or least-cost quantity of stock to re-order taking account delivery costs and stock-holding costs

Buffer stocks: safety stock in case of sudden increases in demand or supply problems

Re-order quantity: the number of units ordered each time

Lead time: the normal time taken between ordering new stocks and their delivery

Top tip

You will not be asked to calculate the optimum order size but it is advised that you remember the costs of stock holding and the costs of being out of stocks – and apply these ideas to the business in question.

Progress Check B

1. Identify three costs associated with holding stocks at an oil refinery.
2. Explain the concept of opportunity cost in relation to stocks.
3. Explain the factors that would determine the maximum stock levels of milk held by a supermarket.
4. Explain the factors that would determine the maximum stock levels of newspapers held by a supermarket.

22.3 Just-in-Time

Just-in-Time is an operating system that includes minimizing stocks as far as possible.

Raw materials

Delivered only when needed.

Work-in-progress

Kept to a minimum by efficient production process.

Finished products

Despatched to customers as soon as completed.

It can also be a system used by retail outlets, for example, supermarkets in terms of products arriving at a supermarket branch from suppliers.

It is difficult to get JIT to work effectively as a number of wide-ranging conditions have to be met:

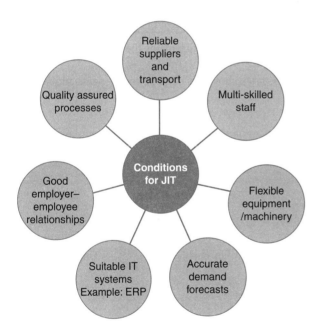

> **Key term**
>
> **Just-in-Time:** this stock control/production method aims to avoid holding stocks by requiring supplies to arrive just as they are needed in production and completed products are produced to order

Situations in which JIT will not work

✗ Some of the conditions are not easy to achieve especially to do with staff and suppliers

✗ Small firms may not be able to afford to implement it

✗ Circumstances (for example, inflation) may make holding stocks attractive

✗ The costs of stock-outs are prohibitively expensive so that buffer stocks are essential.

> **Top tip**
>
> Any question that involves discussing how appropriate JIT is in different business situations could lead to an answer that considers the potential drawbacks of the approach as well as its more obvious benefits.

Progress Check C

1. Why might JIT not be appropriate for a small family business?
2. Explain two conditions for JIT to work effectively.
3. Discuss whether JIT is suitable for a product with falling demand.
4. Should all businesses aim to minimise stocks at all times?

Multiple Choice Questions

1. The following are examples of the costs of holding stock **except:**
   (i) storage cost
   (ii) wastage
   (iii) purchase cost
   (iv) opportunity cost

2. One of the problems of insufficient stock is:
   (i) Lost sales
   (ii) High storage space
   (iii) Small reorder quantities
   (iv) Purchase of more machinery

3. JIT is likely to be of most use in which one of the following situation?
   (i) A product with constant demand
   (ii) A specialised product unique to each customer
   (iii) A product with unpredictable demand

   (iv) A product with long delivery lead time

4. Lead time is determined by which one of the following:
   (i) the amount of storage space
   (ii) the time taken for the supplier to deliver
   (iii) the costs of holding stocks
   (iv) the buffer stock level required

5. Given the following information about a firm's stock levels, what is the reorder level of stocks?
   - Buffer stock is 100
   - Lead time is 3 weeks
   - Stock is used at the rate of 80 units per week
   - Stock deliveries are 500 units at a time.
   (i) 180
   (ii) 340
   (iii) 500
   (iv) 580

Exam-style Question

Mediquip (MQ) manufactures high quality medical equipment for hospitals. Amongst the problems they have is stock levels. The Operations Director of Mediquip has made the following comments:

"Our present system of stock control is not working effectively as we have stock shortages in some components and far too much stock in others."

This is illustrated in the following stock data:

Component	Lead time of component from supplier (weeks)	Components held in stock (weeks)	Supplier of component	Demand for component
A	2	4	Reliable	Rising
B	1	6	Reliable	Constant
C	3	9	Unreliable	Falling
D	4	5	Unreliable	Unpredictable

(a) Explain the term Lead time.   [3]
(b) Why might it be important for MQ to hold stocks of components?   [4]
(c) Discuss the possible usefulness of JIT (Just in Time) to MQ.   [10]

Adapted from Cambridge 9707 Paper 21 Q1(c) November 2009

Student's plan for (c)

Define JIT

Explain MQ's circumstances with regard to product, customer and the need to hold stock.

- Assess product A against the JIT criteria (conclude that about the right level of stock is being held) JIT possible.
- Assess product B against the JIT criteria. Currently far too much stock. Once this is run down could be ideal if costs of running out are not too high.

- Assess product C. Doesn't really seem suitable
- Assess Product D. Unsuitable.

Conclude: Mixed picture, ultimate decision depends on costs of running out of stocks. If disastrous then JIT not suitable.

Authors' Comments
Excellent approach that should produce a good answer. Answer is clearly analytical and since it discusses MQ and each product individually it is clearly in context.

Revision checklist – tick when done and understood!

Topic	Textbook read	Revision complete
Understand the reasons for holding stock		
Explain the types of stock		
Discuss the costs of holding stock		
Interpret a stock holding diagram		
Explain economic order quantity		
Evaluate the usefulness of JIT		

Capacity Utilisation

Revision Objectives

After you have studied this chapter, you should be able to:

☞ Understand how to calculate and interpret capacity utilisation

☞ Explain the reasons for excess capacity

☞ Recommend strategies for solving excess capacity problems

☞ Recommend strategies for dealing with capacity shortage

☞ Evaluate outsourcing.

23.1 What is capacity utilisation?

Capacity utilisation measures one aspect of business efficiency. It measures what percentage of a firm's potential output is actually being achieved.

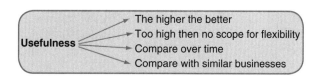

Usefulness → The higher the better
→ Too high then no scope for flexibility
→ Compare over time
→ Compare with similar businesses

$$\text{Capacity utilisation} = \frac{\text{Current output level}}{\text{Maximum possible output level}} \times 100$$

Capacity utilisation up = Average fixed costs down
leading to
Average unit costs down

> **Top tip**
>
> Capacity utilisation relates to a firm's output. If a firm is working at less than maximum capacity, as output increases the business will gain from improved capacity utilisation. Even though unit costs fall, it does not gain from economies of scale.

Working close to 100% utilisation is a trade off:

Benefits of high utilisation

✓ Average costs down
✓ Sign of success
✓ Employees get sense of security.

Disadvantages of high utilisation

✗ Staff under pressure
✗ No flexibility for new orders
✗ Insufficient time for machine maintenance
✗ Greater unreliability.

Key term

Capacity utilisation: the proportion of maximum output capacity currently being achieved

Progress Check A

1. A hotel has 75 rooms. On average 50 rooms are filled each night. What is the average capacity utilisation?
2. The daily overhead cost for the hotel is $500. What is the average overhead cost per room if 50 rooms are occupied?
3. If the hotel could increase its utilisation to 80% what would the average overhead cost become?
4. Why might a restaurant want to increase its capacity utilisation?
5. Explain two reasons why a cell-phone manufacturer might not want to work at full capacity for long periods of time.

23.2 Excess capacity

Key term

Excess capacity: exists when the current levels of demand are less than the full capacity output of a business – also known as spare capacity

Reasons for excess capacity

✓ Product might be seasonal
✓ Demand might have fallen
✓ Efficiency might have increased
✓ Improved technology.

Solutions to excess capacity

See the figure below for solutions to excess capacity.

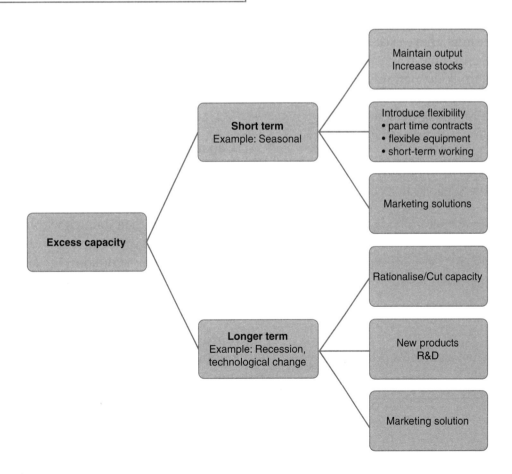

A

Each method will have an impact on staff (directly through lost jobs, shorter working) or indirectly through motivation. The method also depends on the nature of the product. For example, it is not suitable to maintain production for a perishable product.

Top tip

When making decisions about how to deal with excess capacity it is important to consider both the timescale and cause of the problem.

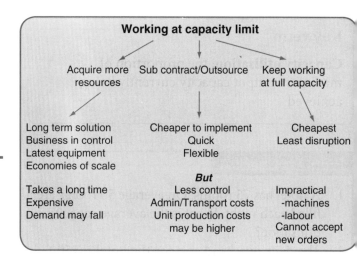

Key term

Rationalisation: reducing capacity by cutting overheads to increase efficiency of operations, such as closing a factory or office department, often involving redundancies

Progress Check B

1. Give two reasons why a greetings card manufacturer might have excess capacity
2. A car manufacturer has 6 assembly plants. What do you think the best way would be to solve overcapacity due to a recession?
3. How realistic is producing new products a way of dealing with excess capacity for a hairdressing business?
4. Explain how marketing might solve the problem of overcapacity in a chocolate factory.

23.3 Working at full capacity/ Capacity shortage

Key term

Full capacity: when a business produces at maximum output

Progress Check 23.3

1. Explain two disadvantages of working at 100 per cent capacity utilisation.
2. Explain two advantages and two disadvantages of sub-contracting as a way of solving capacity shortage for an oil refining company.
3. Why might capacity shortages be dealt with differently if the problem is short term rather than long term?

23.4 Outsourcing

Key terms

Capacity shortage: when the demand for a business's products exceeds production capacity

Outsourcing: using another business (a 'third party') to undertake a part of the production process rather than doing it within the business using the firm's own employees

Business Process Outsourcing (BPO): a form of outsourcing that uses a third party to take responsibility for certain business functions such as HR and Finance

Core activity: activity or activities within a business which are central to the businesses aims and objectives

High capacity utilisation is not the only reason for outsourcing.

Advantages and disadvantages of outsourcing are shown here.

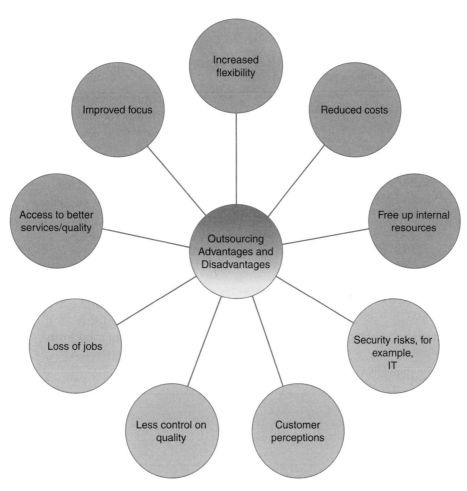

> **Top tip**
>
> You may be asked for your advice on outsourcing an activity.
> Generally the more important an activity is to the overall aims and reputation of the business, the less likely it is that outsourcing will be appropriate.

Progress Check D

1. Would you advise a school to outsource its HRM functions? Explain your answer.
2. Are there some functions that a newspaper business should not consider outsourcing? Explain your answer.
3. Explain two benefits to a bank of outsourcing its customer service call centre.
4. Why might a business outsource to another country?

A

Multiple Choice Questions

1. Which of the following statements about capacity utilisation is true?
   (i) It measures workers' productivity
   (ii) It measures the productivity of machinery
   (iii) It measures current output compared with maximum output
   (iv) It measures the proportion of output that has been outsourced

2. When capacity utilisation increases
   (i) average fixed costs decrease
   (ii) average fixed costs increase
   (iii) average variable costs decrease
   (iv) average variable costs increase

3. Which of the following situations is most likely to lead to rationalisation?
   (i) A short term increase in demand
   (ii) A long term increase in demand
   (iii) A short term decrease in demand
   (iv) A long term decrease in demand

4. Which of the following is an advantage of introducing greater flexibility?
   (i) Flexible equipment might be expensive

   (ii) Staff may not like having flexible working contracts
   (iii) Staff may need to be trained, adding to costs
   (iv) Production can be varied to meet demand

5. Which of the following is an advantage of working at full capacity?
   (i) Staff may feel under pressure
   (ii) Machinery more likely to break down
   (iii) Lower average costs
   (iv) Difficult to cope with unexpected increase in demand

6. Outsourcing is best used for:
   (i) core activities of a business
   (ii) production
   (iii) non-core activities
   (iv) overtime work

7. Which of the following is not a benefit to a firm from outsourcing?
   (i) Increased employment
   (ii) Increased flexibility
   (iii) Improved company focus
   (iv) Reduced overhead costs

Exam-style Question

Mediquip (MQ) manufactures high quality medical equipment for hospitals. Amongst the problems it has is falling capacity utilisation. The Operations Director of Mediquip has made the following comments:
   "Because of falling demand our factories only worked at 75% capacity utilisation. With a recession this year I don't see things getting any better. We have closed one production line but this will only delay a solution to the problem, not solve it."
   The following figures give the trend in production:

	Last year	This year
Output	24 000	12 000
Capacity	32 000	24 000

   (a) Calculate the capacity utilisation for this year. [3]
   (b) Comment on the trend in capacity utilisation. [4]

Student's answers
   (a) Capacity utilisation is 12 000/24 000 = 0.5
   (b) Capacity utilisation has fallen from 75% to 50%. Although the capacity of the business has been reduced from 32 to 24, a 25% reduction, production has fallen even more, from 24 000 to 12 000, a 50% reduction. This is probably because of the recession. However the business produces medical equipment and maybe hospitals will be able to spend more when the recession is over so it may be a temporary problem.

Authors' Comments

(a) The student has the right figures but forgot to multiply by 100.

(b) The student is allowed to carry forward the wrong answer to (b). The commentary is as detailed as it can be, not only commenting on the trend, but also giving clear reasons for it and commenting on what may happen in the future. It clearly uses the context. Good answer.

Revision checklist – tick when done and understood!

Topic	Textbook read	Revision complete
Use the formula for capacity utilisation		
Assess solutions to excess capacity problems		
Assess solutions to working at full capacity		
Use the concept of outsourcing to solve capacity problems		

Lean Production and Quality Management

24

A

Revision Objectives

After you have studied this chapter, you should be able to:

☞ understand the concept of lean production
☞ describe the factors for the success of Kaizen
☞ link lean production concepts with quality issues

☞ distinguish between quality control, quality assurance and TQM
☞ assess costs and benefits of quality improvement methods
☞ choose between quality methods.

24.1 Lean production

The process of lean production aims to minimise waste:

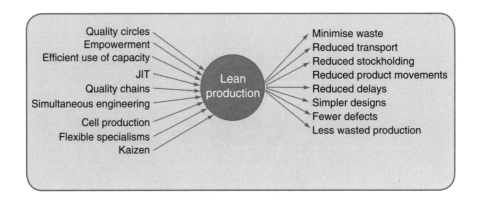

Progress Check A

1. Explain how JIT can contribute to lean production.
2. Classrooms at school are empty during school holidays. How might the school use classrooms to reduce waste?
3. Why might car manufacturers use flexible specialism?
4. Describe the main features of cell production.

Key terms

Lean production: producing goods and services with the minimum of waste resources while maintaining high quality

Simultaneous engineering: product development is organised so that different stages are done at the same time instead of in sequence

Cell production: splitting flow production into groups that are responsible for whole work units

24. 2 Kaizen

The conditions for successful Kaizen (continuous improvement) are:

- ✓ Management culture
- ✓ Team working
- ✓ Empowerment
- ✓ Staff involvement.

But

- ✗ Some changes may need to be radical
- ✗ Resistance from managers and staff
- ✗ Additional costs, for example, training
- ✗ 'Diminishing returns' may lead to abandonment.

> **Key term**
>
> **Kaizen:** Japanese term meaning continuous improvement

Top tip In an examination answer it would be good analysis to link the Kaizen principle to the work of Herzberg on job enrichment.

Progress Check B

1. Why might Kaizen not be suitable in responding to a major change in technology?
2. Why might the impact of Kaizen diminish over time?
3. Explain why involving staff is essential to successful Kaizen.
4. Give three advantages of team-working.

24.3 Quality methods

Table 24.1

Improving quality	
Costs	**Benefits**
Determining customer needs	Increased customer satisfaction/business
Training costs	Good publicity

Table 24.1 (*Continued*)

Rejection costs (materials/products)	Improved reputation
Equipment costs	Easier to launch new products on existing reputation
Inspection costs	Brand building
Reworking faulty products	May allow premium pricing
Tracing problems costly, time consuming	Improves customer loyalty

Table 24.2

Quality methods		
Quality control	**Quality assurance**	**TQM**
Prevention	Setting standards	Culture of quality
Inspection	Checks processes	Interdependencies
Correction/ Improvement	Changes systems	Everyone involved
Based on sampling of finished product	Standards throughout processes	Zero defects
	• Product design • Inputs • Production • Delivery • Customer service	Internal customers
Negative culture	Costly to set up	Completely changes culture
Inspection is tedious	Time consuming setting standards	Whole business needs to be committed
Sampling so failures get through system	What are appropriate standards?	Are workers prepared to accept responsibility?

Key terms

Quality product: a good or service that meets customers' expectations and is therefore 'fit for purpose'

Quality standards: the expectations of customers expressed in terms of the minimum acceptable production or service standards

Quality control: this is based on inspection of the product/service or a sample of products/services

Quality assurance: a system of agreeing and meeting quality standards at each stage of production to ensure customer satisfaction

TQM (Total Quality Management): an approach to quality that aims to involve all employees in the quality improvement processes

Internal customers: people within the organisation who depend on the quality of work being done by others in the organisation

Zero defects: the aim of achieving perfection every time

Top tip

Quality is often viewed by students as an absolute concept and not a relative one. Quality must be explained with reference to the expectations of the target market customers. The level of quality selected by any business must be based on the resources available to it, the needs of the target market and the quality standards of competitors.

Progress Check C

1. Explain the difference between quality assurance and quality control.
2. Explain why improving quality is important for an aircraft manufacturer.
3. Are consumer expectations on the quality of clothes the same for everyone? If not, why not?
4. Why does sampling not lead to zero defects?
5. Why is quality an issue for all businesses, not just manufacturing?

24.4 Other quality issues

ISO9000

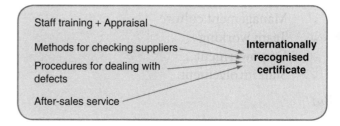

Key term

ISO9000: this is an internationally recognised certificate that acknowledges the existence of a quality procedure that meets certain criteria

Benchmarking

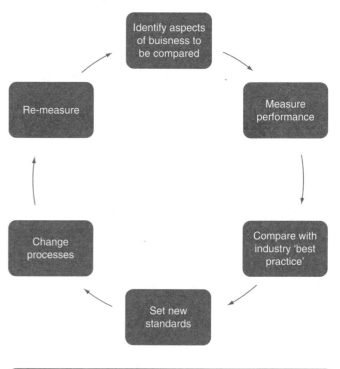

Key term

Benchmarking: it involves management identifying the best firms in the industry and then comparing the performance standards – including quality – of these businesses with their own business

Progress Check D

1. Why is ISO9000 not a guarantee of quality?
2. How could benchmarking discourage innovation?
3. How do quality circles fit in with the ideas of Herzberg?
4. Why could it be difficult to get sufficient information for benchmarking?

Top tip

Quality is not just an issue for large businesses. Small and medium-sized firms also need to give consideration to this vital operations management area. They must ensure that the quality level selected and the quality assurance methods used are within their resources. By reducing waste levels and staff checking quality levels, businesses can save money in the long run.

Multiple Choice Questions

1. Lean production means:
   (i) sampling for defects
   (ii) automated production
   (iii) continuous production
   (iv) reducing waste

2. Which of the following is not involved in Kaizen?
   (i) Sampling products for errors
   (ii) Team-working
   (iii) Empowering workers to manage their own quality
   (iv) Continuous improvement

3. Which of the following is not a requirement of flexible specialism?
   (i) Flexible production systems
   (ii) Flexible employment contracts
   (iii) Flexible workforce
   (iv) Flexible prices

4. A quality product is best described as:
   (i) a product that has passed quality control
   (ii) a product that is good value for money
   (iii) a product that has been made using lean production
   (iv) a product that meets customers' expectations

5. A disadvantage of traditional quality control is that:
   (i) all items have to be inspected
   (ii) it ensures all items are fit for purpose
   (iii) it is based on sampling so failures can get through
   (iv) it requires pre-defined standards at all stages of production

6. Which of the following statements best describes quality assurance?
   (i) A system of agreeing and meeting standards at all stages of the production process
   (ii) A system of checking quality at the end of the production process
   (iii) A system of comparing quality standards with competitors
   (iv) An internationally agreed standard

7. Which of the following is not true about quality assurance?
   (i) It stresses the need to get products right first time
   (ii) It puts the emphasis on the prevention of poor quality
   (iii) It randomly tests products for quality
   (iv) It establishes quality standards for each stage of the production process

8. Which of the following is an incorrect statement about TQM?
   (i) It requires more quality inspectors
   (ii) It involves internal customers
   (iii) It fits in well with Herzberg's principles
   (iv) It means quality is everyone's responsibility

A

Exam-style Question

(a) Evaluate whether adopting TQM would be likely to solve the quality problems of Saucy Choices. [16]

(b) Discuss how the manufacturing company might achieve effective improvements in quality using methods such as TQM. [14]

Part (a) from Cambridge 9707 Paper 31 Section A Q2 November 2009

Student's essay plan for (b)

✓ Introduction to quality control
✓ Explain the meaning of TQM
✓ Describe the problems facing Saucy Choices
✓ Analyse how TQM could address these problems
✓ Analyse other methods that could be used
✓ Assess costs and likely outcomes
✓ Evaluate whether costs exceed likely benefits
✓ Conclude.

Authors' Comments

This answer is likely to be analytical throughout and is prepared to think beyond TQM. There are several potential instances of evaluative comments: judgments about TQM and other methods and which are better suited to this manufacturing situation. Finally concluding whether costs outweigh benefits. Promises a good answer.

Revision checklist – tick when done and understood!

Topic	Textbook read	Revision complete
Lean production		
Kaizen		
Link between quality and lean production		
Quality control		
Quality assurance		
TQM		
ISO9000		
Benchmarking		
Quality circles		

Project Management 25

Revision Objectives

After you have studied this chapter, you should be able to:

☞ understand the reasons for project management
☞ describe the processes involved in project management

☞ draw network diagrams
☞ calculate EST, LFT, project durations
☞ calculate total float and free float
☞ evaluate CPA.

25.1 Managing projects

Projects, large as well as small, need managing.

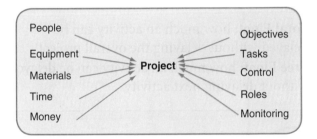

Key terms

Project: a specific and temporary activity with a starting and ending date, clear goals, defined responsibilities and a budget

Project management: using modern management techniques to carry out and complete a project from start to finish in order to achieve pre-set targets of quality, time and cost

There have been spectacular failures in project management, mainly time overruns and cost overruns. For example: Millennium Dome, Wembley Stadium. Can you think of examples in your country?

Progress Check A

1. Why do projects need planning?
2. Why do projects need monitoring?

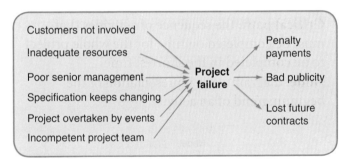

Progress Check B

1. Why is it important to involve customers in a project implementing a new IT system?
2. How could bad publicity affect a building firm involved in a major sports complex project?
3. Why is it important to complete a project on time?
4. Give an example of inadequate resources when building a new airport.

25.2 Critical Path Analysis (CPA)

Network diagram shows:

- ✓ sequence of activities
- ✓ logical dependencies

- ✓ duration of each activity
- ✓ earliest start time of each activity
- ✓ latest finish time of each activity.

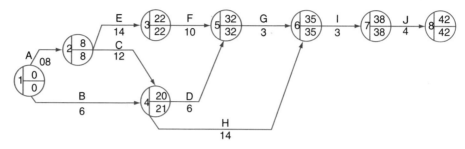

Adding in the activities and durations

Key terms

Critical path analysis: a planning technique that uses a network diagram to identify all tasks in a project, puts them in the correct sequence and allows for the identification of the critical path

Network diagram: the diagram used in critical path analysis that shows the logical sequence of activities and logical dependencies between them

Critical path: the sequence of activities that must be completed on time for the whole project to be completed in the shortest time

Node: diagrammatic representation of the beginning/end of an activity

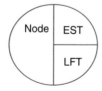

EST (Earliest Start Time): Found by looking at preceding activities. EST for last activity is overall minimum duration of project

LFT (Latest Finish Time): Found by working backwards in time from subsequent activities (only possible to calculate once all the ESTs have been calculated)

'Float' shows how much potential slack there is in the system.

Total float = LFT − duration − EST

Free float = EST of next activity − duration − EST of activity under consideration

Critical activities all have zero float.

Key terms

Total Float: how much an activity can be delayed without delaying the overall project

Free Float: how much an activity can be delayed without delaying next activity

 Top tip
Remember, activities are shown by lines. Nodes are used to help show the logical sequences.

Arrows must be shown on diagrams to show the direction of the logical relationships.

Progress Check C

1. How is the Earliest Start Time calculated?
2. Why is it useful to know the project duration?
3. Why is it more important to monitor critical activities than it is to monitor activities with large floats?
4. What is the free float on a critical activity?
5. Distinguish between free float and total float.

25.3 Evaluating CPA

Advantages and disadvantages of CPA are shown here:

Benefits
- Helps plan completion date
- Floats help ordering equipment, reorganinsing tasks, coping with delays
- Fits in well with ideas of ERP
- Creates a planning culture
- Effective easy analysis of changes in assumptions

Disadvantages
- Can be costly, time consuming
- Relies on assumptions
- Cannot guarantee success, plan is only as good as the management
- No technique can guarantee success

Progress Check D

1. Outline two benefits of using CPA.
2. Outline two limitations of CPA.
3. Why does using CPA not guarantee successful completion of a project?
4. Suggest three real-life situations that would benefit from the use of CPA.
5. Would you use CPA for planning your revision? If not, why not.

Multiple Choice Questions

1. Which of the following statements about project management is not true?
   (i) It needs clearly defined objectives
   (ii) It helps to allocate resources effectively
   (iii) It ensures a product has a market
   (iv) It helps to control a project

2. Which of the following best describes critical path analysis?
   (i) It shows how a project can be completed with maximum labour resources
   (ii) It shows how a project can be completed in the minimum time
   (iii) It takes account of unforeseen events
   (iv) It predicts the success of a project

Questions 3–6 relate to the partial network shown below (time in days):

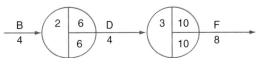

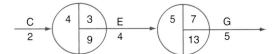

3. Which of the following statements is true?
   (i) *E* cannot start until *D* is completed
   (ii) *B* cannot start until *C* is completed
   (iii) *F* cannot start until *D* is completed
   (iv) *G* cannot start until *E* and *F* are completed

4. Which of the following statements is true?
   (i) *D* is on the critical path
   (ii) *B* is not on the critical path
   (iii) *E* is on the critical path
   (iv) *F* and *G* are on the critical path

5. How much total float does activity *E* have?
   (i) 0 days
   (ii) 2 days
   (iii) 6 days
   (iv) 4 days

6. Which of the following statements about activity *E* is true?
   (i) It is not on the critical path
   (ii) It has free float of 6 days
   (iii) It has a total float of 2 days
   (iv) It is on the critical path

7. Total float is:
   (i) LFT – duration – EST
   (ii) the total of all the free floats
   (iii) the total slack in a project
   (iv) the time an activity can be delayed without delaying the next activity

Exam-style Question

Tanroh Farms is planning to open a safari lodge. Contractors will be used for each stage of the project. It is important that the project is completed before the start of the rainy season in 18 weeks.

Activities for completing the safari lodge project

	Activity	Explanation	Preceded by	Duration (weeks)
	A	Order materials and await delivery	–	3
	B	Prepare land	–	2
	C	Prepare a marketing strategy	–	8
	D	Build lodge bases	A, B	3
	E	Fit walls and windows	D	5
	F	Fit electrical connections	E	2
	G	Install bathrooms	E	4
	H	Fit roofs	E	3
	I	Paint lodges	F, G, H	1

(a) Using the data above construct a network diagram (CPA) for the safari lodge project, showing all earliest start times and latest finish times. [10]

(b) If activity *B* is delayed by two weeks, briefly advise Tanroh on what steps he could take to avoid the project taking longer than 16 weeks. [4]

(c) Discuss the usefulness of this CPA. [8]

Adapted from Cambridge 9707 Paper 3 Section A Q3(a)&(b) November 2008

Student's plan for 1(c)

✓   Discussion of minimum project duration – 20 weeks. This does not compare well with the rainy season. Are there durations that can be reduced/looked at again?

✓   Discussion of which activities are on the critical path *A, D, E, H, I* and what this means for resource allocation and hiring contractors.

✓   Discussion of the nature of the time estimates – how they could differ from those used. The benefits of then doing 'what-if' analysis and making contingency plans based on that.

✓   Discussion of the usefulness of floats – monitoring, reallocating resources, determining priorities.

✓   How good is the management? It's going to be difficult managing all the various subcontractors – this is a farm, not building contractors. Would it be worth employing a project manager?

✓   Draw together strands of argument to conclude that it is potentially an invaluable tool but it does depend on whether the farm has the skills to use it effectively.

Authors' Comments

This answer is analytical throughout and is prepared to think beyond just the results of the CPA. It uses the farm context well. It's worth noting that the project duration was calculated incorrectly in part (a) – it should be 16 weeks not 20 weeks, but the student is allowed to carry forward their wrong answer to this part – indeed will be rewarded for making the judgement about not finishing the project before the rainy season. It should be an excellent answer.

Revision checklist – tick when done and understood!

Topic	Textbook read	Revision complete
Project management		
CPA		
Floats		
Evaluation of CPA		

Business Finance

Revision Objectives

After you have studied this chapter, you should be able to:

☞ explain the need for finance
☞ explain working capital

☞ analyse sources of finance
☞ recommend the choice of finance.

26.1 The need for finance

Start up
- Buildings
- Stock
- Other startup costs

Working capital
- Day to day spending
- Stock
- Expenses
- Bills
- Operating costs

Capital expenditure
- New machinery
- Takeovers
- Research and developments

Contingencies
- Changed economic circumstances
- Unexpected developments
- Cash shortages

Key terms

Start up capital: capital needed by an entrepreneur to set up a business

Capital expenditure: involves the purchase of assets that are expected to last for more than one year, such as buildings and machinery

Revenue expenditure: spending on all costs and assets other than fixed assets. It includes wages and salaries and materials bought for stock.

26.2 Working capital

Finance needed for day to day operations:

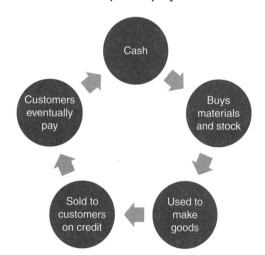

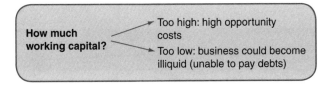

How much
working capital?
- Too high: high opportunity costs
- Too low: business could become illiquid (unable to pay debts)

Key terms

Working capital: the capital needed to pay for raw materials, day-to-day running costs and credit offered to customers. In accounting terms working capital = current assets – current liabilities

Liquidity: the ability of a firm to be able to pay its short-term debts

Liquidation: when a firm ceases trading and its assets are sold for cash to pay suppliers and other creditors

Progress Check A

1. State two needs for finance for a new business.
2. Distinguish between capital expenditure and working capital.
3. Explain why a business may need finance to meet contingencies.
4. Give two examples of capital expenditure.

26.3 Sources of finance

The various sources of finance are discussed here. These are not all suitable for unincorporated businesses who are more likely to borrow from friends, relatives, and sources of micro finance.

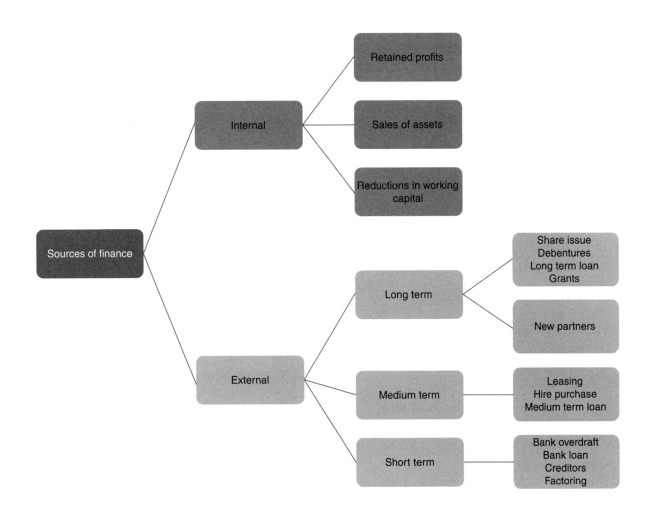

Table 26.1

	Sources of finance	
Source	**Advantages**	**Disadvantages**
Retained profits	Source of permanent finance No interest or other costs	Not suitable for new businesses Needs agreement of owners/shareholders
Sale of assets	Useful for underemployed assets Sale and leaseback may be possible	May be expensive Difficult to identify which assets
Reduce working capital	Relatively easy, increases efficiencies	One off, likely to be small Dangers of reducing too much
Shares • Sell additional shares • Convert to PLC	Low risk – reduces gearing Do not have to be repaid although shareholders will expect higher dividends	Risks takeover Can be expensive Needs agreement of shareholders
Debentures	Similar to loans	Similar to loans
Long term loans	Wide choice of types of loans to suit different situations No loss of shareholder control	May involve collateral Interest payments may be high May be risky – higher gearing
Grants	Do not have to be repaid	Not widely available
Leasing and Hire Purchase	Avoids large cash payments Leasing will reduce maintenance costs One off source, short term only	Can be expensive Less control over leased equipment
Medium term loan	Straightforward way of borrowing from a variety of sources and a wide choice of types of loans	May have stringent conditions May not be available
Bank overdraft	Flexible Easy to arrange	Very expensive Can be 'called in' – high risk to business
Creditors (delay payments for purchases)	Easy way of borrowing if suppliers agree	May be a cost in terms of lost discounts for early payment
Factoring	Guaranteed income from debts	One-off method Can be expensive
Find a partner (sole trader) or introduce a new partner (partnership)	Cheap source of additional finance Brings in expertise	Dilutes ownership Changes nature of business

Progress Check B

1. Explain the difference between short term and long term finance.
2. Why does a business have to be careful selling assets to raise finance?
3. State two drawbacks of overdrafts as a source of finance.
4. Why is trade credit a source of finance?
5. Why do retained profits appear to be a cheap source of finance?
6. Why might a new business decide to lease new equipment rather than buy it?

26.4 The choice of finance

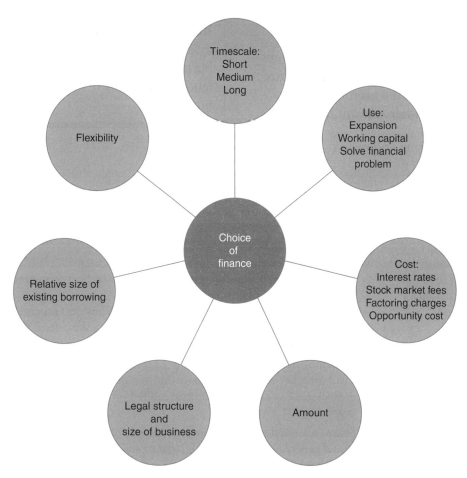

Selling shares is an external source of finance. Although the business is owned by shareholders, the business is a separate legal entity.

Overdrafts can solve cash flow problems in the short term but they do not solve liquidity problems

> **Top tip**
>
> When answering case studies it is important to analyse the legal structure of a business before recommending sources of finance – sole traders, for example, cannot sell shares!

Key terms

Overdraft: bank agrees to business borrowing up to an agreed limit as and when required

Factoring: selling of the claims over debtors to a debt factor in exchange for cash (immediate liquidity) – only a proportion of the value of the debts will be received in cash, the rest is commission to the factor

Long term loans: loans that do not have to be repaid for at least one year

Equity finance: permanent finance raised by companies through the sale of shares

Long term bonds/debentures: bonds issued by companies to raise debt finance, often at a fixed rate of interest

Rights issue: existing shareholders are given the right to buy additional shares at a discounted price

Venture capital: risk capital invested in business start-ups or expanding businesses that have good profit potential but do not find it easy to gain finance from other sources

Top tip

You should be able to recommend appropriate sources of finance for businesses needing capital for different reasons recognising the legal structure of the business, the need for finance, gearing and other relevant factors.

Key term

Business plan: a detailed document giving evidence and forecasts about a new or existing business, and that aims to convince external lenders and investors to extend finance to the business

To raise finance, investors will need to see a business plan. (Chapter 37)

Table 26.2

Factors to be considered in making the 'source of finance' decision	
Factor influencing finance choice	**Why significant**
Use to which finance is to be put – which affects the time period for which finance is required	• It is very risky to borrow long-term finance to pay short-term needs. Business should match the sources of finance to the need for it. • Permanent capital may be needed for long-term business expansion. • Short-term finance would be advisable to finance a short-term need to increase stocks or pay creditors.
Cost	• Obtaining finance is never 'free' – even internal finance may have an opportunity cost. • Loans may become very expensive during a period of rising interest rates. • A Stock Exchange flotation can cost millions of dollars in fees and promotion of the share sale.
Amount required	• Share issues and sales of debentures, because of the administration and other costs, would generally be used only for large capital sums. • Small bank loans or reducing debtors' payment period could be used to raise small sums.
Legal structure and desire to retain control	• Share issues can only be used by limited companies – and only public limited companies can sell shares directly to the public. Doing this runs the risk of the current owners losing some control – except if a rights issue is used. • If the owners want to retain control of the business at all costs, then a sale of shares might be unwise.
Size of existing borrowing	• This is a key issue – the higher the existing debts of a business (compared with its size), the greater the risk of lending more. Banks and other lenders will become anxious about lending more finance. • This concept is referred to as gearing and is fully covered in Chapter 32.
Flexibility	• When a firm has a variable need for finance – for example, it has a seasonal pattern of sales and cash receipts – a flexible form of finance is better than a long-term and inflexible source.

Progress Check C

1. Why would you not recommend shares as a source of finance for a partnership?
2. Give three sources of finance to meet long terms needs of a large public limited company.
3. Give two sources of finance suitable for short term working capital needs of a sole trader.
4. Why is gearing important in considering the suitability of long term loans?

Multiple Choice Questions

1. Which of the following is a permanent source of finance?
   (i) long-term loan
   (ii) retained profit
   (iii) overdraft
   (iv) sale of stock

2. Which of the following best describes working capital?
   (i) Capital needed for capital expenditure
   (ii) Capital needed to start a business
   (iii) Capital spent on wages
   (iv) Capital needed for day-to-day expenditure

3. Which of the following statements is true?
   (i) Businesses should aim to increase their working capital
   (ii) Businesses need working capital to impress investors
   (iii) Businesses need working capital because cash inflows and cash outflows happen at different times
   (iv) None of the above

4. Increasing credit terms to customers are likely to:
   (i) upset customers
   (ii) please customers
   (iii) decrease working capital
   (iv) provide additional long term finance

5. Which is the most likely use for Debt factoring?
   (i) Providing small amounts of finance for one-off problems
   (ii) Providing regular large amounts of finance
   (iii) Providing permanent finance
   (iv) To finance major long term projects

6. Which of the following statements best describe debentures?
   (i) Long term bonds issued by businesses
   (ii) Short term loans by banks to businesses
   (iii) A type of overdraft
   (iv) A loan that is secured against an asset

7. A public limited company wants to take over a competitor. This will involve a large amount of finance. The best source is likely to be:
   (i) an overdaft
   (ii) debt factoring
   (iii) taking on a new partner
   (iv) a share issue

8. A sole trader wants to increase the stock of products in his shop. The best source of finance is likely to be:
   (i) a long term bank loan
   (ii) trade credit
   (iii) debentures
   (iv) mortgage

9. An advantage of taking on a new partner is that:
   (i) it reduces the risk of a takeover
   (ii) it ensures the business will be able to get a loan
   (iii) the partner will bring additional finance
   (iv) the other partners will now have limited liability

Exam-style Question

The *ABC* bus company started with just one bus five years ago. Joe, the owner, is a sole trader. The business has enjoyed rapid growth and Joe now owns four buses. There is the opportunity to expand into new routes which will require the purchase of three new buses; however he does not have the money to buy them. Joe's profits grew steadily in the first five years, and all these profits have been re-invested to buy new buses. Next year he does not expect profits to be so great. Joe currently has no loans, although he is worried that his overdraft is getting higher – diesel prices have gone up rapidly and he has to pay his suppliers quicker than he used to. This is a worry to him. So far Joe has managed to run the business on his own. He is, however, finding it increasingly difficult to run the larger business, especially the personnel side of the business. Joe expects interest rates to rise following poor economic news. He was approached recently by a venture capitalist who was looking for opportunities to invest, however Joe did not really understand the proposal that was made to him. He did wonder about some wealthy relatives.

Evaluate possible sources of finance for Joe. [14]

Student's answer

Joe has two needs for finance. He clearly has a working capital problem and he needs long term finance if he wants to expand his business with the new routes.

Dealing with the working capital problem first, Joe seems not to be handling cash flow well. Although the business is profitable he is unable to mange payments to his suppliers of diesel and his overdraft is increasing. We do not know the size of the overdraft relative to the business income but we do know it is a worry which suggests a significant problem. The overdraft does solve the immediate cash flow problem but it does not solve the underlying problem. A solution might be to go to his suppliers and explain that their new credit terms have caused him a problem. They may, then be prepared to renegotiate their credit terms. If they fail to he could try other suppliers. If that doesn't work he will have to look elsewhere for an injection of capital.

As far as the long term needs are concerned he needs a significant amount of finance to purchase three buses. He is a sole trader so that share issues are out of the question. A bank loan is possible because of the zero gearing ratio. However the market seems uncertain and buses may not supply much security for the bank. The venture capitalist is a possibility but it would not be good for Joe to do something he is not comfortable with.

It is interesting that he is having problems running his expanded business and that he does lack certain skills. That suggests he needs some help so that a new partner may be a possibility worth considering. He has some wealthy relatives who may be able to help, either through lending or by becoming a partner. The latter would depend on the skills they could bring, but if they had the right skills and could put a significant amount of money into the business that would seem an ideal way to grow for Joe.

Authors' Comments

This is a good answer despite being brief. Not only has the student shown clear understanding of both long and short term finance, this knowledge has been applied very effectively in context. The judgement at the end is largely convincing and seems very sensible given the situation of Joe's business.

Revision checklist – tick when done and understood!

Topic	Textbook read	Revision complete
The need for finance		
Working capital		
Sources of finance		
The choice of finance		

Forecasting Cash Flows 27

Revision Objectives

After you have studied this chapter, you should be able to:

☞ understand the meaning of cash flow
☞ distinguish between cash and profit
☞ explain the uses and limitations of cash flow forecasts
☞ produce cash flow forecasts
☞ recognise causes of cash flow problems

☞ recommend solutions to cash flow problems
☞ recognise the link between cash flow and working capital
☞ recommend solutions to working capital problems.

27.1 Cash flow

Cash flows in (Example: from sales) → Cash is used → Cash flows out (Example: on buying raw materials)

Key terms

Cash: money in the form of notes or coins or other methods of immediate payment such as cheques, bankers drafts etc.

Cash flow: the sum of cash payments to a business (inflows) less the sum of cash payments made by the business (outflows)

Cash inflows: payments in cash received by a business such as those from customers or from the bank (when receiving a loan)

Cash outflows: payments in cash made by a business, such as those to suppliers, workers

Keeping a check on cash flow is important because workers and suppliers have to be paid, even though

customers may not yet have paid for products they have bought.

27.2 Difference between cash and profit

Cash = difference between money coming in and money going out

Profit = difference between sales revenues and costs

Products sold on credit are included in 'sales revenue' even though the cash has not been recieved.

Raw materials bought on credit are included in 'costs' even though they have yet to be paid for.

A firm can make a profit (it is earning more than it is spending) but may still become insolvent and face liquidation because of timing problems between cash inflows and cash outflows. This is the most common reason for businesses to fail.

Key terms

Liquidation: when a firm ceases trading and its assets are sold for cash to pay suppliers and other creditors

Insolvent: when a business cannot meet its short-term debts

Top tip

When given the opportunity, emphasise the importance of having enough cash in the short-term. Profit can wait to be earned in the long-term – but cash payments always have to be made!

27.3 Uses and limitations of cash flow forecasts

Uses

- ✓ Planning when setting up a business
- ✓ Convincing investors that an enterprise is worth investing in
- ✓ Setting targets
- ✓ Identifying possible future cash flow problems
- ✓ Aid decision making
- ✓ 'what if' analysis can identify key issues.

Limitations

- ✗ The future cannot be predicted with certainty, for example, competitor's new products might reduce the sales and cash inflow of a business
- ✗ Unforeseen developments, for example, the credit crunch can make outcomes significantly different from forecasts
- ✗ Only as good as initial assumptions.

Top tip

Remember, cash flow forecasts are forecasts, not actual accounts.
    They are estimates based on assumptions.
    They can neither be 'right' nor 'wrong' but they can be good forecasts or forecasts based on poor assumptions.

Progress Check A

1. Why are cash flow forecasts useful when setting up a business?
2. Why are assumptions needed for cash flow forecasts?

3. Give two reasons why is it important to identify possible future cash flow problems.
4. Why might a sudden change in oil prices affect the cash flow forecasts of a taxi firm?
5. Explain how a business can have a cash flow problem but still make a profit.

27.4 Forecasting cash flows

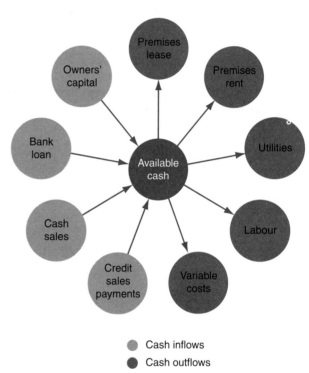

- ● Cash inflows
- ● Cash outflows

Table 27.1

Easy to forecast (fixed or agreed)	Difficult to forecast
Owners' capital	Cash sales
Bank loan	Credit sales
Property payments (lease/rent)	Utilities
	Labour
	Variable costs

Key terms

Cash flow forecast: estimate of a firm's future cash inflows and outflows

27.5 Presenting cash flow forecasts

There is no single agreed format for cash flow forecasts. Here are examples of the two most common methods:

Table 27.2

Method 1	Method 2
Cash inflows	**Opening balance**
Owners' capital	
Cash sales	**Cash inflows**
Payment from credit sales	Owners' capital
Total cash in	Cash sales
	Payment from credit sales
Cash outflows	**+ Total cash in**
Lease	
Rent	**Cash outflows**
Materials	Lease
Labour	Rent
Other costs	Materials
Total cash out	Labour
Net cash flow	Other costs
Opening balance	**– Total cash out**
Closing balance	
	= Closing balance

Progress Check B

1. What is meant by the term 'opening balance'?
2. What would happen to cash flow if a business bought its premises rather than renting them?

Key term

Overtrading: expanding a business rapidly without obtaining all the necessary finance so that a cash flow shortage develops

Progress Check C

1. Explain how poor credit control can affect cash flow.
2. Give examples of unexpected events that might have an effect on the cash flow of a farm.
3. Explain how a recession might affect the cash flow of a car manufacturer.

Top tip

Cash flow forecasts do not solve cash flow problems, but they do help identify problems.

They are part of financial planning and can help prevent cash flow problems from developing.

27.6 Causes of cash flow problems

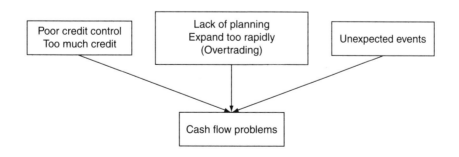

27.7 Improving cash flows

Ways of increasing cash inflows:

Table 27.3

Method	How it works	Possible drawbacks
Overdraft	Flexible loans on which the business can draw as necessary up to an agreed limit.	• Interest rates can be high – there may be an overdraft arrangement fee • Overdrafts can be withdrawn by the bank and this often causes insolvency.
Short-term loan	A fixed amount can be borrowed for an agreed length of time.	• The interest costs have to be paid • The loan must be repaid by the due date.
Sale of assets	Cash receipts can be obtained from selling off redundant assets, which will boost cash inflow.	• Selling assets quickly can result in a low price • The assets might be required at a later date for expansion • The assets could have been used as collateral for future loans.
Sale and leaseback	Assets can be sold, for example, to a finance company, but the asset can be leased back from the new owner.	• The leasing costs add to annual overheads • There could be loss of potential profit if the asset rises in price • The assets could have been used as collateral for future loans.
Reduce credit terms to customers	Cash flow can be brought forward by reducing credit.	• Customers may purchase products from firms that offer extended credit terms.
Debt factoring	Debt-factoring companies can buy the customer's bills from a business and offer immediate cash – this reduces risk of bad debts too.	• Only about 90–95% of the debt will now be paid by the debt-factoring company – this reduces profit • The customer has the debt collected by the finance company – this could suggest that the business is in trouble.

Ways of reducing cash outflows:

Table 27.4

Method	How it works	Possible drawbacks
Delay payments to suppliers (creditors)	Cash outflows will fall in the short term if bills are paid after, say, three months instead of two months.	• Suppliers may reduce any discount offered with the purchase • Suppliers can either demand cash on delivery or refuse to supply at all if they believe the risk of not being paid is too great.
Delay spending on capital equipment	By not buying equipment, vehicles, etc., cash will not have to be paid to suppliers.	• The efficiency of the business may fall if outdated and inefficient equipment is not replaced • Expansion becomes very difficult.
Use leasing, not outright purchase, of capital equipment	The leasing company owns the asset and no large cash outlay is required.	• The asset is not owned by the business • Leasing charges include an interest cost and add to annual overheads.
Cut overhead spending that does not directly affect output, for example, promotion costs	These costs will not reduce production capacity and cash payments will be reduced.	• Future demand may be reduced by failing to promote the products effectively.

Key terms

Debtors: customers who have bought products on credit and will pay cash at an agreed date in the future

Creditors: suppliers who have agreed to supply products on credit and who have not yet been paid

Progress Check D

1. Explain how debt factoring could improve the cash flow of a steel manufacturer.
2. Explain why increasing credit given to customers will have an adverse affect on cash flow.
3. Explain how suppliers reducing their credit period would affect cash flow.
4. Give one reason why overtrading might cause cash flow problems.

Top tip

Just writing 'the firm should increase sales' does not demonstrate true understanding of the difference between sales revenue and cash flow, any extra sales would have to generate extra cash to help with a cash flow problem.

Any suggestion for increasing inflows or reducing outflows has to be thought about carefully in the context of the business. So a suggestion of 'reducing outflows by cutting staff costs' could well have a negative impact on output, sales and eventually future cash inflows.

27.8 Relationship between cash flow and working capital

Working capital and cash flow are closely related.

Cash flow describes the *flows* of cash in and out of the business. So, for example, a bank statement shows this for a bank account.

Working capital is the *stock* of cash (and near cash) within the business for use in the day to day running of the business. A personal equivalent is a purse full of money able to be spent.

Working capital is needed because the flows of money into and out of the business never match up nicely in time.

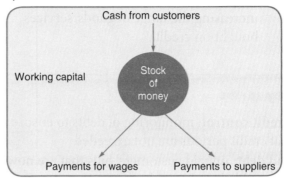

27.9 Managing working capital problems

Working Capital too high means there is a stock of cash (and other near cash assets) tied up which the business could use more productively elsewhere.

Working capital insufficient means that the business has insufficient in its stock of cash/near cash to meet its obligations – liquidation threatens.

Sources of working capital

Cash can be released through debtors by:

- ✓ making credit periods for customers shorter
- ✓ not giving credit to new customers
- ✓ ensuring creditworthiness of customers so fewer 'bad debts'
- ✓ offering discounts for prompt payments
- ✓ employing debt factors for bad debts
- ✓ improved credit control.

Cash can be released through stocks (inventories) by:

- ✓ keeping smaller inventory levels
- ✓ improving stock control efficiency, for example, through use of computers
- ✓ using lean systems such as Just-In-Time.

Cash can be managed better by:

- ✓ using cash flow forecasts to predict problems/excesses
- ✓ putting cash to use at times of surplus
- ✓ effective planning.

Cash needs can be reduced through creditors by:

✓   negotiating longer credit terms with suppliers

✓   increasing the range of goods/services bought on credit.

Key terms

Credit control: monitoring of debts to ensure that credit periods are not exceeded

Bad debt: unpaid customers' bills that are now very unlikely to be paid

---

Progress Check E

1. Explain the difference between working capital and cash flow.
2. Why might reducing credit period for customers have a negative impact on the sales of a car retailer?
3. A holiday firm has excess cash at the end of the holiday season.
   Give two examples of how this cash could be employed more effectively.
4. Give two disadvantages of using a debt factor for improving cash flow.

Multiple Choice Questions

1. Which of the following is an example of a cash inflow?
   - (i)   A new asset
   - (ii) The value of stocks
   - (iii) Cash sales
   - (iv) Cash purchases

2. Which best describes a firm in liquidation?
   - (i)   It has an excess of liquid assets
   - (ii) It has ceased trading so that creditors can be paid through the sale of assets
   - (iii) It cannot meet its short term debts
   - (iv) Its sales are falling

3. Which one of the following is true?
   - (i)   Profit is revenue less costs
   - (ii) Profit is what is left after cash outflows are deducted
   - (iii) Profit is the same as net cash flow
   - (iv) Profit is always bigger than net cash flow

4. Which one of the following is true?
   - (i)   Depreciation is an item in cash flow forecasts
   - (ii) Depreciation is not an item in cash flow nor is it considered in calculating profit
   - (iii) Depreciation is part of the profit calculation
   - (iv) Depreciation is added to profit

5. Which of the following best describes a cash flow forecast
   - (i)   It forecasts future profits
   - (ii) It compares future inflows with revenues
   - (iii) It compares future outflows with revenues
   - (iv) It forecasts future cash inflows and outflows

6. A small retail business has made the following forecasts for its next month:
   Loan from bank: $50 000

   Cash sales: $50 000
   Cash purchases: $30 000
   Payment for purchases on 1 month credit: $5000
   Receipts from sales on 2 months credit $10 000.
   Total cash inflow for the business for next month will be:
   - (i) $145 000
   - (ii) $80 000
   - (iii) $110 000
   - (iv) $75 000

7. Total cash outflow from the business in Question 6 next month will be:
   - (i) $35 000
   - (ii) $30 000
   - (iii) $80 000
   - (iv) $5 000

8. The owner of a fashion shop believes the business has too much working capital. Which of the following might be a solution to the problem?
   - (i)   Repay loans
   - (ii) Increase prices
   - (iii) Reduce wages costs
   - (iv) Take out a short term loan

9. A retailer of computers has decided to improve its credit control. Which of the following is likely to be the reason?
   - (i)   It is finding it difficult to find suppliers
   - (ii) It is finding customers are late with their payments
   - (iii) It has a cash flow surplus
   - (iv) It has too much inventory

Exam-style Question

Eldorado Gold (EG) has discovered gold in a remote region of the country. It is planning to develop a gold mine and has produced the following cash flow forecast for the next 5 years:

Table 1

Cash flow forecast ($m)					
Year	2012	2013	2014	2015	2016
Opening balance	−10	−90	−95	−85	+5
Sales of gold	0	0	20	100	X
Development costs	80	5	0	0	0
Operating costs	0	0	10	10	10
Closing balance	−90	−95	−85	+5	+295

(i) Using the information in the Table, calculate the value of X (the sales of gold in 2016).   [2]

(ii) Comment on the usefulness to EG of this cash flow forecast.   [6]

Adapted from Cambridge 9707 Paper 23 Q2(b) (I)&(II) June 2011

Student's answer

(i) Closing balance = opening balance + cash inflows – cash outflow
So +295 = +5 + X – 10 so X = 295 – 5 + 10 = $310 million

(ii) The cash flow forecast shows the largest negative balance to be –$95 million. This shows, based on the assumptions, that the firm will have to arrange for a large amount of finance. After 3 years of production the firm is showing $295 million closing balance. This looks very favourable compared with the development costs of $85m. This helps the firm with the decision to go ahead with the project. However, the cash flow forecast is only based on assumptions. It is very difficult to forecast for this type of project especially 5 years ahead. So although there are clear uses for the cash flow forecast it ought to be compared with forecasts using other assumptions, most notably the price of gold which will affect the sales figures.

Authors' Comments

(i) The student made a good attempt at the calculation and quoted the formula correctly. Unfortunately there was a mistake in the calculation. The right answer is $300 million.

(ii) The student has clear understanding of cash flow forecasts and their usefulness, and the answer used the context effectively.

Final revision checklist – tick when done and understood!

Topic	Textbook read	Revision complete
Meaning of cash flow		
Cash versus profit		
Prepare cash flow forecasts		
Solutions to cash flow problems		
Working capital		
Solutions to working capital problems		

Costs 28

After you have studied this chapter, you should be able to:

☞ understand the importance of cost information
☞ classify various types of cost
☞ understand and use break-even analysis
☞ evaluate results from break-even analysis
☞ understand different costing methods
☞ use costing methods to make decisions
☞ evaluate costing methods.

28.1 Importance of costs

Cost information is important for the reasons given here.

✓ Key factor in determining profits
✓ Informs pricing decisions
✓ Informs production decisions
✓ Allows monitoring/comparisons
✓ Helps set budgets and targets
✓ Helps decisions about resource allocations
✓ Essential for decision making.

28.2 Classifying costs

Costs need to be classified for the purposes of analysis such as break-even, costing, pricing and other decisions.

Key terms

Direct costs: these are costs that can be clearly identified with each unit of production and can be allocated to a cost centre

Indirect costs: costs that cannot be identified with a unit of production or allocated accurately to a cost centre

Fixed costs: costs that do not vary with output (in the short term)

Variable costs: costs that vary with output

Top tip

Direct costs are similar but not the same as variable costs. Not all direct costs are variable costs.

If a firm decided to produce a special order for a supermarket, and if the variable costs are $10 per unit and it costs $20 000 to change the packaging for an order of 20 000 units (i.e. $2 per unit) to change the packaging, then the direct costs are $12 per unit.

Classifying costs can be difficult:

✓ purchase of equipment – fixed
✓ raw materials – variable
✓ promotion – usually fixed
✓ rent – usually fixed
✓ labour – can be either (fixed salaries + variable payments)
✓ energy – can be either (heating + powering machines)
✓ Internet services can be either.

28.3 Break-even

Break-even analysis is a useful decision tool. Break-even can be determined graphically:

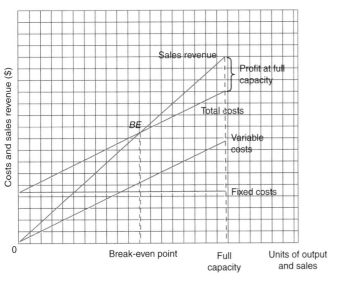

A typical break-even chart

Or mathematically:

$$\text{Break-even} = \frac{\text{Fixed costs}}{(\text{Unit price} - \text{Variable cost})^{*}}$$

* This is contribution per unit.

Key terms

Break-even point of production: the level of output at which total costs equal total revenue – neither a profit nor a loss is made

Margin of safety: the amount by which the sales level exceeds the break-even level of output

Note: Break even is measured in units of production.

Table 28.1

Break-even analysis	
Uses	**Limitations**
Price decisions	Assumptions may not be realistic
Purchasing new equipment	Costs etc. may not be linear
Choosing between locations	Costs difficult to identify for new projects
Performing 'what if' analysis	Costs difficult to classify
Which project to invest in	Assumes all units sold

28.4 Uses of costing information

Business managers need to know and understand costs to make a wide range of important decisions. They not only need to know the costs of running a business but also need to know the costs of individual products. Some examples of decisions involving costs include:

- ✓ setting prices
- ✓ increasing production
- ✓ reducing production
- ✓ stopping production
- ✓ monitoring
- ✓ accepting special offers
- ✓ controlling costs
- ✓ calculating profits.

Cost centres are used to monitor costs. It is easy to identify direct costs but more difficult to know the impact of the other costs on a product or service. For example, costs of running an A level Business Studies Departmental cost centre are:

- ✓ teachers' salary – mainly direct
- ✓ text book – direct
- ✓ materials used in class – direct
- ✓ photocopy machine – shared with rest of college
- ✓ other college services – shared with rest of college
- ✓ heating and lighting – shared with rest of college.

Key terms

Cost centre: a section of a business, such as a department, for which costs can be identified and allocated

Profit centre: a section of a business to which both costs and revenues can be allocated – so profit can be calculated (based on assumptions about overheads)

Although profits can only really be calculated for a business as a whole it is useful to create cost and profit centres to provide:

- ✓ targets to work for
- ✓ the ability to monitor and control
- ✓ assess performance
- ✓ make decisions.

But

- ✗ allocation of overheads is arbitrary
- ✗ it distorts the holistic nature of the business by breaking it up for costing purposes
- ✗ not all influences on a centre are within the control of the centre.

Key term

Overheads: an alternative term for indirect costs

Top tip

It is easy to confuse indirect costs (overheads) with fixed costs.

Indirect costs are costs that are shared with other parts of the business. Fixed costs may, or may not be shared. For example, a business studies teacher's salary is usually a fixed cost but it is not an indirect cost of the business studies course.

Progress Check C

1. Distinguish between a profit centre and a cost centre.
2. Explain why the concept of 'profit' does not directly apply to an individual product.
3. Explain two advantages of using cost centres.
4. Explain two difficulties of using profit centres.

28.5 Costing methods

Decisions relating to products and profit centres can be made using a variety of costing methods.

Full costing/Absorption costing

For a profit centre:
Profit = Revenue for the centre – direct costs – allocated indirect costs

The profit for the whole business is the total of the individual profits.

Contribution costing

It is sometimes known as marginal costing.
For a cost centre:
Contribution = Revenue for the centre – direct costs

The profit for the business is the total of the contributions less the indirect costs.

Features and disadvantages of costing methods

The disadvantages of costing methods are highlighted in italics.

Table 28.2

Features and *disadvantages* of costing methods		
Full costing	**Absorption costing**	**Contribution costing**
Allocates overheads in a simplistic, uniform way	Allocates overheads in a more rational way	Does not allocate overheads
Easy to calculate and understand	More work in allocating overheads	*More difficult to understand as it appears to overlook overheads*
But allocation of overheads will not reflect reality	*But how do you decide a more rational approach? Floor space? Amount of machinery? Workforce?*	Does recognise that it is a **business** that makes a profit/loss and that a cost/profit centre makes a contribution to the overall business
Enables 'profit' to be estimated at a detailed level in an organisation Particularly relevant to a single product business Overhead costs do not risk being overlooked		*Full costing better for single product firms*
Easy to use for pricing decisions if allocation of fixed costs is appropriate. If not it's useless! *But arbitrary allocation may lead to inconsistencies between cost/profit centres* *Allocation has to be consistent over time, and may have to change if level of output changes*		*Can be misleading when indirect costs (overheads) are confused with fixed costs (which are not necessarily overheads)*

Progress Check D

1. Distinguish between full costing and contribution costing.
2. A profit centre has:

Sales revenue	$15 000
Direct materials	$7 000
Direct labour	$6 000
Allocated overheads	$5 000.

   Calculate the profit for the profit centre.
   Calculate the contribution for the profit centre.

   Is it right to conclude that the cost centre is performing poorly?
3. Explain the usefulness of the contribution costing method.
4. Explain why full costing might not be appropriate for a car manufacturer with many different models of car.
5. Explain why a supermarket might want to keep open a department even when full costing shows it is making a loss.

28.6 Using contribution costing

Stop making product

Does it make a positive contribution? If so continue.
   (If absorption costing were used it might show the product making a loss, but the allocated overheads would still have to be paid for by the remaining products.)

Does it make a negative contribution? If so:

✓ Is it an important part of a product range? Then maybe continue.

✓ Might there be a better future for the product? Then maybe continue.

Accept a contract or special order at below full cost/customary price

✓ Does it make a positive contribution?

✓ What might be the response of existing customers?

✓ Is there enough capacity to avoid adverse impact on existing products/services?

✓ Is a lower price consistent with brand image and other aspects of marketing?

✓ Is there a risk of resale into a higher price market?

✓ If the answer to these is favourable then accept.

Common example is producing 'own brand' products for supermarkets.

Sell a product/service at a discount to particular customers

Same process as accepting a contract.
Common examples:

- ✓ discounted fares on trains and planes at off-peak times
- ✓ discounted hotel room rates
- ✓ cheaper off-peak electricity charges.

Make or buy in (Outsource)

- ✓ Which makes the greater contribution?
- ✓ What would be the impact of 'buy in' on the workforce?

28.7 Full costing versus contribution costing

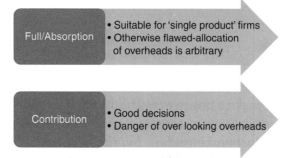

| Full/Absorption | • Suitable for 'single product' firms
• Otherwise flawed-allocation of overheads is arbitrary |
| Contribution | • Good decisions
• Danger of over looking overheads |

Progress Check E

1. Explain why qualitative factors are important in 'special order' decisions.
2. Why might it make sense to continue making a product even when it does not make a positive contribution?
3. A firm makes lorries. It has been approached for a special order of 100 lorries for a supermarket company. Each ordinary lorry costs $50 000 to make. The extra cost of meeting the supermarket's requirements is $10 000 dollars per lorry. There is a one-off extra cost of $50 000 to change the machinery to make the lorries. The supermarket firm has offered £75 000 per lorry for the order and the firm usually charges $90 000 per lorry.
   Should the firm accept the contract?
4. Explain why railway companies may sell tickets at below full cost.

Multiple Choice Questions

1. Which of the following is not a reason for keeping cost information?
   - (i) It is a legal requirement
   - (ii) It helps decision making
   - (iii) It is important for setting targets
   - (iv) It helps in setting budgets

2. Which of the following is not a variable cost?
   - (i) Raw materials for making soft drinks
   - (ii) Wages of a head teacher
   - (iii) Commission paid on sales
   - (iv) Electricity to power a piece of production machinery

3. A direct cost is one that:
   - (i) is variable
   - (ii) is fixed
   - (iii) cannot be identified with a unit of production
   - (iv) can be identified with a unit of production

Questions 4–6 relate to the data given here.

The following information relates to a pen manufacturer:
Material costs $0.60 per pen
Direct labour costs $0.10 per pen
Selling price $1.50
Fixed costs $800 per day
Current production 1500 pens per day

4. What is the break-even level of output?
   - (i) 500
   - (ii) None of these
   - (iii) 1500
   - (iv) 1000

5. What is the margin of safety?
   - (i) 100
   - (ii) 500
   - (iii) 1000
   - (iv) 1500

6. What is the profit at the current level of production?
   (i) $1000
   (ii) $2000
   (iii) $3000
   (iv) None of these

7. A feature of contribution costing is that:
   (i) decisions are made on the basis of profits
   (ii) decisions should also take account of quantitative factors
   (iii) decisions are made on the basis of contribution
   (iv) decisions take account of the allocation of overheads

8. Which of the following statements about making decisions using costing methods is true?
   (i) There is only one right method of costing
   (ii) Decisions should also involve qualitative data
   (iii) Contribution costing is wrong because it ignores fixed costs
   (iv) Decisions should only involve consideration of quantitative data

Exam-style Question

Radar cosmetics have a range of products called Aquaskin. Aquaskin is a new product and little marketing has been done on it so far. It is designed to complement the range of products with one targeted at young people. The Chief Executive has been presented with cost information about the product range:

Table 1

2010 cost and sales figures				
	Aquaskin Junior	**Aquaskin Cream A**	**Aquaskin Cream B**	**Aquaskin Cream C**
Labour costs per 100 items	$40	$60	$30	$80
Material costs per 100 items	$200	$300	$100	$600
Allocated fixed factory and Head Office costs	$190 000	$250 000	$450 000	$350 000
Selling price per 100 items	$400	$500	$250	$900
Sales (boxes of 100 units)	1000	12 000	20 000	6000

The Chief Executive responded to these figures by saying, "These are bad results for the Aquaskin Junior range. I believe we should stop making this product immediately. This would increase our annual profit by $30 000".

Do you agree with the Chief Executive that the company should stop producing the Aquaskin Junior cream? Use the quantitative data in Table 1, relevant calculations and qualitative data to justify your answer. [16]

Adapted from Cambridge 9707 Paper 31 Section A Q2 November 2010 (Read case study on page 113)

Student's answer

If Aquaskin Junior is stopped, lost revenue is $400 × 1000 = $400 000.
   Direct cost savings are $(200 + 40) ×1000 = $240 000
   So lost contribution would be $160 000.
The Chief Executive seems to have assumed that the allocated fixed and Head Office costs would also disappear giving the CEO's figure of a gain of $30 000. However, it is likely that these indirect costs would remain and have to be recovered by the remaining products.

I think it should not be cancelled because it makes a positive contribution and this would be lost, putting the firm in a worse position.

In addition, because it is a complementary product, stopping production may have an impact on other products. It is also a new product with little marketing.

Authors' Comments

In terms of quantitative information the student has done very well, calculating contribution correctly, unravelling the CEO's calculation and drawing a justified conclusion. In terms of qualitative data the answer is less good. Although three factors have been identified they have not been well developed in terms of their influence on the decision. The student needs to develop these points in much more detail and give a justified recommendation.

Final revision checklist – tick when done and understood!

Topic	Textbook read	Revision complete
Types of costs		
Break-even		
Costing methods		
Using costing methods		
Evaluating costing methods		

Accounting Fundamentals

29

Revision Objectives

After you have studied this chapter, you should be able to:

☞ know what business accounts contain
☞ explain the differences between income statement and balance sheet
☞ understand the key items that appear on these accounts
☞ calculate liquidity and profit margin ratios, and explain what results mean
☞ evaluate usefulness of accounts and ratios.

29.1 Need for keeping accounting records

The various stakeholders in a business have differing uses for accounts. Typically:

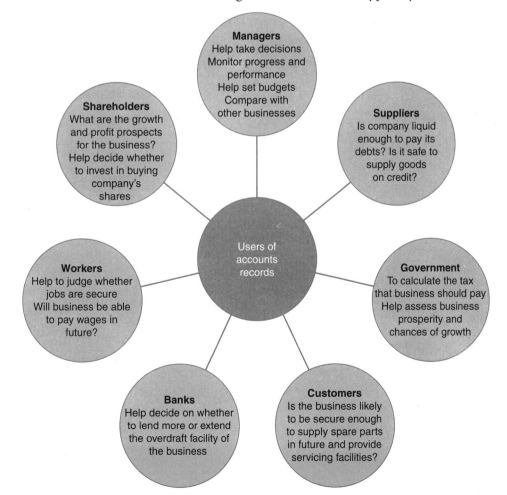

Managers
Help take decisions
Monitor progress and performance
Help set budgets
Compare with other businesses

Shareholders
What are the growth and profit prospects for the business?
Help decide whether to invest in buying company's shares

Suppliers
Is company liquid enough to pay its debts? Is it safe to supply goods on credit?

Users of accounts records

Workers
Help to judge whether jobs are secure
Will business be able to pay wages in future?

Government
To calculate the tax that business should pay
Help assess business prosperity and chances of growth

Banks
Help decide on whether to lend more or extend the overdraft facility of the business

Customers
Is the business likely to be secure enough to supply spare parts in future and provide servicing facilities?

29.2 Income statement?

This is a very important accounting record. It tells managers and other stakeholders whether a business is making a profit or not.

What are the major items on an income statement?

The major items on an income statement are:

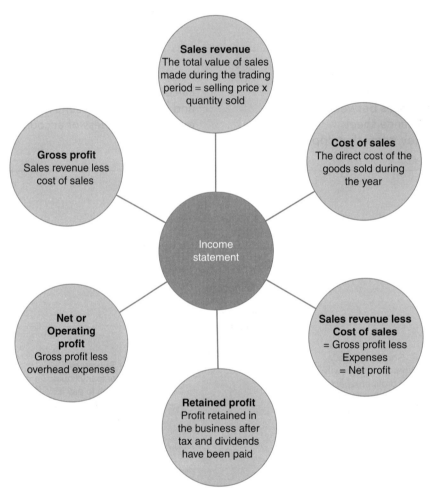

In the year to 31/12/2009, Coca Cola recorded the following (simplified) data on the company Income Statement:

	($million)
Sales revenue	30 990
Cost of sales	11 088
Expenses	11 671
Tax paid	2 040
Dividends paid	3 800

(a) Calculate the company's:
  (i) gross profit
  (ii) operating/net profit
  (iii) retained profit.

(b) Assess whether Coca Cola's stakeholders should be pleased with the company's recent performance if its retained profit was $4872 million in the year ending 31/12/2005.

29.3   What is a balance sheet?

This tells managers and stakeholders what the 'net worth' of the business is. This can be compared with past years and other similar businesses.

What are the major items on a balance sheet?

Here is a simplified version of the Balance Sheet for Coca-Cola for year ending 3/4/09.

> **Key term**
>
> **Balance sheet:** an accounting statement that records the values of the business assets, liabilities and shareholders equity at one point in time

Table 29.1

	$m	Note/Definition
Assets *Non-current (Fixed) assets:*		**Non-current assets:** assets to be kept and used by the business for more than one year
Property, plant and equipment	8 425	
Intangible assets (including trademarks and goodwill)	14 414	**Intangible assets:** items of value that do not have a physical presence such as patents and trademarks
Other assets including investments in other companies	7 550	
Total non-current assets	30 389	
Current assets:		**Current assets:** assets that are likely to be turned into cash before the next balance sheet date
Inventories	2 298	**Inventories:** stocks held by the business in the form of materials, work in progress and finished goods
Debtors (trade receivables) and other current assets	3 600	**Debtors (trade receivables):** the value of payments to be received from customers who have bought goods on credit
Cash	6 816	**Note:** Also called 'cash and cash equivalents'.
Total current assets	12 714	
Total assets	**43 103**	**Note:** This total will balance with Equity and Liabilities – hence the 'Balance Sheet'.
Equity and liabilities		
Current liabilities:		**Current liabilities:** debts of the business that will usually have to be paid within one year
Creditors (Trade payables)	5 651	**Creditors (Trade payables):** value of debts for goods bought on credit payable to suppliers.
Short term loans	7 518	**Note:** These loans will include the company's overdraft with the bank. Other current liabilities might include provisions to pay for tax and dividends.
Total current liabilities	13 169	
Non-current liabilities:		**Non-current liabilities:** value of debts of the business that will be payable after more than one year
Long term loans	8 826	**Note:** Other non-current liabilities might include debentures issued by the company.

(Continued)

Table 29.1 (*Continued*)

	$m	Note/Definition
Total liabilities	21 995	**Note:** If these actually equalled total assets there would be no shareholders equity in the company at all!
Shareholders equity:		The net worth of the company owned by the shareholders (Total assets – Total liability)
Share capital	880	
Retained earnings and other surpluses	20 228	**Note:** Also referred to as retained profits. These are owned by shareholders, not the business.
Total Shareholders Equity	21 108	
Total equity and liabilities	**43 103**	**Note:** This *does* balance with total assets!

Top tip

It is not essential to learn the precise layout of this Balance Sheet – companies may vary the format anyway. If you have a question that requires you to change or adapt a Balance Sheet just follow the exact layout given to you on the examination paper.

Progress Check B

1. Why do you think the value of Coca Cola's intangible assets is so high?
2. Why do you think Coca Cola offers credit to its retail customers (creating debtors or accounts receivable)?
3. Do you think Coca Cola managers should be worried about the level of long term loans taken out by the company? Explain your answer.
4. If Coca Cola made the following transactions during the year, indicate which category these would appear on in the balance sheet. (The first has been done for you.)

(i) Purchase of property with a mortgage: Non-current assets UP and Long term liabilities UP
(ii) Increased inventories financed by short term loans
(iii) Sale of a trademark and the proceeds used to repay 5 year bank loan.

29.4 Why calculate ratios?

Ratios allow much easier analysis of company performance than the 'raw' financial data shown in the income statements and balance sheet. Using ratios allows:

✓ two values to be compared with each other, for example, current assets and current liabilities
✓ ratio results can be compared easily with past years
✓ ratio results can also be compared to those of other companies in the same or similar industry and with 'rule of thumb' values in some instances
✓ analysing accounts using ratios can indicate potential problem areas that company management may need to focus on.

How is liquidity measured?

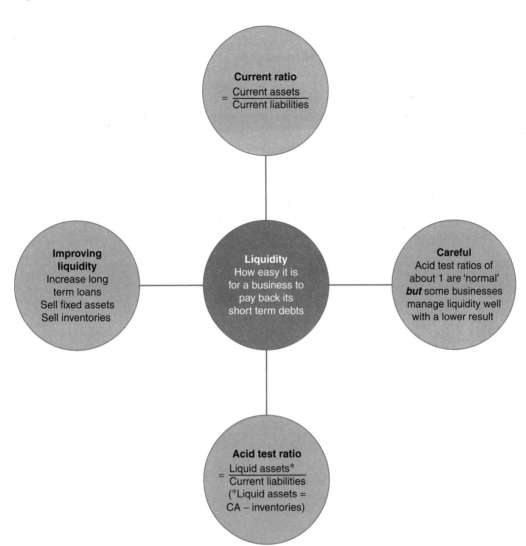

Current ratio
$= \dfrac{\text{Current assets}}{\text{Current liabilities}}$

Improving liquidity
Increase long term loans
Sell fixed assets
Sell inventories

Liquidity
How easy it is for a business to pay back its short term debts

Careful
Acid test ratios of about 1 are 'normal' *but* some businesses manage liquidity well with a lower result

Acid test ratio
$= \dfrac{\text{Liquid assets*}}{\text{Current liabilities}}$
(*Liquid assets = CA – inventories)

Top tip

Raising cash by selling inventories will improve the acid test ratio – but it will keep the current ratio about the same as both cash and inventories are current assets.

Progress Check C

1. Calculate the current ratio for Coca Cola in 2009.
2. Calculate the acid test ratio for Coca Cola in 2009.
3. Comment on this company's liquidity.

29.5 How is profitability measured?

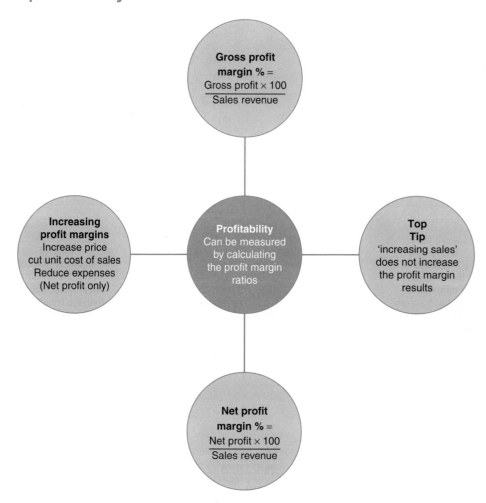

When discussing ways in which a business might increase its profit margins do not forget to evaluate. For example: will increasing prices be a good idea if the demand is very price elastic? Will cutting the cost of sales by using cheaper materials lead to a lower quality product?

Progress Check D

1. Calculate Coca Cola's gross profit margin for 2009.
2. Calculate Coca Cola's net profit margin for 2009.
3. Discuss the usefulness of comparing these results with two other companies: Pepsi Cola and Toyota.

29.6 Are accounts and accounting ratios useful?

As we saw earlier all stakeholders have an interest in companies published accounts – and ratio analysis makes the information they contain even more revealing. However, when analysing accounts and using ratio results you should remember that:

- the 'latest' data might already be several months out of date
- the accounts might have been made to appear more attractive, i.e. window dressed
- different companies may have different 'year endings' so direct comparisons over the same time period become difficult
- the external environment can have a major impact on company performance – not just managers decisions

- ratios differ between industries so difficult to compare
- ratio results may highlight problems – but they do not suggest solutions! This is down

to managers to choose the most effective strategies for improving performance.
- the past may not be a good guide to the future.

Multiple Choice Questions

1. Which one of the following stakeholder groups is likely to be most interested in analysing company accounts to determine liquidity?
   (i) Shareholders
   (ii) Local community
   (iii) Suppliers
   (iv) Government

2. The most likely reason why a business has recorded an increased net profit margin is that:
   (i) prices have been reduced
   (ii) cost of sales increased
   (iii) dividends have been reduced
   (iv) overhead expenses have fallen

3. One of the main differences between an income statement and a balance sheet is that:
   (i) income statements record the value of a business during the year but balance sheets record profit at one time period
   (ii) income statements record the profit made at one moment in time but balance sheets show the value of the company during the year
   (iii) income statements show the profit made over a

period, usually one year but balance sheets show the value of shareholders stake in the business
   (iv) income statements show the profit ratios of the business but balance sheets show the liquidity ratios of the business

4. A likely decision a manager would take to improve the liquidity of a business would be:
   (i) buy more non-current assets to expand the business
   (ii) pay staff higher wages to encourage increased production
   (iii) sell off assets not needed
   (iv) reduce the long term loans of the business

5. One of the possible limitations of using ratios to compare the performance of two businesses is that:
   (i) net profit margin may be higher than the gross profit margin for some businesses
   (ii) the businesses may be in completely different industries
   (iii) ratios are based on forecasts that can never be completely accurate
   (iv) some public limited companies will not publish their accounts so ratios cannot be calculated

Exam-style Question

Tivoli Fashions makes expensive wedding dresses. Each one is a unique design and they are all hand made using old fashioned sewing machines. Materials such as ribbons, semi-precious stones and silk are bought in from several suppliers. The Managing Director recruited two designers last year and this means that designs do not have to be 'bought in' from other businesses. For the first time the business promoted itself at a major wedding fair which was also attended by many of the growing number of rival businesses. Even though this was expensive for Tivoli, there was much interest from potential customers. The following table shows an extract from Tivoli Fashions latest accounts:

As at 31/5/11	$
Non current assets	12 000
Current assets	7 000
Inventories	3 000
Current liabilities	8 000
For year ending 31/5/11	
Sales revenue	45 000
Cost of sales	15 000
Expenses	25 000

(a) What is meant by the term 'non-current assets'?   [3]
(b) Calculate for Tivoli Fashions:
    (i) Gross profit margin   [4]
    (ii) Net profit margin   [4]
    (iii) Current ratio   [3]
    (iv) Acid test ratio   [3]
(c) Last year, the net profit margin ratio was 15%. Analyse *two* likely reasons for the change in this ratio for the year
    ending 31/5/11.   [6]
(d) Discuss *two* ways in which this business could improve its liquidity position.   [10]

Student's answer to (c)

The net profit margin has fallen from 15% to 11%. This means that on each $1 worth of sales the net profit earned has fallen by nearly $0.04 in just one year. Two possible reasons for this are expenses rising at a faster rate than sales or prices being reduced.

Expenses include overhead or fixed costs such as management salaries, rent and promotion costs. Tivoli Fashions increased promotion costs in 2011 by attending a wedding fair, in order to increase demand, but this may have increased expenses by more than the increase in sales then the net profit margin would fall.

If the selling price to retailers was reduced, perhaps because of the increased competition in this market, Tivoli would have cut both its gross profit and net profit margins.

Authors' Comments

The student clearly understands profit margins – two appropriate suggestions are made, these are both explained briefly and applied to Tivoli Fashions.

Final revision checklist – tick when done and understood!

Topic	Textbook read	Revision complete
Users of accounts: who they are and what they are looking for		
The main published accounts: Income statements		
Balance sheets		
Profit margin ratios: How to calculate		
Profit margin ratios: How to improve		
Liquidity ratios: How to calculate		
Liquidity ratios: What they mean		
Liquidity ratios: How to improve		
Using accounts and ratios: Uses and limitations		

Budgets

Revision Objectives

After you have studied this chapter, you should be able to:

☞ understand the reasons for budgeting
☞ describe the stages in producing a budget
☞ explain different types of budget

☞ discuss the usefulness of budgets
☞ understand and explain variance analysis.

30.1 Why budgets are needed

A budget is a plan for the future, which an organisation aims to fulfil. It differs from a forecast in that a forecast is prepared based on assumptions.

Budgets are used to:

✓ plan
✓ allocate resources
✓ set targets
✓ co-ordinate
✓ monitor and control
✓ assess performance
✓ improve plans.

Key terms

Budget: detailed plan for the future
Budget holder: individual responsible for the initial setting and achievement of a budget
Delegated budget: giving some delegated authority over the setting and achievement of budgets to junior managers

Top tip

Delegated budgeting ties in with motivational theories of Herzberg – making work more challenging and rewarding.

Progress Check A

1. Explain the difference between a forecast and a budget.
2. Explain why a firm manufacturing shoes should prepare a budget.
3. Explain how a budget could be used to monitor performance in a hospital.
4. Why might a delegated budget improve motivation?

A **30.2** Stages in preparing budgets

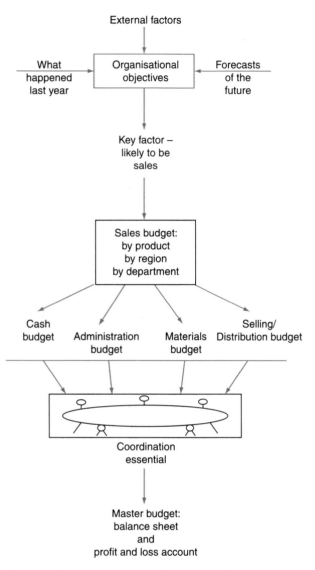

How budgets are commonly prepared

30.3 Types of budget

> **Key terms**
>
> **Incremental budgeting:** budgeting that uses last year's budget as a basis for the next year and adjustments are then made
>
> **Zero budgeting:** all budgets are set to zero and budget holders have to argue their case from a 'clean sheet'
>
> **Flexible budgets:** once set, expenses are allowed to vary as sales or production vary

30.4 Usefulness of budgets

Advantages	Disadvantages
Provide a means of controlling income/expenditure	May lack flexibility
Allow for review of performance	Focused on short term
Clarifies responsibilities	May lead to unnecessary spending
Allow for delegation of financial responsibilities	May require significant training
Increase capital efficiency	Difficult for new situations
Help coordination between departments	
Provide clear targets	

> **Top tip**
>
> Remember budgets are plans not forecasts although they may be based on, for example, sales forecasts. Budgets are targets for departments and people in the organisation.

Progress Check B

1. Explain three advantages to a new business of setting budgets.
2. Explain the benefits of setting financial targets to the manager of a supermarket.
3. Why might there be a need for training in a school for knowing how to produce and use budgets?
4. Why might setting a spending budget lead to more spending than necessary in a large organisation?

30.5 Budgetary control – variance analysis

Variance analysis:

✓ measures differences between actual values and outcomes
✓ helps explain why the outcome is different from the plan
✓ helps in setting future budgets.

Key terms

Variance: the difference between a planned value and the actual outcome

Favourable variance: difference between actual and budget value that leads to a higher than expected profit, for example, sales are higher than budgeted or costs are lower

Adverse variance: difference between actual and budget value that leads to a lower than expected profit for a business, for example, lower sales or higher costs

Progress Check C

1. Distinguish between 'favourable' and 'adverse' variances in relation to costs.
2. Distinguish between 'favourable' and 'adverse' variances in relation to revenues.
3. Give one benefit of variance analysis.
4. How would knowing about variances help the manager of a hotel?

Multiple Choice Questions

1. Which of the following statements about budgets is correct?
   (i) Budgets are forecasts
   (ii) Budgets are part of the published accounts of a business
   (iii) Budgets aid planning
   (iv) Budgets solve liquidity problems

2. Which of the following is not a benefit of budgeting?
   (i) It informs shareholders of the businesses performance
   (ii) It helps planning
   (iii) It can be used for monitoring
   (iv) It is useful for setting targets

3. Which is likely to be the first stage of a budgeting process?
   (i) Coordinating departmental budgets
   (ii) Forecasting sales
   (iii) Setting a budget for materials
   (iv) Identifying external factors

4. Incremental budget means:
   (i) ensuring next year's costs are higher than this year's
   (ii) ensuring next year's revenues are higher than this year
   (iii) basing next year's budget on this year's
   (iv) none of the above

5. A business manufactures computers. It has the following budget and outcome information:

	$m	
	Budget	Outcome
Sales	50	48
Materials	10	9
Labour	20	21
Overheads	15	15

   Which of the following statements is true?
   (i) 'Materials' is the only favourable variance
   (ii) All variances are adverse
   (iii) All variances are favourable
   (iv) 'Sales' is the only favourable variance

Exam-style Question

Media International produces and publishes a range of newspapers and magazines. Some titles have been doing well while others have struggled against competition. The following cost data has been collected:

Table 1

Sales Information for MI's publications					
Product	Budget	Actual	Variance		Relative price to competitors
A	120 000	95 000	−25 000	Adverse	Very High
B	76 000	80 000	+4 000	Favourable	Same
C	55 000	56 000	+1 000	Favourable	Same
D	1 000	2 000	+1 000	Favourable	High
E	50 000	60 000	+10 000	Favourable	Low
F	100 000	110 000	+10 000	Favourable	Same
G	60 000	57 000	−3 000	Adverse	High

Explain, using the information in Table 1, how MI could use variance analysis to make decisions about its products. [8]

Student's answer

The two products of immediate concern are the two with negative sales variances, products A and G. It is noticeable that both products have relatively high prices. It is also noticeable that the variance for product G is small both relative to the sales and to product A. Product A has very high prices. It is also notable that all the products that have positive variances have prices similar or lower to competitors except product D.

This strongly suggests that an important issue in determining the sales is the price of the magazine, which might be expected.

It may be that A and G have higher production costs, or simply that the price has been set too high. In either case, the business could take policy decisions to make the situation less adverse.

Product D behaves completely differently to the others and suggests a new product at its introductory stage which has done better than originally budgeted. It will be important to monitor this product to see if the positive outlook for the product continues.

At this stage there is no evidence to suggest stopping the production of any particular product but it would be useful to explore further pricing decisions for products A and G with particular emphasis on product A.

Authors' Comments

The student clearly understands the concepts of favourable and unfavourable variances. They have used and analysed the information effectively and demonstrated the usefulness of variance analysis through decision making.

Final revision checklist – tick when done and understood!

Topic	Textbook read	Revision complete
Why budgets are needed		
Stages in preparing budgets		
Types of budget		
Usefulness of budgets		
Budgetary control – Variance analysis		

Contents of Published Accounts

Revision Objectives

After you have studied this chapter, you should be able to:

☞ know why accounts are amended
☞ understand the impact of key amendments on the accounts
☞ explain how goodwill is used
☞ understand the impact of other intangible assets
☞ undertake depreciation calculations
☞ interpret the impact of depreciation on the accounts of a business
☞ undertake stock valuation.

31.1 Amending income statements

Most items in the balance sheet are self explanatory. Assets are items the business *owns*, liabilities are what the business *owes*.

Some items need further explanation in order that you can amend accounts.

Accounts often need amendment:

✓ new/revised data becomes available
✓ accounts are needed for a different time period.

Progress Check A

1. Why is it important to start with the accounts for the end of the current year when producing accounts for next year?

31.2 Common amendments

Common amendments include:

Table 31.1

Cause	Impact on balance sheet	Double entry
Sale of inventories for cash	Inventories fall	Cash increases
Creditors ask for early payment	Accounts payable decreases	Cash decreases
Additional shares sold and capital raised is used to buy property	Share capital rises	Fixed assets rise
Equipment depreciated	Fixed assets fall	Profits fall and so shareholder equity (retained profits) falls

31.3 Valuing items on the balance sheet

Key terms

Goodwill: arises when a business is valued at or sold for more than the balance-sheet value of its assets

Intellectual property: an intangible asset that has been developed from human ideas and knowledge

Market value of company: the estimated total value of a company if it were taken over

Capital expenditure: any item bought by a business with the intention of retaining for more than a year, that is the purchase of fixed or non-current assets

Revenue expenditure: any expenditure on costs other than non-current asset expenditure

Depreciation: the decline in the estimated value of a non-current asset over time

Net realisable value: the amount for which an asset (usually an inventory) can be sold minus the cost of selling it. It is only used on balance sheets when NRV is estimated to be below the cost of purchase of the asset.

Table 31.2

	Value on Balance sheet	Comment and Impact
Goodwill – arises from extra value in the business beyond measurable fixed assets, for example, a strong customer base	Usually only valued when a company is bought/taken over. Appears under fixed/non-current assets. Needs to be depreciated as impact of goodwill falls.	Difficult to value – value may decline over time so if it appears it is depreciated – and is then an expense in the income statement
Other intangible assets • Brands • Patents (intellectual property) • Copyrights • R&D	Not usually given a value although there is an increasing trend to valuing brand names. Appears under fixed/non-current assets. Needs to be depreciated.	Difficult to value — where it does appear, it is depreciated. Depreciation appears as an expense in the income statement.
Capital expenditure, for example, spending on fixed assets	Appears as fixed/non-current asset and then depreciated	Depreciation (the use of the asset) appears as an expense on the income statement
Inventories	Appears as a current asset	Valued at purchase price unless the value of the asset has fallen below this. They are then valued at net-realisable value.
Revenue expenditure	Appears only as an expenditure on Income statement	

Progress Check B

1. Explain why depreciation has an impact on shareholders' equity.
2. Why does an increase in depreciation have an impact on the Income Statement.
3. A business buys a new lorry with a loan. The useful life is three years. Explain the impact of this event on the accounts of the business over the three years.
4. Why is it difficult to put a value on the brand name Nike?
5. Should a football club put a value on its best player? How might the club determine a value?

31.4 Depreciation

There are several methods of depreciation but at A level you only need to consider straight line depreciation.

Straight line depreciation

In this method an asset is depreciated in equal amounts each year over its useful life.

Each year of the asset's life it is depreciated by an amount equal to:

$$\frac{\text{Original cost of asset} - \text{Expected residual value}}{\text{Expected useful life of asset (years)}}$$

Next years' net book value of asset =
Current year net book value of asset – Depreciation

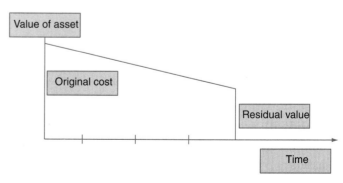

Depreciation of an asset has an impact on profit and value of assets but not on cash.

Key terms

Straight line depreciation: a constant amount of depreciation is subtracted from the value of the asset each year

Net book value: the current balance sheet value of a non-current asset = original cost − accumulated depreciation

Top tip Other methods of depreciation are not tested by Cambridge

31.5 Valuation of inventories

Inventories are recorded at either purchase price or net realisable value, whichever is smaller.

Multiple Choice Questions

1. Brands are an example of:
   (i) intangible assets
   (ii) current assets
   (iii) share capital
   (iv) current liabilities

2. Goodwill is best described as:
   (i) the attitude of a successful business to its employees
   (ii) the increase in business value resulting from research and development
   (iii) the value of a business over and above the value of its physical assets
   (iv) the price another business is prepared to pay for a business

3. A business has to sell its inventories quickly to raise cash. The amount of cash raised is likely to be:
   (i) the book value of the inventories
   (ii) less than the book value of the inventories
   (iii) more than the book value of the inventories
   (iv) none of the above

4. Asking debtors to make much speedier payments will:
   (i) increase the cash in the business
   (ii) reduce the cash in the business
   (iii) leave the cash in the business the same
   (iv) reduce accounts payable

5. A company sells more shares. The impact of this on the balance sheet will be:
   (i) more inventories in the business
   (ii) less share capital in the business
   (iii) an increase in assets
   (iv) an increase in cash and share capital

6. A fixed asset is depreciated because:
   (i) it enables accountants to make the profits more for tax purposes
   (ii) the business will pay a lower dividend
   (iii) it will increase the book value of the business
   (iv) the asset will eventually need to be replaced

7. Accountants will use the Net Realisable Value (NRV) of inventories when:
   (i) NRV is larger than the original cost of the stock
   (ii) NRV is smaller than the original cost of the stock
   (iii) inflation has increased the value of the stock
   (iv) there is a high opportunity cost of holding stock

Exam-style Question

A business buys a piece of machinery for $70 000. The machinery is estimated to have a useful life of 4 years, after which it can be sold for $10 000.

    (a) Calculate the annual depreciation charge using straight line depreciation.   [2]
    (b) How much will the asset be worth after 3 years?   [2]
    (c) What would happen to the accounts if the firm decided that the useful life was only 3 years, but with the same residual value?   [6]
    (d) Explain the impact on the firm's cash flow.   [2]

Student's answer to (c)

If the firm decided the useful life was only 3 years then annual depreciation would increase from $15 000 per year to $20 000 per year. The value of the asset in the balance sheet would decrease by $5 000 a year more and reach $20 000 in 3 years. Correspondingly net profits would fall more quickly meaning $5 000 less each year would be put into reserves. So net profit would be lower, but the balance sheet would still balance.

Authors' Comments

The student clearly understands depreciation and has given an excellent explanation, with correct calculations, of its impact on all parts of the accounts of the firm.

Revision checklist – tick when done and understood!

Topic	Textbook read	Revision complete
Why accounts are amended		
The impact of key amendments on the accounts		
Goodwill valuations		
Depreciation		
Undertake depreciation calculations		
The impact of depreciation on the accounts of a business		
Undertake stock valuations		

Revision Objectives

After you have studied this chapter, you should be able to:

- ☞ calculate and interpret profitability ratios
- ☞ calculate and interpret liquidity ratios
- ☞ calculate and interpret financial efficiency ratios
- ☞ calculate and interpret shareholder ratios
- ☞ calculate and interpret the gearing ratio
- ☞ use ratio analyse to improve business performance
- ☞ assess the practical uses and limitations of ratios.

32.1 Uses of ratios

Accounts are very detailed documents. Business decision makers want quick and easy ways of getting a 'picture' of the main financial features of a business. Ratios will tell them about:

- ✓ how good the business is at generating profits
- ✓ how effective the business is at managing its working capital
- ✓ how sound the business is going to be as a potential investment (both to potential shareholders and lenders)
- ✓ how risky the business is with regards to its financial structure.

The use of ratios, together with assessing trends, help in answering these issues.

Types of ratio:

Progress Check A

Also refer back to Chapter 29

1. Why might the owners of a car manufacturer want to analyse the accounts of a competitor?
2. How would ratios help the owners analyse the financial position of their competitor?
3. Give reasons why the accounts of a business are difficult to interpret.
4. How do ratios help people who are interested in the financial situation of a business?

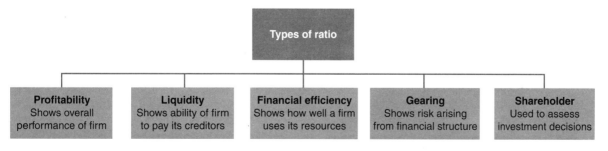

| **Profitability**
Shows overall performance of firm | **Liquidity**
Shows ability of firm to pay its creditors | **Financial efficiency**
Shows how well a firm uses its resources | **Gearing**
Shows risk arising from financial structure | **Shareholder**
Used to assess investment decisions |

A   **32.2** The ratios

Profitability ratios: Used to assess the firm's ability to translate sales into profits

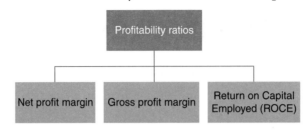

	Formula	Interpretation	Caution	How ratio can be improved
Return on Capital Employed (ROCE)	$\dfrac{\text{Net or Operating profit} \times 100}{\text{Capital employed}}$	The higher the better Compare with other businesses Compare with interest rates Unit: %	Several methods used – confusing Not related to risks	Improve by increasing profits (for example, increasing prices) or reducing capital employed
Gross profit margin	$\dfrac{\text{Gross profit} \times 100}{\text{Sales revenue}}$	The higher the better Trend very useful to monitor Unit: %	Industry dependent	Reduce COGS Increase sales revenue by more than COGS
Net Profit Margin	$\dfrac{\text{Net profit} \times 100}{\text{Sales revenue}}$	The higher the better Trend very useful to monitor Unit : %	Industry dependent	Reduce overhead expenses Increase gross profit margins

Liquidity ratios: Used to assess the firm's ability to pay its short term liabilities

Current ratio	$\dfrac{\text{Current assets}}{\text{Current liabilities}}$	Trend more useful than actual value For some businesses range 1.5 to 2 thought suitable Unit: no units	Ideal level is industry dependent	Better management of: • stock levels • cash • accounts receivable • trade payables.
Acid test ratio	$\dfrac{\text{Current assets} - \text{Stocks}}{\text{Current liabilities}}$	Trend more useful than actual value For some 1 thought suitable Unit: no units	Ideal level is industry dependent	Better management of: • cash • accounts receivable • trade payables.

Efficiency ratios: Used to assess the firms' ability to manage its current assets

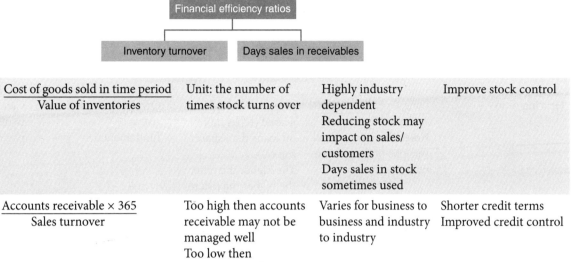

Inventory turnover	$\dfrac{\text{Cost of goods sold in time period}}{\text{Value of inventories}}$	Unit: the number of times stock turns over	Highly industry dependent Reducing stock may impact on sales/customers Days sales in stock sometimes used	Improve stock control
Days sales in receivables	$\dfrac{\text{Accounts receivable} \times 365}{\text{Sales turnover}}$	Too high then accounts receivable may not be managed well Too low then customers might want more credit Unit: days	Varies for business to business and industry to industry	Shorter credit terms Improved credit control

Shareholder ratios: Usually used by investors to assess the suitability of the firm for investment

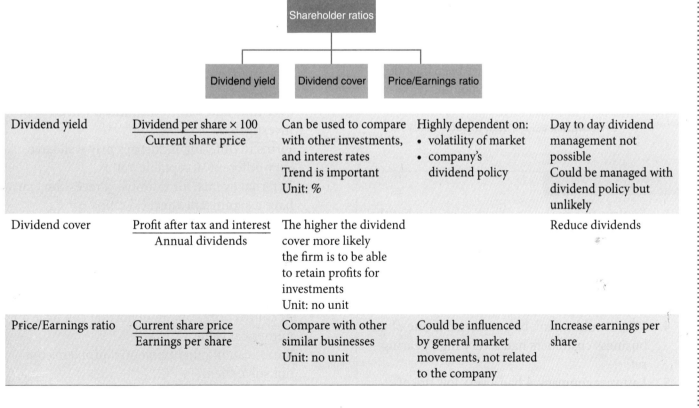

Dividend yield	$\dfrac{\text{Dividend per share} \times 100}{\text{Current share price}}$	Can be used to compare with other investments, and interest rates Trend is important Unit: %	Highly dependent on: • volatility of market • company's dividend policy	Day to day dividend management not possible Could be managed with dividend policy but unlikely
Dividend cover	$\dfrac{\text{Profit after tax and interest}}{\text{Annual dividends}}$	The higher the dividend cover more likely the firm is to be able to retain profits for investments Unit: no unit		Reduce dividends
Price/Earnings ratio	$\dfrac{\text{Current share price}}{\text{Earnings per share}}$	Compare with other similar businesses Unit: no unit	Could be influenced by general market movements, not related to the company	Increase earnings per share

Financial gearing: Used to measure risk associated with financing the business

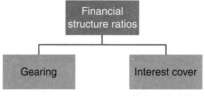

Gearing ratio	$\dfrac{\text{Long-term loans} \times 100}{\text{Capital employed}}$ **Note:** There are several versions of the gearing ratio.	Over 50% = highly geared (relies more on loans than share capital) The higher the ratio, the higher the risk to investors Low = safe and unambitious	Owners' attitude to risk is fundamental	Can be reduced by issuing more shares, or paying back loans
Interest cover	$\dfrac{\text{Operating profit}}{\text{Annual interest paid}}$	The higher the ratio the lower the risk to investors Unit: no unit		Reduce dependency on long term loans (Decrease gearing)

Top tip

The Cambridge syllabus will only require you to calculate some of the ratios above. Other ratios have been included to aid students' understanding of the analysis of accounts and to provide more complete assessment of ratio analysis.

Progress Check B

1. Explain to a manager of a shoe shop what the liquidity ratios tell him about the business.
2. Why might a supermarket be able to do well with a very low current ratio?
3. How might the manager of a restaurant improve its profitability ratios?
4. Why would a bank be concerned if one of its business customers had a very high gearing ratio?
5. Last year company *A* had a very low price/earnings ratio. There are rumours that it might be taken over by a competitor which has pushed the share price up. What would you expect to happen to the price/earnings ratio? Why?

32.3 Limitations of ratio analysis

- Accounts are historical. Forecast accounts are based on the past. The future may well be different from the past.
- Ratios cannot be looked at in isolation. Trends over time and within the industry need to be investigated.
- Firms in differing industries may well have very different 'acceptable' ratios.
- External events, for example, a recession can have a significant effect on ratios.
- There is a range of different formulae for some ratios.
- Accounts can, within limits, be adjusted to make some ratios look favourable (window dressing).
- Accounts only contain items that can have a numerical value.
- Ratios can highlight potential problems but not solve them.

Progress Check C

1. The following is an extract from the published accounts of a car manufacturer.

$m	Year ending December 2010	Year ending December 2011
Sales revenue	800	700
Gross profit	100	70
Net operating profit	30	20
Inventories	60	80
Accounts receivable	40	30
Current assets	120	130
Current liabilities	80	130
Non-current liabilities	100	120
Capital employed	400	400
Number of shares issued	80m	85m
Share price at year end	$6.00	$3.00

(a) Calculate the gross profit margin, net profit margin and return on capital employed for each year. Comment on the trend in the firm's profitability.

(b) Calculate the current ratio, the acid test ratio, days sales in receivables and stock turnover ratio. Comment on the trend in the firm's liquidity.

(c) Calculate the gearing ratio. Comment on the usefulness of this ratio to a potential lender to the firm.

(d) Calculate the shareholder ratios.

2. Explain how an increasing gearing ratio in a business affects the risk to a lender to the business.

3. Explain, with examples, why ratio results are often industry dependent.

4. How might having a sale to reduce stocks (inventory levels) affect the current ratio?

Multiple Choice Questions

1. The current ratio compares:
   (i) current assets relative to sales
   (ii) current assets relative to current liabilities
   (iii) liquid assets relative to current liabilities
   (iv) long term assets relative to current assets

2. The gearing ratio is useful to assess:
   (i) a firm's ability to repay its debtors
   (ii) the risk of a liquidity problem
   (iii) the risk to a long term creditor
   (iv) the dividend a shareholder is likely to receive

3. Which statement best describes the results of 'Days sales in receivables' calculation for a firm?
   (i) It depends on the industry the firm is in
   (ii) It is better if the result increases over time
   (iii) It should be around 30 days
   (iv) It depends on the size of the business

4. Net profit margin is:
   (i) always greater than or equal to gross profit margin
   (ii) sales less expenses
   (iii) always less than or equal to gross profit margin
   (iv) net profit less expenses

5. Which of the following types of business often operates successfully with a low current ratio?
   (i) A shop which is owned and operated by a family
   (ii) A firm making seasonal products
   (iii) A large supermarket chain
   (iv) Ship building firm

6. Which of the following is a limitation to using published accounting information?
   (i) Business always exaggerate in their accounts
   (ii) Accounts are only based on historical information
   (iii) Most people don't understand accounts so they are deliberately misleading
   (iv) They do not allow trends to be analysed

Exam-style Question

The Board at Sam's Fashions (SF) are anxious about the next annual general meeting of shareholders. There has been considerable speculation in the financial press that investors, particularly large shareholders, are going to upset the meeting. At the last Annual General Meeting of this public limited company, many shareholders had been disappointed about the falling profits. They were worried about the proposal to reduce dividends and the impact this could have on the share price of the company.

The decision to cut retail prices last year by 5% on average had helped sales volume in the short term – but with the result of reducing profit. Because of difficult global trading, Sam, the Managing Director believes that the only way forward is through rapid expansion. The board will be presented with the following financial information:

Appendix A: Financial data on Sam's Fashions Financial Year ending 31st May

	2009	2010
Total dividends	$70m (paid)	$60.2m (proposed)
Dividend per share	$0.50 (paid)	$0.43 (proposed)
SF's share price at end of year	$5.00	$3.50
Net profit	$200m	$150m
Capital employed	$1 000m	$990m
Retained profits	$45m	$15m

(a) Using data in Appendix A, calculate for **both** financial years 2009 and 2010:
  (i) the return on capital employed   [3]
  (ii) the dividend yield.   [3]
(b) Would you advise Sam to reduce the level of dividends more than has been proposed? Justify your answer.   [10]

Adapted from Cambridge 9707 Paper 33 Q1 June 2010

Student's plan

- Dividend yield up because of fall in share price – this is not necessarily a good sign! Will share price fall further if dividends are further reduced?
- ROCE suggests that performance of business has declined – do Directors want to reflect this in dividends or do they want to keep shareholder happy in short term hoping that performance will soon improve?
- Increasing retained profits and liquidity of the business by reducing dividends further could be a real benefit to the business **but** will it be wisely invested? Are Sam's ambitious plans sensible in a difficult market?
- If dividend yield remained at 10%, i.e. $0.35 then SF would retain an extra $11.2m.
- Overall judgement may depend on how important it is to stop shareholders taking drastic action at the next AGM or discourage them from selling shares. This seems quite likely. In the light of difficult trading conditions it may be better to keep shareholders happy than expand.

Authors' Comments

The student plans to use all of the calculated ratios, and wants to use them effectively to build up a picture of the present financial position of the firm. The student has also recognised the key attitudes of shareholders as well as the current economic situation of the firm.

The student intends to discuss the conditions for a judgement and has then proceeded to make a judgement which is supported by earlier analysis.

This should lead to the student demonstrating all of the key examination skills.

Revision checklist – tick when done and understood!

Topic	Textbook read	Revision complete
Profitability ratios		
Liquidity ratios		
Financial efficiency ratios		
Shareholder ratios		
Gearing ratio		
Using ratio analyse to improve business performance		
Uses and limitations of ratios		

Investment Appraisal

Revision Objectives

After you have studied this chapter, you should be able to:

☞ understand the concept of investment
☞ assess the factors influencing an investment decision
☞ apply and interpret the concept of payback
☞ apply and interpret ARR
☞ explain the reasons for discounting the future
☞ apply and interpret NPV
☞ interpret IRR
☞ assess an investment.

33.1 Investment

Investment is spending money now with the hope of an improved return in the future. In this context it could be spending on new machinery, new factories, major marketing campaigns and so on.

Key term

Investment appraisal: evaluating the profitability or desirability of an investment project

Factors influencing investment decisions

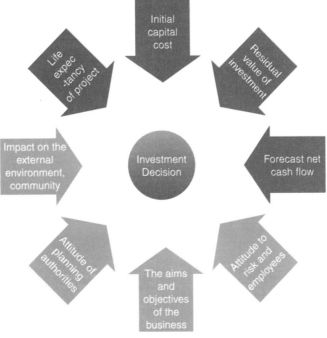

Dark brown arrow: Quantitative factors
Light brown arrow: Qualitative factors

Top tip

For any investment it is important to identify the key features of the context within which an investment decision is to be made. For example: the size of the business, the relative size of the investment required, the firm's situation with regard to risk, the difficulties in forecasting the future in the given situation etc.

Progress Check A

1. Is spending money on staff uniforms an investment?
   Explain your answer.
2. Give three examples of likely investments by a software company.
3. Explain the term 'annual net cash flow' in the context of a new piece of machinery.
4. Explain why actual annual net cash flows for a new oil refinery might be different from those forecast.

33.2 Investment appraisal: non-discounting methods

Method	How calculated	Advantages	Disadvantages
Payback	Length of time it takes for the net cash inflows to pay back the original capital cost of the investment	• Easy to compare projects • Will want short payback if borrowing for project, maybe less than criterion level • Short payback reduces opportunity cost • Long payback increases uncertainty, risk • Quick, easy to calculate, understand • Widely used	• No discounting of the future • Simplistic • Disregards cash flow beyond payback period (focuses on short term rather than long term)
Average Rate of Return(ARR)	P/C×100 where P is annual average profit (net cash flow) of project, C is capital cost of project	• Compare with ARR of other projects, prevailing interest rates • Some business set a minimum acceptable rate for projects, the criterion rate • It focuses on profit • Easily understood, relatively easily calculated and compared to criterion rate	• Ignores timing of cash flows • Includes cash flows from towards the end of the life of the project – more uncertainty • No discounting of the future

Key terms

Criterion rate: the minimum rate set by management for investment appraisal results for a project to be accepted
Criterion level: the maximum payback period set by management for investment appraisal results for a project to be accepted

Progress Check B

1. Why might a business buying a new computer system be concerned if the payback period is 4 years?
2. State three reasons why a business manufacturing cell phones might want a short payback for a new factory project.

3. Explain any one of these reasons.
4. Explain one limitation of using the ARR method to appraise a project.
5. Why might you reject a project that gives an ARR 0.5% less than the prevailing interest rate in your country?

33.3 Discounting the future

There is always an opportunity cost in investing in a project. This is reflected in the discount rate.

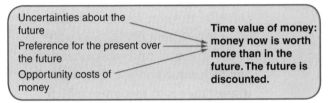

Uncertainties about the future
Preference for the present over the future
Opportunity costs of money

Time value of money: money now is worth more than in the future. The future is discounted.

Progress Check C

1. Why is there a need to discount the future?
2. What factors would a business consider when choosing a criterion discount rate?
3. Why is the prevailing interest rate in a country important in choosing the discount rate?

33.4 Net Present Value (NPV)

Key terms

Net Present Value: today's value of the estimated cash flows resulting from an investment

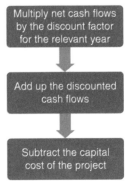

Multiply net cash flows by the discount factor for the relevant year

↓

Add up the discounted cash flows

↓

Subtract the capital cost of the project

Net Present Value

Advantages	Disadvantages
It considers both size and timing of cash flows	Some managers find it difficult to understand
Discount rates can be chosen for different economic circumstances	Depends on choice of discount rate. What should it be?
It considers the time value of money which includes an element of risk	May be difficult comparing projects with different capital costs

Progress Check D

1. Explain what a positive Net Present Value means.
2. A project lasts five years. In a cash flow forecast, a business has been optimistic about the residual value of an investment at the end of the five year period. Explain the impact on Net Present Value if a more realistic forecast is used.
3. The future for the retail sector has become less predictable due to long term economic conditions. Should the discount rate for a retail business increase? Explain your answer.
4. Why might a business use a criterion rate rather than the prevailing interest rate?

33.5 Other methods

Internal Rate of Return (IRR)

An NPV of zero indicates the point of indifference:

Greater than zero: the project is worth considering
Less than zero: the project is not worth considering

The discount rate that gives a zero NPV for a project is known as Internal Rate of Return (IRR).

The question then becomes 'Is the IRR acceptable to the business?' You will not be required to calculate IRR.

Advantages	Disadvantages
The IRR can easily be compared with prevailing interest rates or the criterion rate	The calculation is more complex than other methods
It avoids the need to choose an actual discount rate	It is more difficult to understand
It is easy to compare different projects	It might give a spurious sense of precision – other factors are involved in the decision

A

> **Key term**
>
> **Internal Rate of Return:** the rate of discount that gives a Net Present Value of zero – the higher the IRR the more profitable the investment

Discounted payback

Similar to Payback but instead of using cash flows the calculation uses discounted cash flows. This method recognizes that cash flow may overstate future benefits of a project because of the time value of money.

> **Progress Check E**
>
> 1. Project *A* has an IRR of 10% while project *B* has an IRR of 20%. All other things being equal, which project would you chose? Explain your reason.
> 2. What would happen to the IRR for a project if all future cash flows for a project were projected to increase?
> 3. Why might using discounted payback be preferable to using payback for a project requiring borrowing.

33.6 Limitations of investment appraisal

- Numerical methods only consider 'measurable' features of a decision. There are other important factors to consider.

- Calculations are only as reliable as the data used. Forecasts can only be, at best, opinions about the future.
- Each method has its own shortcomings. Results between methods may give contradictory messages.
- Risks are difficult to assess and attitudes to risk can vary considerably both within an organisation and between organisations.

> **Top tip**   Unless the question only asks for calculations it is important to consider the non-numerical features of an investment decision as well as the strengths and weaknesses of any technique you use. Of particular importance is to recognise which aspects of forecasts are critical to the decision and how different assumptions about these might affect the decision.

> **Progress Check F**
>
> 1. Explain how the views of a local community might affect an investment decision.
> 2. Explain why qualitative factors might influence the decision of a newspaper to replace its printed version with an online version.
> 3. What qualitative factors would be involved in the decision to replace software in a retail outlet?

Multiple Choice Questions

1. What distinguishes an investment from other forms of spending?
   - (i)   It is money spent on machinery
   - (ii) It is money spent now with the aim of a return in the future
   - (iii) It is money spent where it is needed
   - (iv) It is money spent on attracting customers

2. Investment appraisal is best described as:
   - (i) a technique for assessing share price movements
   - (ii) a technique to help a business decide where to invest its profits
   - (iii) a technique for assessing whether a business investment is worthwhile or not
   - (iv) none of the above

3. An investment has a cost of $25 000. The net cash flows are, in the first 4 years:
   $10 000
   $12 000
   $12 000
   $20 000

The payback period is:
(i) 2 years
(ii) 2 years and 2 months
(iii) 2 years and 3 months
(iv) 3 years

4. With the above information the Accounting Rate of Return (ARR) is:
(i) 10%
(ii) 19%
(iii) 29%
(iv) 30%

5. With the information in Question 3, the NPV will be
(i) More than $29 000
(ii) $29 000
(iii) Less than $29 000

(iv) It is not possible to say without discount factors

6. Which of the following statements about Payback is true?
(i) Payback takes into account all cash flows
(ii) Payback takes into account the time value of money
(iii) Payback does not take into account the time value of money
(iv) Payback needs a calculation of the average net cash flow

7. Which of the following statements about Net Present Value is not true?
(i) It takes account of the time value of money
(ii) It uses discount factors
(iii) It only takes account of some of the net cash inflows
(iv) It looks at all net cash inflows

Exam-style Question

Radar Cosmetics
New factory location could reduce costs
Radar has always manufactured its products in country P. However, wage rates and land prices are at least 50% higher than in countries R and S. The directors plan to establish a new factory abroad to manufacture products under the 'Aquaskin' brand. This would lead to the closure of one of the two existing factories in country P. The Operations Director had produced a report about two possible factory sites – one in country R and one in country S. Here is some of his report.

- The employment laws in country R are the same as in country P.
- Country R is in a large free trade area with many other countries and is a well-known tourist destination.
- The opportunities for joint ventures and accepting sub-contracted work are likely to be higher in country S due to the huge cosmetics industry already based there. This would offer opportunities for economies of scale.
- The initial investment in country R for the factory capacity required would be at least $3.5m, based on a five year lease of the property.

Table 1

The expected cash inflows from the country R location over this time period are forecast to be					
	Year 1	Year 2	Year 3	Year 4	Year 5
Expected cash inflows	2.5	2.5	3.0	4.0	6.0

- Cash outgoings are expected to be 50% of cash inflows in any one year.

Table 2

Results for country S are			
ARR	Payback	NPV	Capital cost
40%	3 years	$3.6m	$8m

(a) Calculate for the country R location:
(i)   Average Rate of Return (ARR)   [3]
(ii) Payback period   [3]
(iii) Net Present Value (NPV) at 10% discount rate.   [4]

A

(b) Using your results from part (a), data in Table 2 and other information, recommend the country in which Radar should locate its new factory.

[14]

Adapted from Cambridge 9707 Paper 32 Q4 November 2010

Student's answer

(a) (i)   31.4 %
     (ii) 2 years and 8 months
     (iii) $3.02m

(b) *Essay plan only*

- Country *R* – lower capital cost and quicker payback, important for this business with falling net profits (but no actual data on this given). Lower ARR but still high, as suits quite a high risk venture into a foreign country.
- Country *S* – higher ARR with potential for further profits from economies of scale in future. Higher capital cost could be a problem – Government grants available (no information on this).
- Qualitative: which location represents more of a culture shock? Managers prepared to move to either location? *But* country R might be more attractive if tourists find it appealing. Language and distance problems? Huge industry in country S could give cheap components. Country R will ensure no trade restrictions, unlike country S location.
- More information would have been helpful, for example, actual estimated unit costs in each location.
- Final choice Country *S* because of key issue of falling profits and higher capital cost in Country *S*.

Authors' Comments

(a) All calculations are correct.
(b) The student plans to answer this in a very logical way. Provided there is depth of analysis and discussion, as promised, it should achieve high marks.

Revision checklist – tick when done and understood!

Topic	Textbook read	Revision complete
The concept of investment		
Investment appraisal: non-discounting methods		
Discounting the future		
NPV		
Other methods		
Limitations of investment appraisal		

What is Strategic Management **34**

Revision Objectives

After you have studied this chapter, you should be able to:

☞ know the factors that determine corporate strategy
☞ distinguish between strategic decisions and tactical decisions
☞ understand the need for strategic management

☞ understand how strategy and organisational structure can be linked
☞ assess the importance of competitive advantage for a business and how it might be achieved.

34.1 What is meant by 'corporate strategy'?

A strategy is a 'way of achieving an objective'. The importance of corporate aims and objectives was revised in Chapter 4. This chapter revises the meaning and importance of corporate strategies.

> **Key term**
>
> **Corporate strategy:** a long term plan of action for the whole organisation aimed at achieving a particular corporate objective

An objective without a strategy – or plan – to achieve it will never be reached. It is like having a target without any arrows!

Review success of this strategy by assessing whether the corporate objective is being achieved

Corporate objective
To increase return on capital by 15% in 3 years

Divisional and departmental objectives
For example, Marketing dept: increase market share in Asia by 5% for each of next 3 years

Corporate strategy
To pursue market development into emerging market countries – one new market entered each year for next 3 years

A Influences on strategy formation

Corporate strategic decisions are influenced by:

1. **Objectives** – as explained above
2. **Resources available** – a small business may not have the finance or skilled management required to develop a high technology product
3. **Competitive environment** – are competitors innovative? Are they entering new markets? Are they cutting costs to be more competitive? A business is likely to respond to each of these situations with a different strategy of its own.
4. **Strengths of the business** – focusing on existing strengths to develop new strategies is likely to be more successful than trying to develop new strengths.

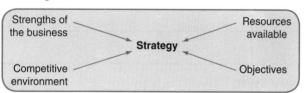

34.2 Strategy and tactics – what are the differences?

Key term

Tactical decision: short term decisions aimed at meeting a specific part of the overall strategy

The key differences between strategic decisions and tactical decisions are:

Table 34.1

	Strategic decisions	Tactical decisions
Time period	Long term	Short term
Resources required	Many (usually)	Few (usually)
Taken by	Directors/ Senior managers	Middle / Junior managers
Reversing the decision, for example, if it is a bad one	Difficult	Relatively easy
Impact usually on	Whole organisation	One department

Progress Check A

1. "We intend to improve returns to our shareholders over a five year period". Quote from a company CEO. Is this an objective or a strategy?
   Explain your answer.
2. "We will focus on research and development of new products to create more consumer interest". Quote from a company CEO.
   Is this an objective or a strategy? Explain your answer.
3. "Our aim is to penetrate the markets we are in to gain further market share". Quote from a company CEO. Outline one strategy that the business might adopt to achieve this objective.
4. Outline the difference between a marketing strategy for the launch of a new product and the marketing tactics that might be used to apply the strategy.
5. "The furniture company today announced that it will offer three special discount deals for customers as well as a trial of a new colour material for its dining chairs." Quote from a newspaper article.
   Are these tactical or strategic decisions? Explain your answer.

34.3 The need for strategic management

Senior management in any business needs to develop strategies for the future.

Key term

Strategic management: the role of management when setting long-term goals, taking and implementing strategic decisions that should enable a business to reach these goals.

Each stage of strategic management brings benefits to the organisation (Table 34.2).

Table 34.2

Stage of strategic management	Benefit
Analysing current position of business – Strategic Analysis (Chapter 35)	Helps in the process of making appropriate decisions – identifies strategic opportunities
Setting appropriate objectives (Chapter 4)	To give the business focus and direction
Taking the appropriate strategic decision(s) (Chapter 36)	Effective decision making should choose the 'best' option for the business
Implementing the decision(s) (Chapter 37)	Integrating and coordinating departments, allocating sufficient resources – should increase chances of strategic decision being successful
Evaluating success of decision(s) against the preset objectives	Have the objectives been met? If not, another decision may be necessary

34.4 How strategy can influence organisational structure?

Chandler considers that 'structure follows strategy'. This means that the organisational structure of a company should be based on the strategies it is following.

You might want to revise organisational structure again – refer to Chapter 12. The three clearest examples are:

Table 34.3

Strategy	Impact on organisational structure
Rationalisation (for example, cost cutting to gain competitive advantage)	Delayer the organisational structure. By removing layers of 'middle managers', overhead costs can be reduced and communication improved
Market development – expansion into other countries markets	Geographical divisions with considerable decentralisation; for example, S.E. Asia, USA, Europe, Rest of World. Locally made decisions may be more effective than centralised decisions
Expansion into different product areas	Divisional structure so that each range of products has its own divisional head and becomes a profit centre of the business

If organisational structure does not 'follow strategy' then the wrong structure may be used, possibly leading to:

- ✓ higher overhead costs
- ✓ no separate and accountable profit centres
- ✓ centralised decision making when decentralisation might be better.

34.5 Competitive advantage – what it is and how to achieve it?

> **Key term**
>
> **Competitive advantage:** superiority of an organisation over rivals gained by providing products of same value but at lower prices or by charging higher prices for differentiated goods of higher value

Competitive advantage means that a business has a clear benefit over its rivals – increasing the chances of sales and profits growth.

Michael Porter states that competitive advantage can be gained in one of two ways and that this decision is a central component in a firm's competitive strategy:

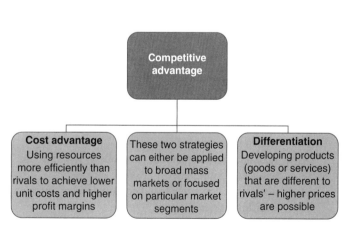

Progress Check B

1. Why do you think it is important for a manager to follow the stages of strategic management when developing a range of new products?

2. Why do you think it is important to implement an important strategic decision carefully?

3. Why is it important to review the impact of a strategic decision against the original corporate objective?

4. Outline how a computer manufacturing company's decision to attempt to become the lowest cost producer in the industry might impact on its organisational structure.

5. Why might it be an advantage to create a decentralised organisational structure when a company starts operating in more than one country?

6. Explain, with business examples, the difference between the two approaches to competitive advantage: cost advantage and differentiation advantage.

Multiple Choice Questions

1. A strategic decision is one which:
   (i) involves many resources yet is easy to reverse
   (ii) is so important that it is usually taken by senior management
   (iii) is similar to other decisions so can be taken by junior managers
   (iv) involves few resources and has no long term consequences

2. The decision by Apple to develop a range of new advanced technology products was influenced by all of the following factors *except*:
   (i) The finance and other resources that the company had available
   (ii) The strategic decisions of the company's competitors
   (iii) The skills and experience that the company's research teams have developed
   (iv) Governments making it a legal requirement for companies to spend resources on new products

3. Typically, the correct order for the stages of strategic management is:
   (i) analysis of company; implement decision; take decision; review success
   (ii) take decision; implement decision; review success; analysis of company
   (iii) analysis of company; take decision; implement decision; review success
   (iv) review success; analysis of company; take decision; implement decision

4. According to Michael Porter the *two* main ways for a business to gain competitive advantage are:
   (i) cost reductions and cheaper products
   (ii) differentiated products and new developments
   (iii) cost reductions and increased prices
   (iv) differentiated products and cost reductions

5. Which of the following is an example of a business gaining a competitive advantage?
   (i) Cutting costs of production to allow for lower prices
   (ii) Attempting to sell the same products as competitors but at higher prices
   (iii) Setting higher prices than competitors for products that are clearly inferior
   (iv) Cutting costs of production to make the company seem different to competitors

6. Which one of the following is a potential advantage for a fashion clothing business in pursuing a 'differentiation' strategy?
   (i) Lower prices could be charged as costs of production would be below competitors'
   (ii) No promotional costs would be needed as the products would 'sell themselves'
   (iii) Consumers might be prepared to pay higher prices for better designed clothes
   (iv) Design and production costs would be minimised allowing the business to become more profitable

Exam-style Question

Read again the Case Study from Chapter 7 Page 42 (TeenPrint)

(a) Discuss whether the decision to start an additional magazine, focused at a particular age group, is a strategic decision or a tactical decision.   [10]

Additional case study material:

Several months after this decision was taken, Ahmed and the other directors decided to start up a new magazine in a foreign market, country B. This meant setting up printing facilities abroad as well as employing writers and production staff. This as a major strategic decision for TeenPrint but Ahmed considered it essential if the company was to continue to expand. The economic conditions in country B were much more favourable.

(b) Evaluate ways in which TeenPrint could attempt to establish a competitive advantage over rival businesses.   [16]

Case study based on Cambridge 9707 Paper 31 June 2010

Student's answer to (a)

A strategic decision is one that has a big impact on a firm's long term success in meeting its overall objectives. A tactical decision is one that concerns the short term and is just one part of an overall strategy.

Starting a new magazine will need a lot of resources, even for an existing publishing company. The market segment will need to be researched and this will take time and money. New printing machines might be needed, if there is no excess capacity. A new marketing strategy will be needed because the new magazine will not be aimed at the same type of consumers as the existing one. This suggests that the decision is a strategic one.

Also, this is a big decision that should be taken by senior managers. It would not be normal for junior managers to take a decision like this because if it fails it could lead to the company going out of business. Finally, the decision would be difficult to reverse as once the new workers had been employed and the new machines purchased, it would be unwise to decide not to produce the magazine after all.

Therefore, even though this decision does not diversify the business into a completely new industry or country's market it is a strategic one and not a tactical decision. An example of a tactical decision could be whether to sell the magazine from just newspaper shops or petrol stations too.

Authors' Comments

Quite a brief answer but contains good definitions; application to the case; analysis of what strategic decisions are and a final judgement.

The student could have referred to the 'cross-functional' nature of most strategic decisions, i.e. the fact that the new magazine will have an impact on the finance, HR, marketing and ops man departments – suggesting that it truly is strategic in nature.

Revision checklist – tick when done and understood!

Topic	Textbook read	Revision complete
Factors that determine corporate strategy		
Differentiating between strategic and tactical decisions		
The importance of strategic management		
Linking 'strategy to structure'		
Competitive advantage and how it can be achieved		

Strategic Analysis 35

35.1 How strategic analysis helps a business?

By undertaking effective strategic analysis a business should obtain answers to three important questions.

1. Where is the business now – in terms of its products and main markets?
2. How might external events impact on the business?
3. How might the business respond to these events?

The answers to these questions will help business managers decide on the most effective future strategies the business should adopt.

35.2 SWOT analysis

Key term

SWOT analysis: a form of strategic analysis that identifies internal strengths and weaknesses and external opportunities and threats

This is part of the process of determining:

| Where are we now? | → | Where do we want to be? |

Benefits

✓ SWOT analysis is useful to managers when planning a new strategy. It helps to match the firm's resources and strengths to the opportunities available – whilst identifying the major external risk factors
✓ The process of undertaking the SWOT analysis can promote discussion and cooperation between senior managers
✓ Inexpensive – it is usually undertaken by business managers – not expensive external consultants.

Limitations

✗ It is often over simplified – it can just lead to lists being created with no priority or quantitative measure given to each factor
✗ To be more effective much more detailed analysis of each strength, weakness, opportunity and threat will be needed – especially before a major strategic decision is taken
✗ It is often subjective – based on the views of the analyst. Another manager might arrive at a different SWOT list

✗   Different weights might be applied to the various issues identified by different managers.

Top tip

Strengths and Weaknesses should be *internal*, Opportunities and Threats are *external*.

Progress Check A

1. Explain why SWOT analysis requires both internal analysis of the business and external analysis beyond the business.
2. Should a business decide to take advantage of every 'opportunity' identified? If not, why not?
3. Undertake a simple SWOT analysis of a well known business in your country that is planning to expand its operations.
4. Explain why your SWOT analysis might be different from someone else's SWOT analysis of the same business.

35.3 PEST analysis

Key term

PEST analysis: the strategic analysis of a firm's macro-environment – political, economic, social and technological factors

The macro-environment means the important external issues that affect business performance and future strategies. Some business analysts refer to PESTLE analysis by separating out two further external factors: Legal and Environmental.

An example outlining PEST analysis for Toyota setting up operations in a country for the first time is shown below:

Benefits

✓   Provides an understanding of wider business environment

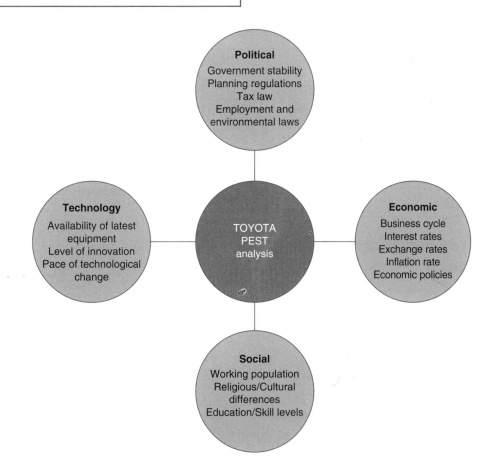

A

✓ Encourages analysis of the business environment in setting future business objectives and strategies

✓ Helps to identify future problems and take action to avoid them or minimise their effects

✓ Different PEST analyses for each country a business operates in will highlight political, economic, social, cultural and legal differences.

Limitations

✗ A list of points needs further critical analysis

✗ May need to be updated regularly given the pace of external changes

✗ Some information may be based on inaccurate forecasts, for example, economic changes

✗ Only considers the external environment

✗ Judgements still need to be made about the relative importance of each factor to the business.

Progress Check B

1. Why might 'Political' factors (including legal factors) be different in differing countries?
2. Explain how the 'Economic' environment might change quickly.
3. Suggest three 'Social' factors for a multinational soft drinks business to analyse before starting operations in your own country.
4. Give examples of businesses likely to be greatly affected by technological change in the next few years – examples should include both negative and positive effects.

35.4 Vision statements and mission statements

Key terms

Vision statement: what the organisation would like to achieve or accomplish in the long term

Mission statement: the business's core purpose and focus to be communicated to stakeholders

Benefits

✓ Help provide decision makers with focus and direction – 'will this new strategy help us achieve our vision/mission?'

✓ Sense of purpose is provided to decision makers – 'we may need new strategies if we are to attain our vision/mission'.

Limitations

✗ Often rather general and ill-defined so of limited use when taking specific decisions

✗ May need to be constantly reviewed to meet changing circumstances and new challenges.

35.5 Boston Matrix Analysis

Key term

Boston Matrix: a method of analysing the product portfolio of a business in terms of market share and market growth

The Boston Matrix in the figure given below shows:

- four products sold by one business
- the size of each circle represents the value of sales for each product
- the four products are in different markets with different rates of sales growth
- the products have either high or low market share.

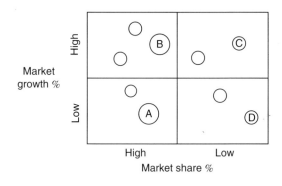

The four Boston Matrix product classifications are:

Product A – 'Cash cow' – low market growth but high market share

Product B – 'Star' – high market growth and high market share

Product C – 'Problem child' (or question mark) – high market growth but low market share

Product D – 'Dog' – low market growth and low market share.

Uses of Boston Matrix analysis

✓ Analyses the performance and current market position of existing products

✓ Encourages managers to take strategic decisions about existing products, such as:
  (i) 'Divest' dog products
  (ii) 'Build' problem children, for example, with cash obtained from 'cash cows'
  (iii) 'Hold' or support a star product to lengthen the period of its success

✓ Encourages managers to take decisions about developing new products, for example, to replace a 'dog'.

Limitations of Boston Matrix analysis

✗ It provides information and some analysis but it does not explain *why* a product is in the position it is

✗ It cannot forecast what might happen with each product – other information might be needed, such as market research

✗ It assumes that high market shares are always more profitable than low market shares – may not be the case if a higher profit margin is made on a low volume product.

Progress C

1. Suggest a possible vision statement and mission statement for your school or college (or find out what they are!). Differentiate between vision and mission statements.
2. Explain what action a business might take if one of its products has low market share but is in a high growth market.
3. Which products, according to the Boston Matrix, should a business aim to replace with new products as soon as possible?
4. Explain what measures a car manufacturing business might take to keep one of its 'star' products successful.

35.6 Porter's Five Forces

Diagram of Porter's Five Forces is given below:

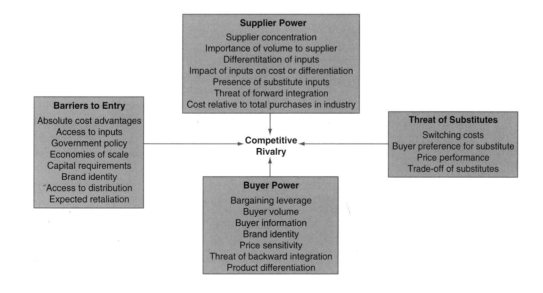

By understanding the forces that determine competitive rivalry, the following types of strategic decisions could be made more effectively.

- ✓ Which markets to enter?
- ✓ Do we stay in existing markets?
- ✓ What actions can be taken to improve our competitive position?

35.7 Core competences

> **Key terms**
>
> **Core competence:** an important business capability that gives a firm competitive advantage
>
> **Core product:** a product or process based on a firm's core competence

Core competences include unique sets of skills or production techniques. Examples include:

- ✓ *Microsoft* – set of software patents and skills that are difficult for other firms to duplicate
- ✓ *Toyota* – hybrid technology engines that can be adapted to many types of vehicles
- ✓ *Walmart* – low cost logistical system that gives the firm a substantial cost advantage for entering new markets.

To be of commercial value to a business, a core competence should:

- ✓ be able to offer recognisable benefits to consumers
- ✓ not be easy for other firms to copy
- ✓ be applicable to a range of products and markets.

Once a core competence has been established, it opens up strategic opportunities for developing new core products and consumer products.

> **Progress Check D**
>
> **For Questions 1–5 base your answers on any business of your choice.**
> 1. Explain two factors that increase 'supplier power'.
> 2. Explain two factors that increase 'buyer power'.
> 3. Explain two possible 'barriers to entry' into market the business operates in.
> 4. Explain two factors that increase the 'threat of substitutes'.
> 5. Explain four factors that determine a firm's competitive rivalry.
> 6. Explain how a core competence in making efficient and patented wind turbines could give a business a competitive advantage.

Multiple Choice Questions

1. Which one of the following statements is correct?
   (i) SWOT analysis is a technique used to take important business decisions
   (ii) SWOT analysis helps managers decide 'where the business is now'
   (iii) SWOT analysis sets business objectives for the future
   (iv) SWOT analysis considers only the external environment of business

2. Which one of the following statements is correct?
   (i) PEST analysis is an internal audit of a business's current strengths and weaknesses
   (ii) PEST analysis is sufficient to allow managers to make important strategic decisions
   (iii) PEST analysis outlines some important external influences on a business

   (iv) PEST analysis assesses the performance of each of a business's products

3. One of the uses of the Boston Matrix is:
   (i) to indicate strategic decisions that could be taken with the businesses product portfolio
   (ii) to indicate which products are profitable and which are not
   (iii) to increase the motivation of both managers and workers
   (iv) to identify the level of competitive rivalry that exist in each of the markets the firms operates in

4. Porter's Five Forces analysis aims to help managers:
   (i) identify the market shares and market growth in each of the markets a business operates in
   (ii) analyse the performance and current market position of existing products

(iii) analyse, for each business unit or division, the level of competitive rivalry

(iv) choose which strategies should be adopted to improve the power of a business

5. According to Porter's Five Forces analysis, competitive rivalry depends on:
   (i) supplier power, firm's market power, barriers to entry and buyer power
   (ii) supplier power, buyer power, barriers to entry and threat of substitutes
   (iii) threat of substitutes, threats from suppliers, buyer power, barriers to competition

(iv) firm's market power, consumer power, supplier power, threat of substitutes

6. According to Hamel and Prahalad, a core competence will:
   (i) offer a business a competitive advantage if it is easy for other firms to copy
   (ii) increase the firm's competitive advantage if it can develop core products from it
   (iii) increase competition as the business cannot differentiate itself from rivals
   (iv) only exist if it can be used to develop a single differentiated product

Exam-style Question

Forest Paper Products (FPC)

FPC is a public limited company. It owns forests in several low-income developing countries. It cuts down trees to produce timber. Most of this timber is sold to other users but FPC also has a factory producing wooden furniture, using its own timber.

This furniture is traditionally designed and is sold through 'low price' retailers. Consumers' incomes have been rising in recent years and demand for imported furniture has increased. Imported furniture is often made of new technology materials plastic not wood and is based on modern designs. Lower import tariffs and an appreciating exchange rate have made imports more competitive.

Several pressure groups are angry that FPC destroys large areas of woodland each year – often in areas of great natural beauty. FPC has responded by stating that they plant one new tree for every one cut down. The organisational structure of FPC is a hierarchical one – in the factory, for example, there are seven levels of hierarchy with an average span of control of 3. All of the company's sawmills are operating at full capacity – reflecting the high level of demand for its timber which is sold at very competitive prices. The company recorded a net profit margin of 14% in the last financial year.

The directors of FPC are about to choose one of two strategic options:

Option 1: Expansion of furniture making by a takeover of a large Asian furniture manufacturing firm. This might lead to economies of scale in furniture making and allow FPC to import furniture from a low cost factory.

Option 2: Exploitation of other primary products. Much of the land where the forests were is still owned by FPC. This land could contain metals such as copper and lead. These could be mined to earn additional revenue. FPC has no experience of this industry and mines would lead to local residents being relocated.

Evaluate the importance of both SWOT and PEST analysis to FPC's directors as they analyse the two strategic options. [20]

Adapted from Cambridge 9707 Paper 33 Section B Q6 June 2011

Student's plan

Define SWOT and PEST

- Give examples of what would be included in both forms of strategic analysis – relevant to FPC and taken from the case study
- Explain the benefits of SWOT – applied to this case, for example, company is profitable (strength) but has no experience of mining (weakness) *so* does this indicate that profits would be better invested in expanding existing operations?
- Explain the benefits of PEST – applied to case, for example, high exchange rate at present is a positive factor for taking over.
- Asian furniture maker and importing products: new technology in furniture making/designs means competitors have a competitive advantage.
- Limitations of both SWOT and PEST – both need to be updated frequently, for example, due to changes in primary product prices, can be subjective (who within FPC is going to undertake them?) and they are not sufficient forms of strategic analysis on their own.
- Evaluation: Useful – but other forms of analysis required too. For example, Boston Matrix for furniture and timber products; Porter's 5 Forces for identifying the levels of competitive rivalry in the markets FPC operates in (and might operate in, say, mining); identifying core competence.

A

Authors' Comments

- Has clear structure and demonstrates appropriate knowledge
- Clear attempts to apply to this business – good
- Recognises that both SWOT and PEST have benefits – but limitations too
- The student seems to understand the importance of this strategic choice for FPC which suggests that other forms of strategic analysis are needed too – and explains why. This has the potential to be an excellent answer.

Revision checklist – tick when done and understood!

Topic	Textbook read	Revision complete
Strategic analysis – Why is it important?		
SWOT – Benefits and limitations		
PEST – Benefits and limitations		
Vision and missions statements		
Boston Matrix – Product classifications; uses and limitations		
Porter's Five Forces model		
Core competences and core products		

Strategic Choice 36

Revision Objectives

After you have studied this chapter, you should be able to:

☞ understand strategic choice as part of strategic management
☞ know what Ansoff's Matrix shows and how it helps strategic choice
☞ know how to use Force-Field analysis

☞ understand how to use decision trees when making strategic decisions
☞ be able to evaluate strategic choice techniques.

36.1 What is meant by strategic choice?

Strategic choice means deciding between future strategies.

Strategic choice is necessary because:

✓ limited resources mean that a business cannot pursue all possible strategies
✓ even if there is only one possible new strategy, the choice still exists of not pursuing it.

Strategic decisions can be so vital to the future success of a business that the choice of which one(s) to pursue is very important.

36.2 Ansoff's Matrix and making strategic choices

Key term

Ansoff's Matrix: a model used to show the degree of risk associated with the four growth strategies: market penetration; market development; product development and diversification

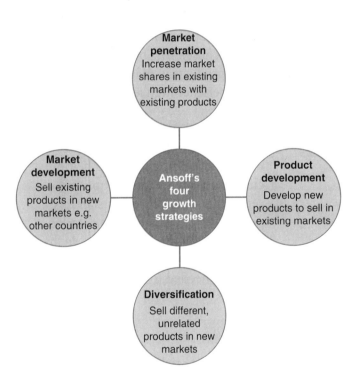

According to Ansoff, the main classifications for different growth strategies that a business can choose are:

1. *Market penetration* – As both the product and the market are known to the business this is the least risky strategy.

Tactics that can be used as part of this strategy include: lower prices, increased advertising and sales promotion, development of brand image.

2. **Market development** – The existing products are well known to the business but there might be substantial differences between existing and new markets. For example, business customers may have different requirements to those of consumers. Consumers in different countries may have different tastes and cultural influences.

3. **Product development** – The existing markets are offered new products – or developments of existing ones. This requires research and development and there is often a considerable risk that this could prove to be unsuccessful or ineffective if competitors launch an even better product.

4. **Diversification** – Often the riskiest strategy in the short term because both the performance of the product and the exact needs of consumers in new markets are unknown. This might be the strategic option chosen by a business that has uncompetitive products in markets that are either saturated or experience high levels of competition.

Top tip

Although Ansoff's Matrix can be useful in assessing risk, and helping choose between strategic options, remember that it is only a starting point for strategic choice – detailed use of quantitative techniques such as investment appraisal and decision trees are needed to give more depth of analysis.

Progress Check A

1. Why is it often quite risky for a business to enter new markets?
2. Why is the result of research and development into a new product never certain?
3. Give an example of a diversification strategy that could be adopted by a banking business operating in your country.
4. A supermarket chain in your country wants to pursue a market penetration strategy. Explain two ways in which this could be carried out.

36.3 Force-Field analysis and making strategic choices

Key term

Force-field analysis: identifies and analyses the positive factors (driving forces) that support a decision and negative factors that restrain it

Kurt Lewin suggested using this model before making important strategic decisions. If the restraining forces are much more significant than the forces for change, it could be better not to take this strategic decision. If, however, management action can reduce the restraining forces and/or increase the forces for change, the decision might be worthwhile.

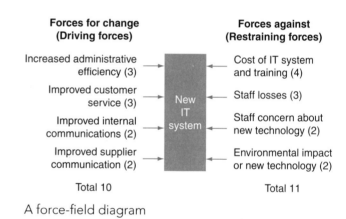

A force-field diagram

Steps to take

1. Analyse current business position and where it 'hopes to be'
2. Identify all restraining forces and driving forces
3. Allocate a number to them indicating the significance of each force (1–10)
4. Total both sets of scores – decide whether to proceed with the strategy
5. If the strategy is decided on but restraining forces still exceed driving forces how can restraining forces be reduced and driving forces increased?

Limitations of force-field analysis

- Not all of the restraining/driving forces might be identified

- Numerical values are entirely subjective
- Gives a numerical result which seems to suggest great accuracy in assessing success/failure of the new strategy.

Expected value: the likely financial result of an outcome = probability x forecast economic return

Progress Check B

1. Identify *two* possible driving forces and *two* possible restraining forces in a decision to relocate production of computers to a low cost country.
2. Suggest numerical values for these forces (scale: 1–10; where 1 = very weak) to indicate their relative strength/weakness.
3. If the total numerical value for restraining forces is greater then driving forces, suggest any *two* actions managers might take to reverse this.

36.4 Decision trees and making strategic choices

Key terms

Decision tree: a diagram that sets out the options connected with a decision and the outcomes, probabilities and economic returns that may result

Constructing a decision tree

1. Information required
- ✓ All possible outcomes from a decision
- ✓ Estimated probability of each outcome occurring
- ✓ Estimated economic return from each outcome.

2. Method of construction
- ✓ Work from **left** to **right**
- ✓ Square nodes for each decision point
- ✓ Round nodes for each set of outcomes
- ✓ Add in probabilities and economic returns.

3. Calculating expected values
- ✓ Work from **right** to **left**
- ✓ Multiply each probability of an outcome by its economic return
- ✓ Add these results at round nodes
- ✓ Take the best result at each square node
- ✓ Subtract cost of decision to calculate the best expected value and therefore the most beneficial decision.

Worked example

Forecasted probabilities and economic pay-offs from alternative marketing strategies:

	Probabilities of success/failure	Forecasted economic pay-off
Option A Capital cost $5m	0.70 probability of success	$12m gain
	0.30 probability of failure	$2m loss
Option B Capital cost £3m	0.50 probability of success	$10m gain
	0.50 probability of failure	$1m loss

(a) Draw a decision tree based on this data. [4]
(b) Calculate the expected monetary values of Option A and Option B. [4]

Solution

(a)

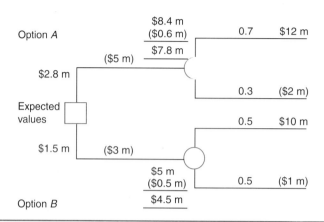

> **Top tip**
>
> You may be asked to calculate expected values from a decision tree given to you – but you may also be asked to draw the decision tree first.

✗   The results obtained are 'average' results that would be obtained if the decision was taken on several occasions. The expected monetary values will not be the exact results from making a decision once.

Limitations of decision trees

✗   High margin of error (especially with 'one-off' projects) as the probabilities and economic returns are estimated or based on assumptions

✗   Qualitative factors – such as objectives of the business and ethical considerations – are not allowed for on a decision tree

Strengths of decision trees

✓   Systematic approach that requires managers to consider all options and outcomes

✓   Identifies key aspects of a decision

✓   Can be used to assess key assumptions through 'what if' analysis. Example: By changing probabilities.

Multiple Choice Questions

1. Which one of the following could be classified as a 'market penetration' strategy for a chain of supermarkets?
    (i)   Taking over an existing food supplier
    (ii) Introducing a loyalty card scheme to provide incentives such as discounts to existing customers
    (iii) Opening up branches in another country for the first time
    (iv) Working closely with a new supplier to introduce a range of goods for the first time

2. According to Ansoff's Matrix, which one of the following strategies would be the most risky for a furniture retailing business?
    (i)   Opening more stores selling furniture and reducing prices

    (ii) Introduce a new range of furniture to encourage existing buyers to spend more
    (iii) Starting up a chain of furniture shops in another country for the first time
    (iv) Opening stores selling televisions in another country

3. If the senior managers of a hotel business were not prepared to take high risks the most likely growth strategy they would choose would be to:
    (i)   open a hotel in another country
    (ii) open a car hire business to tourists and travellers
    (iii) open another hotel in the same country
    (iv) open a hairdressing business in another country

4. Lewin's Force Field analysis suggests that, if a strategic decision was made:
    (i) Constraining forces would always equal driving forces
    (ii) The profit from a new project can be calculated by using this model
    (iii) The decision to proceed should be taken if the driving forces are less than the restraining forces
    (iv) After identifying positive and restraining forces, managers could try to increase the chances of the decision being successful

5. One of the claimed benefits of decision trees is that:
    (i) they accurately predict the expected payoffs/profits to be made from different strategic options
    (ii) they lead to calculations of the expected financial values of each decision being considered
    (iii) they are the only decision making technique that managers choosing between strategies will need
    (iv) they include a consideration of qualitative factors as well as quantitative ones

6. What is the expected payoff/value from a decision, costing $3000, that is expected to have a 0.6 chance of success, with expected profits of $5000 if successful and $2000 if not successful?
    (i) $300
    (ii) $800
    (iii) $3000
    (iv) $3800

Exam-style Question

Re-read the exam case studies at the end of Chapters 7 and 34

Additional case study material for TeenPrint

Ahmed has decided to use the decision tree technique to help him make the choice between launching a new magazine for 20–35 year olds or a new magazine for 56–70 year olds. The decision tree he constructed below shows the forecast probabilities and possible pay-offs from the magazine as well as the internet versions of the magazines which Ahmed wants to consider crating too. In addition to the decision tree below he has undertaken some secondary market research and the results of this are shown in Table 1.

Table 1

Data for the country (2012 and 2014 are forecasts)			
	2010	2012	2014
% increase in consumer spending by 20–35 year olds	6	4	2
% increase in spending by 56–70 year olds	6	5	5
% of population aged 20–35	10	11	11
% of population aged 56–70	15	18	19

Decision tree constructed by Ahmed to help make the choice between the two magazines (all financial data in $000s):

Ahmed's decision tree (All financial data $000's)

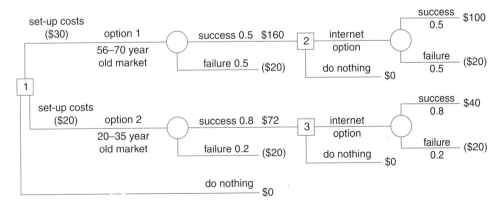

(a) Use the decision tree to calculate the expected monetary values of the two magazine options. [10]

(b) For which age range would you recommend TeenPrint to launch a new magazine? Use your results to Question (a) and any other information to support your recommendation. [16]

Cambridge 9707 Paper 32 Section A Q5(a)&(b) June 2010

Student's answer to (a)

(All values in $000)

Value at Node 2 = $(0.5 \times \$100) + (0.5 \times -\$20) = \$40$

So, if the magazine for 56–70 year olds is decided on the internet version will also be profitable so this expected value can be **added** to the pay-offs of the paper based magazine.

Value at Node 3 = $(0.8 \times \$40) + (0.2 \times -\$20) = \$28$

So, if the magazine for 20–35 year olds is decided on the internet version will also be profitable so this expected value can be **added** to the pay-offs of the paper based magazine.

Value of Option 1 before subtracting set-up costs
= $(0.5 \times \$200)^* + (0.5 \times -\$20) = \$90$

Value of Option 2 before subtracting set-up costs
= $(0.8 \times \$100)^* = (0.2 \times -\$20) = \$76$

* These pay-offs include the expected values from the internet options.

Expected monetary values at Node 1 after set-up costs deducted = $60 Option 1
$56 Option 2

Authors' Comments

A correct (and very well laid out) answer. Now try to answer (b).

Final revision checklist – tick when done and understood!

Topic	Textbook read	Revision complete
What 'strategic choice' means		
Ansoff's Matrix – Uses and limitations		
Force-Field analysis – Uses and limitations		
Decision trees – Uses and limitations		

Strategic Implementation

Revision Objectives

After you have studied this chapter, you should be able to:

☞ know what strategic implementation means
☞ understand the importance of business plans and corporate planning
☞ recognise different types of business culture and be able to evaluate the impact of culture on strategic implementation

☞ understand the problems of establishing a 'change culture'
☞ evaluate the importance of managing change and the ways this can be done
☞ understand what contingency planning and crisis management mean.

37.1 Strategic implementation

Once strategic decisions have been made – action needs to be taken to put them into effect. This is what strategic implementation means – ensuring the organisation is prepared to accept and action the major decisions that have been made.

> **Key term**
>
> **Strategic implementation:** the process of allocating and controlling resources to support chosen strategies

Factors that need to be considered within strategic implementation:

✓ plan of action
✓ adequate resources
✓ preparing workforce for change
✓ appropriate business culture and leadership style
✓ control and review system – is the chosen strategy leading to the desired results?

37.2 Business plans

Starting a new business – or developing an existing business in a major way – should be planned for. Planning should always be the first stage of the strategic implementation process.

> **Key term**
>
> **Business plan:** a document describing a new business or a development of an existing business, its objectives and strategies, the market it is in (or plans to be in) and financial forecasts

Contents of a business plan

Entrepreneurs setting up a new business will be asked by potential investors for a detailed business plan. Existing businesses use business plans too when planning to implement major strategic changes.

Progress Check A

1. Why would a potential investor – such as a bank – be unlikely to invest in an entrepreneur's new business if a Business Plan had not been written?
2. Why would an existing business be advised to develop a Business Plan for a strategic decision such as entering an export market for the first time?

37.3 Corporate plans

Corporate plans are the route map that a business intends to follow over the medium to long term (more than one year). Typically, corporate plans include details of:

1. long term objectives of the business – SMART aims for the next few years
2. the business strategies to be introduced to achieve these objectives
3. the department/divisional objectives and strategies based on those for the whole business.

Benefits of corporate plans

✓ Managers have to consider the strengths and weaknesses of the business and how to implement the strategic decisions made in drawing up the plan
✓ Clear plans provide focus, direction and a clear plan of action to managers for the coming years
✓ Help to coordinate the work of all functional departments towards commonly agreed goals
✓ Provide a control and review stage to allow checking of performance against original targets
✓ *Most useful* when flexibility and contingency planning are built into the plan.

Limitations of corporate plans

✗ Based on forecasts of the future (for example, interest rates, GDP growth, company sales and competitors actions) that may prove to be unrealistic
✗ Take time and resources to develop – for example, these may be in short supply for small businesses
✗ Managers can become so 'tied to the plan' that they fail to adapt and respond to changing internal and external circumstances.

The main influences on a company's long term plan are internal and external:

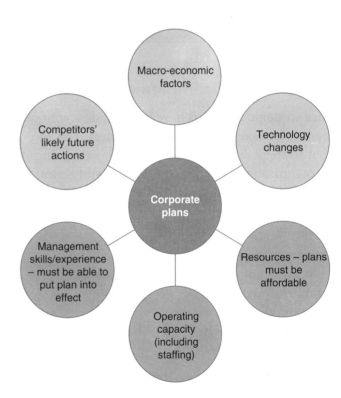

Progress Check B

1. If corporate plans have to be often changed – due to external and internal forces – is there any point in preparing them? Explain your answer.
2. Why would it be important to coordinate the work of all functional departments when developing a corporate plan?

3. Explain how any one external economic factor could affect the corporate plan of a large exporting business operating in your country.

37.4 Corporate culture

Difficult to measure and define – but every business has one! How does a business really operate? What standards and ethical position does a business take? How are workers treated and managed? Once all of these questions have been answered it is possible to have an idea about a firm's corporate culture.

> ### Key term
>
> **Corporate culture:** the values, attitudes and beliefs of the people working in an organisation that control the way decisions are taken and how the business interacts with stakeholders

Types of corporate culture

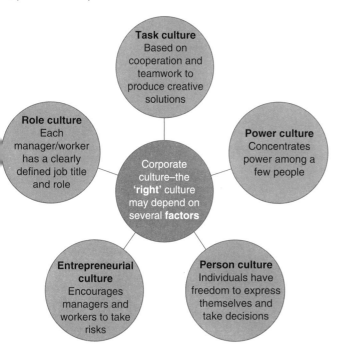

Changing corporate culture

Changing corporate culture can result in changes to senior staff, job descriptions, ethical stance of the business and working practices.

Some key steps that managers should follow are:

- ✓ focus on developing the positive aspects of the business
- ✓ obtain full commitment of senior staff to the change – their behaviour and attitudes are crucial
- ✓ establish new objectives and mission statement
- ✓ encourage participation of all staff in changing culture
- ✓ train staff in new procedures
- ✓ change the staff reward system – appropriate behaviour under the new culture should be appropriately rewarded.

The corporate culture of a business can have an impact on many factors:

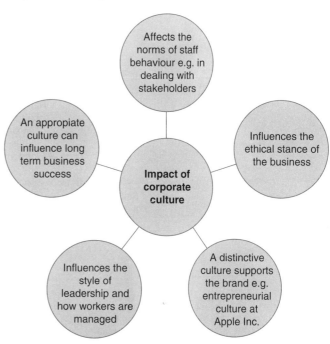

> ### Progress Check C
>
> 1. Government departments and organisations often operate with a role culture but research and development companies (for example, in I.T.) often operate with task or entrepreneurial culture. Explain the possible reasons for these differences.
> 2. If a family owned food retailing business, with loyal staff and a 'person' culture, is taken over

by a large public limited company with the objective of driving through major changes, do you think that a change in culture might be necessary? Explain your answer.

3. The major shareholders in an oil producing company with a poor environmental and ethical record want to change the company's ethical stance and attitude to social responsibility. What changes might have to be made within the business to achieve this?

Top tip

As with leadership styles, there is no one 'perfect' corporate culture for all business organisations and at all times.

37.5 Change management

Key term

Change management: planning, implementing, controlling and reviewing the movement of an organisation from its current state to a new one

Major change is an important feature of modern business life.

✓ Changes can be slow and occur over a period of time – incremental change
✓ Some changes are much more sudden and significant – revolutionary change
✓ Dramatic, revolutionary change often causes more problems to business than incremental change

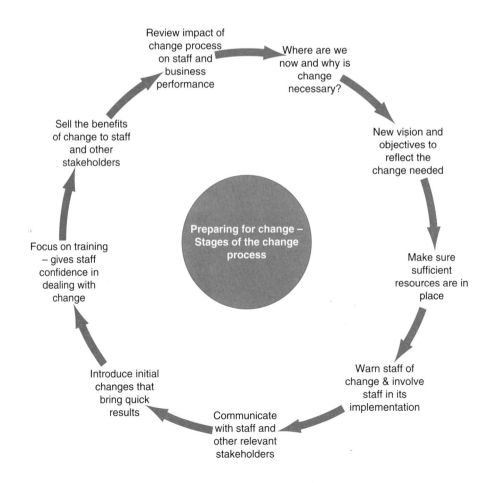

Review impact of change process on staff and business performance

Where are we now and why is change necessary?

New vision and objectives to reflect the change needed

Sell the benefits of change to staff and other stakeholders

Preparing for change – Stages of the change process

Make sure sufficient resources are in place

Focus on training – gives staff confidence in dealing with change

Warn staff of change & involve staff in its implementation

Introduce initial changes that bring quick results

Communicate with staff and other relevant stakeholders

✓ It cannot be prevented – some forces external to any business are always greater then the power of the business to prevent them. Dramatic change often causes more problems to business than incremental change

✓ Change has to be planned for – hence the need for corporate planning – and it needs to be prepared for.

Change management – other factors

Lead change – do not just manage it

This means that managers should not just 'get resources ready for change' but should be dynamic and proactive in selling the benefits of change and making sure that the whole organisation accepts it.

Use project champions and project groups to help drive change forward

> **Key terms**
>
> **Project groups:** these are created by a business to address a problem – such as a major change – that requires input from different specialists
>
> **Project champions:** a person assigned to support and drive a new project forward – they explain the benefits of change and support the project team putting change into effect

Promote the need for and advantages of change at every opportunity

Despite the best efforts of leaders promoting change management, there could be resistance to change due to:

✓ fear of the unknown, for example, new technology

✓ fear of failure, for example, not being able to cope with new work techniques

✓ losing something of value such as the previous business culture

✓ lack of trust, for example, if managers have not been open and communicated well

✓ inertia – some people just do not like change!

Top tip   There is scope to refer to leadership styles when discussing management of change – who would make more effective 'change managers' – autocratic or participative leaders?

> **Progress Check D**
>
> 1. What do you think the main difference is between 'managing change' and 'leading change'?
> 2. Give two examples of incremental changes that have affected businesses in your country.
> 3. Give two examples of revolutionary changes that have affected business in your country.
> 4. Assume that your school or college is aiming to relocate to another part of the city/country. Explain how this major change could be managed most effectively.

37.6 Contingency planning

> **Key term**
>
> **Contingency planning:** preparing an organisation's resources for unlikely events

Disasters and other unforeseen events occur – fires, floods, IT 'crash', oil tanker explosions and so on – and if businesses **did not** plan to cope with these there could be major problems.

✓ Bad publicity – because the business was not ready with resources or people to deal with the emergency

✓ Loss of worker and consumer confidence, for example, lack of safety equipment or no response to dangerous products being sold

✓ Business is unable to continue operations for long period of time, for example, premises destroyed

✓ Legal claims – because damage caused to other people or businesses.

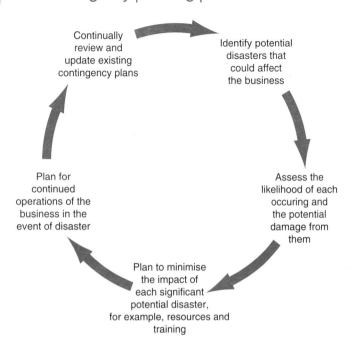

The contingency planning process

- Continually review and update existing contingency plans
- Identify potential disasters that could affect the business
- Assess the likelihood of each occuring and the potential damage from them
- Plan to minimise the impact of each significant potential disaster, for example, resources and training
- Plan for continued operations of the business in the event of disaster

Limitations of contingency planning

- ✘ Time consuming to identify each potential risk and assess the likelihood of occurrence and potential impact on business

- ✘ Must be constantly updated – to take new risks into account and to take account of new developments, for example, in fire-fighting techniques
- ✘ Cannot always identify or assess the degree of risks involved
- ✘ Staff training costs increase if labour costs are high.

Progress Check E

1. One form of contingency planning is sometimes referred to as 'business continuity planning'. Explain what this means.
2. Explain why not all business risks can be planned for.
3. Explain, with an example, how contingency planning might give workers and consumers greater confidence.
4. Explain, with an example, how contingency planning could reduce the bad publicity for a business following a disaster or accident.

Multiple Choice Questions

1. Strategic implementation means:
   (i) deciding on which strategies to follow in future years
   (ii) making sure that the strategies that are being followed are certain to be successful
   (iii) preparing people and resources for changes resulting from strategic choices
   (iv) finding out how the company currently stands in the markets it operates in

2. A business plan should contain all of the following *except*:
   (i) forecasted cash flows for future months/years
   (ii) objectives of the business
   (iii) last years cash flow forecast
   (iv) details of management skills

3. One of the main reasons why businesses have a corporate plan is to:
   (i) eliminate the impact of external forces on the business
   (ii) give a clear direction to management and workers

   (iii) reduce the need to take important strategic decisions to reach corporate objectives
   (iv) reduce the need for long term corporate objectives

4. A business that specialises in producing innovative and creative promotion schemes for other companies is most likely to adopt which one of the following types of corporate culture?
   (i) Task culture
   (ii) Power culture
   (iii) Role culture
   (iv) Authoritarian culture

5. It may be necessary to replace senior managers in a business that is trying to change its overall corporate culture. The most likely reason for this is:
   (i) to cut costs as management salaries are often very high
   (ii) to ensure that managers have attitudes and beliefs that do not conflict with new corporate culture

(iii) to set a good example to all staff so that they know they will lose their jobs if they do not work hard

(iv) to create a culture of fear within the business – even the senior managers can lose their jobs

6. All of the following are major causes of external change that will impact on a business *except*:

(i) new technologies in the industry mean that significant product changes will be needed

(ii) competitive rivalry increases as several new entrants into the market have appeared in recent months

(iii) fear of an inflationary boom has led to the government increasing taxes and interest rates

(iv) the business has recently merged with a larger business in the same industry

7. Four of the main stages of the change process are often placed in the order:

(i) train staff, review the impact of change; establish why change is necessary; new vision for the business

(ii) new vision for the business; train staff; establish why change is necessary; review the impact of change

(iii) establish why change is necessary; train staff; review the impact of change; new vision for the business

(iv) establish why change is necessary; new vision for the business; train staff; review the impact of change

8. Which of the following statements about contingency planning is correct?

(i) Contingency planning focuses on the key risks to a business and prepares resources to deal with them

(ii) Contingency planning identifies the key risks to a business and develops strategies to prevent them happening

(iii) Contingency planning prepares resources to deal with any emergency

(iv) Contingency planning is only effective if all of the potential risks can be identified and prepared for

Exam-style Question

Asia Clothing (AC) manufactures fashion clothing for women. Increased competition has led to major retailers insisting that AC reduce prices so that their shops can become more competitive. AC's directors take pride in their ethical policies.

AC has a strict quality system. However, last year a batch of cloth was received from a supplier that was wrongly marked: 'Fire resistant – ideal for children's clothes'. However it was just ordinary cotton cloth. AC used it to make childrens' clothes and then disaster struck. A child was badly burned when she stood close to a fire wearing one of AC's skirts that caught alight. The newspapers condemned both AC and the shop. AC followed a pre-prepared plan and withdrew all similar clothes, offering shops and consumers compensation. AC paid for the girl's medical treatment and donated $1m to a children's charity. The cloth maker was removed from AC's approved suppliers list. Sales of AC's clothes fell by only 3% over two months and then increased again.

1. Discuss the importance of contingency planning to AC.   [20]

Cambridge 9707 Paper 31 Section B Q7 June 2011

FitsU own 500 shops selling women's fashionable shoes. Recent rapid growth has led to several problems: limited working capital, increased loans and poor communication. The directors are thinking of opening FitsU's first factory to make shoes using latest technology machinery. The Chief Executive believes that vertical integration will give cost savings and good communication between the shops and the factory so that the right styles are stocked. The Marketing Director is opposed to this strategy: "Consumers prefer to buy well known global shoe brands. Just selling our own branded products will not succeed. Instead we should focus on selling shoes online through a new website. This could double our sales." The Finance Director is worried about the financial impact of further growth and the need to increase loans further. The directors agree that careful planning will be needed for making any decision.

2. Discuss the importance of effective management of change to the future of FitsU.   [20]

Cambridge 9707 Paper 32 Section B Q7 June 2011

Student's answer to Question 2

Effective management of change is a key factor to help the business succeed in future. Effective change management comprises of many aspects. Management has not been effective in this case as it seems to use autocratic leadership. This creates a negative atmosphere and leads to staff being treated badly. This will not encourage them to accept the changes that the business is considering such as opening a new factory. Change occurs when the business realises that it has to adapt and be flexible to changing conditions.

For example, FitsU has been a rapidly expanding business that is currently experiencing some difficulties. If the managers continue to take decisions and implement them in the same way as before then the business will be in trouble. The only way management of change will be effective in FitsU is if there is cooperation between all of the departments. This will make sure that, when the plans for the new factory are being discussed, all of the departments are ready for the change. There needs to be clear objectives and the Chief Executive of FitsU needs to suggest a clear vision and sense of direction for the business.

It is the adaptability of everyone in the organisation that will be important. The marketing department needs to come up with a clear strategy for the sport shoes. If this product is dropped then it could have big effects on some of the shop staff – some might even be made redundant. How will the managers deal with this major change? Judging by the way they have upset staff so far, not very well is the answer.

Businesses cannot stay still as they need to respond to outside changes such as new production technology. This might affect FitsU in its new factory. Staff will need training and they will need to be told what is expected of them when changes occur – and how they will be affected, both positively and negatively. FitsU marketing director is planning a new website and this will be a major change for the business. New staff will be needed and if existing staff are afraid of the new technology they might have to be made redundant. So managing this change will have a big impact on staff morale. The best way would be to involve the staff in the decision and ask them to help implement it. However, with the existing senior managers at Fitsu this seems very unlikely.

In conclusion, FitsU is about to experience many changes and managing these well will help the business maintain its level of success. Existing managers though do not seem to be able to do this. Perhaps a complete change of business culture is needed, to a person culture, which will encourage workers to take part in decisions and give them an opportunity to be involved in the process of change.

Authors' Comments

Good effort – but this essay is rather jumbled and would have benefited from a clearer plan such as explaining in turn why each of the changes planned for FitsU need effective management of change.

Good knowledge of change management is shown. Excellent use of the case study is made. There could have been more analysis of how 'leading change' effectively results in more effective implementation of change. Also, the evaluation could have included an assessment of one or two other factors that will determine the future success of FitsU apart from change management – the state of the economy or the level of competitive rivalry, for example.

Revision checklist – tick when done and understood!

Topic	Textbook read	Revision complete
What strategic implementation means		
Business plans – Major contents		
Corporate plans – Usefulness and limitations		
Causes of business change and how change can be effectively managed		
Contingency planning – Importance and limitations		

Answers and Tips

Answers to Multiple Choice Questions

Chapter	1	2	3	4	5	6	7	8	9
1	(iii)	(ii)	(iv)	(i)	(iv)	(iii)			
2	(iii)	(ii)	(ii)	(iv)	(iii)	(ii)			
3	(ii)	(iii)	(i)	(iii)	(iv)	(iii)			
4	(iii)	(iv)	(i)	(iii)	(i)	(iii)			
5	(iii)	(iii)	(iv)	(ii)	(iv)	(ii)			
6	(ii)	(iii)	(iv)	(iii)	(iv)	(i)			
7	(iv)	(iii)	(i)	(iii)	(ii)	(i)			
8	(ii)	(iv)	(iii)	(iii)	(iii)	(iii)	(i)		
9	(ii)	(i)	(iii)	(iv)	(i)	(iv)	(i)		
10	(iii)	(iii)	(iii)	(iii)	(iii)	(ii)	(iv)	(ii)	(i)
11	(ii)	(iv)	(iii)	(iii)	(i)	(iv)	(ii)		
12	(iii)	(ii)	(ii)	(iv)	(ii)	(i)	(iv)	(iv)	
13	(ii)	(iii)	(ii)	(iii)	(iii)	(i)	(ii)		
14	(iii)	(i)	(iv)	(ii)	(iii)	(i)			
15	(iii)	(ii)	(ii)	(iv)	(i)	(ii)			
16	(ii)	(ii)	(iii)	(i)	(iv)	(iii)			
17	(iii)	(iv)	(i)	(ii)	(i)	(ii)			
18	(ii)	(iii)	(ii)	(ii)	(iii)	(iv)			
19	(iii)	(iv)	(ii)	(iv)	(i)				
20	(iii)	(ii)	(ii)	(iv)	(ii)	(iii)	(iv)	(iii)	(i)
21	(i)	(ii)	(iii)	(ii)	(ii)	(iii)	(iv)	(iv)	
22	(iii)	(i)	(i)	(ii)	(ii)				
23	(iii)	(i)	(iv)	(iv)	(iii)	(iii)	(i)		
24	(iv)	(i)	(iv)	(iv)	(iii)	(i)	(iii)	(i)	
25	(iii)	(ii)	(iii)	(i)	(iii)	(i)	(i)		
26	(ii)	(iv)	(iii)	(ii)	(i)	(i)	(iv)	(ii)	(iii)
27	(iii)	(ii)	(i)	(iii)	(iv)	(iii)	(i)	(i)	(ii)
28	(i)	(ii)	(iv)	(iv)	(ii)	(iv)	(iii)	(ii)	
29	(iii)	(iv)	(iii)	(iii)	(ii)				
30	(iii)	(i)	(iv)	(iii)	(i)				
31	(iii)	(iii)	(ii)	(i)	(iv)	(iv)	(ii)		
32	(ii)	(iii)	(i)	(iii)	(iii)	(ii)			

Chapter	1	2	3	4	5	6	7	8	9
33	(ii)	(iii)	(iii)	(iii)	(iii)	(iii)	(iii)		
34	(ii)	(iv)	(iii)	(iv)	(i)	(iii)			
35	(ii)	(iii)	(i)	(iii)	(ii)	(ii)			
36	(ii)	(iv)	(iii)	(iv)	(ii)	(ii)			
37	(iii)	(iii)	(ii)	(i)	(ii)	(iv)	(iv)	(i)	

Tips for Paper 1

- ✓ This is worth 40 per cent of the AS qualification and 20 per cent of the A level qualification.
- ✓ It has two sections.
- ✓ Section A contains 4 compulsory short answer questions.
- ✓ Most of these are 'structured' – which means they have a part (a) and a part (b)
- ✓ Specific and accurate knowledge and understanding is the main skill being examined on this section – learning all of the key definitions will help you gain high marks on this section.

Top tip

Do not spend too long on each of these questions. They carry relatively few marks each. It is important that you spend no more than 30 minutes on this section.

- ✓ Section B requires you to answer **one** essay question from a choice of 3.
- ✓ Most of these questions are again structured – with parts (a) and (b) although some will be a single part.
- ✓ Where there are **two** parts, part (a) usually examines skills of knowledge, application and analysis – but part (b) will also be examining your skills of evaluation.
- ✓ So, do not forget to include judgement and a conclusion to your essay answer. This will also be the case where there is only one part.

Top tip

You should spend around 45 minutes on Section B – including the time taken to read and analyse all three questions carefully before making your choice. Do not try to answer all three essay titles! Remember to use any context that you are given.

Tips for Paper 2

- ✓ This is worth 60 per cent of the AS qualification and 30 per cent of the A level qualification.

Top tip

You are advised to spend 45 minutes on each question – every year some students do badly on the second question because they have spent too long on the first question!

- ✓ If you ignore the data – the information about the business provided to you – then you will score very low marks. The data is meant to encourage you to apply your answers to the business and the features of it and problems that it faces.
- ✓ Many students ignore the key prompt word in the question – see the advice given in the Introduction. Many students fail to show judgement or skills of evaluation when the question asks them to 'discuss' or 'evaluate'. Many marks are lost by overlooking this important fact.

✓ Other students may waste time writing 'evaluation' in their answers to a question that asks them to 'analyse' only.

Top tip Try to get into the minds of the main stakeholders of the business when writing your answers.

Tips for Paper 3

✓ This is worth 50 per cent of the A level qualification.

✓ All of the questions are based on a detailed case study that provides background information about a business, data on its current position and external factors influencing it and strategic options that the managers of the business have to choose between. You are expected to use this data.

✓ The questions are divided into 2 sections. The 5 questions of Section A are all compulsory and will include at least two calculation questions. Section A is worth 80% of the total marks. Section B gives students a choice of questions, 1 must be answered from 2.

✓ The Section B essay questions demand extensive, detailed and evaluative responses that should, again, be based on the case study business.

✓ Many of the Section B questions will focus on Unit 6 of the specification – Strategic Management.

Top tip At least one question on Paper 3 will ask you to make a justified decision for the business, for example, a new location or the most appropriate source of finance. Students often lose marks by concluding their answers with a statement such as: 'so the managers of the business should consider all of these factors before making a final decision'. Instead, they should come to a clear conclusion which is supported by their analysis of the data, such as: 'so despite the high rental costs, site A is preferred to site B because, most importantly, it offers potential for further growth of the business'.

Over to you!

We have explained to you:

✓ the subject knowledge you need to understand and recall

✓ the skills you will need to demonstrate in your answers

✓ the key revision and examination tips that will help you achieve high marks.

It's over to you to produce the examination performance of a lifetime! And remember, no matter how many books you own or how good your school or college is, in the end, your success on the Business Studies course is down to you.

"Recipe for success: Study while others are sleeping; work while others are loafing; prepare while others are playing and dream while others are wishing."

William A Ward (1922–1994)

Index